TRANSFORMATION OF THE SELF IN THE THOUGHT OF FRIEDRICH SCHLEIERMACHER

Transformation of the Self in the Thought of Friedrich Schleiermacher

JACQUELINE MARIÑA

OXFORD
UNIVERSITY PRESS

OXFORD
UNIVERSITY PRESS

Great Clarendon Street, Oxford OX2 6DP

Oxford University Press is a department of the University of Oxford.
It furthers the University's objective of excellence in research, scholarship,
and education by publishing worldwide in

Oxford New York

Auckland Cape Town Dar es Salaam Hong Kong Karachi
Kuala Lumpur Madrid Melbourne Mexico City Nairobi
New Delhi Shanghai Taipei Toronto

With offices in

Argentina Austria Brazil Chile Czech Republic France Greece
Guatemala Hungary Italy Japan Poland Portugal Singapore
South Korea Switzerland Thailand Turkey Ukraine Vietnam

Oxford is a registered trade mark of Oxford University Press
in the UK and in certain other countries

Published in the United States
by Oxford University Press Inc., New York

British Library Cataloguing in Publication Data

Data available

Library of Congress Cataloging in Publication Data

Mariña, Jacqueline.
Transformation of the self in the thought of Friedrich Schleiermacher / Jacqueline Mariña.
p. cm.
Includes bibliographical references and index.
ISBN–13: 978–0–19–920637–7 (alk. paper) 1. Schleiermacher, Friedrich, 1768–1834.
2. Ethics. I. Title.
BX4827.S3M37 2008
230′.044092—dc22 2007045026

Typeset by SPI Publisher Services, Pondicherry, India
Printed in Great Britain
on acid-free paper by
Biddles Ltd., King's Lynn, Norfolk

ISBN 978–0–19–920637–7

1 3 5 7 9 10 8 6 4 2

For Curtis, Katie, and Gabe,
and Franklin, too.

Contents

Acknowledgments   viii

Introduction   1
1. The Philosopher's Stone   15
2. The Principle of Individuation   43
3. Personal Identity   76
4. The World is the Mirror of the Self   109
5. The Highest Good   146
6. Individual and Community   164
7. Transformation of the Self through Christ   186
8. Outpourings of the Inner Fire: Experiential Expressivism
   and Religious Pluralism   221
Concluding Remarks   247

Bibliography   249
Index   259

Acknowledgments

I have incurred numerous debts in the writing of this book, which would not have been written were it not for the help and support of many persons. Robert Adams first suggested I write the book and commented on drafts of many of the chapters; this book would not exist were it not for his support and encouragement. Karl Ameriks also read and commented on parts of the manuscript, as did George di Giovanni, Paul W. Franks, and my Purdue colleague Dan Frank, with whom I have had many fascinating conversations about Spinoza, religion, and ethics. I am grateful to Manfred Frank for his generous e-mail correspondence with me on Schleiermacher's relation to Kant and Leibniz; his own work on Schleiermacher has been a source of inspiration for many of the ideas in this book. Peter Byrne commented on an early draft of the last chapter in this book; his comments spurred me to think further about the implications of the material. A conversation with Fred Beiser at the Schleiermacher conference at Drew University in 2000 helped me to focus more deeply on key issues in Schleiermacher's reception of Kant.

I am grateful to my friends and colleagues at the Schleiermacher Group at the AAR with whom I have interacted on a regular basis throughout the years. Richard Crouter has been a generous and supportive conversation partner who has led me to think differently about Schleiermacher in important ways. I have been very lucky to have colleagues such as Julia Lamm, Brent Sockness, and Christine Helmer, with all of whom I have had numerous conversations throughout the years; their own work on Schleiermacher has influenced my own in subtle and not so subtle ways, even when I have come to disagree with some of their conclusions. Francis Fiorenza has been unstintingly generous with his time and intellectual energy; I have learned much from him about Schleiermacher's theology. I have had animated and stimulating discussions of Schleiermacher's philosophy with Andrew Dole. We disagree on fundamental points of interpretation, and he has challenged me to think more deeply about my own claims, putting forward important objections I needed to consider. These conversations have been truly enjoyable, and I hope to have many more. I have presented early drafts of three of the chapters at the Schleiermacher Group in 1997, 2002, and 2005, and benefited from many excellent comments; an early draft of Chapter 7 was presented at Marquette University in the spring of 2006.

Five persons to whom I owe an enormous debt of gratitude are the late Hans Frei, Nicholas Wolterstorff, Manfred Baum, Henry Allison, and Terrence Tice. I first started my study of Schleiermacher in the late 1980s at Yale University with Hans Frei; Nicholas Wolterstorff, who became my adviser after his death, suggested that I work on Kant. Both Nick and Henry Allison played an important role in my study of Kant. I particularly learned a great deal about Kant from Manfred Baum. This earlier work proved key to my interpretation of Schleiermacher, and it would not have been possible without their help. Nick has been a continuous source of encouragement and support throughout the years, and for his presence in my life I am deeply grateful. Terrence Tice, whose tenacity in encouraging me to work on Schleiermacher played a significant role in the direction of my research, has been, as always, generous with his time and spirit.

Here at Purdue, my colleagues Bill McBride, Charlene Seigfried, Martin Matustik, Don Mitchell, Leonard Harris, and Dan Smith have been especially supportive throughout the years; my work with them on different philosophical projects and projects in religious studies has contributed to my thinking about Schleiermacher in subtle and subterraneous ways. Conversations with Pat Curd on the dangers of religion spurred me to think about the philosophical significance of Schleiermacher for contemporary problems.

I also owe a debt of gratitude to colleagues in History and English: Tithi Bhattacharya and Sue Curtis for their unfailing friendship and moral support throughout the writing of the book; Sally Hastings, Ann Astell, Elena Benedicto, Gerry Friedman, and Aparajita Sagar for animated conversations on all and sundry. For my many colleagues at Purdue, I am deeply grateful.

Preparatory work on the manuscript was made possible by an appointment to the Center for Humanistic Studies at Purdue University in the Fall of 2004; a large part of the manuscript was written during my Spring sabbatical in 2006. I am thankful to Purdue University for this time to devote to research.

I am grateful for the work of Lucy Qureshi, Tom Perridge, and an anonymous reviewer through Oxford University Press; Lucy helped during the beginning stages of the project, and Tom has seen the project through to completion. The reviewer made some very helpful suggestions. I am thankful for their efforts.

Finally, I would like to thank my family and close friends. For many profound conversations on religion and ethics, I am grateful to my husband, Franklin Mason. My children, Katie, Curtis, and Gabriel have been an unfailing source of joy in my life and my deepest inspiration; without them this book would certainly not have been written. My mother, Carmen Mariña, who died too early, taught me how to think about ethics. My in-laws, Peggy and Curtis Mason, and my sister-in-law, Mary Lou McCauley, have been a bedrock of support. For all the good things they have contributed to my life, I thank my father José Mariña and his wife, Lizzie. Tatiana Garmendía, José Balido, and David Appell have been steadfast friends throughout the years. For the presence of all of these lights in my life I am deeply thankful.

Earlier versions of two chapters have appeared elsewhere: Chapter 1 appeared as "Schleiermacher on the Philosopher's Stone: the Shaping of Schleiermacher's Early Ethics by the Kantian Legacy," in the *Journal of Religion* 79, No. 2 (April 1999): 193–215 (© 1999 The University of Chicago); an earlier version of Chapter 8 appeared as "Schleiermacher on the Outpourings of the Inner Fire: Experiential Expressivism and Religious Pluralism," in *Religious Studies* 40, (2004): 125–43 (© 2004 Cambridge University Press). Material from these earlier versions has been incorporated into this book with kind permission of the publishers.

Introduction

The question of the value of religion presses upon us today more than ever. On the one hand there are those who question its validity from the standpoint of an extreme scientific naturalism. For them religion is an atavistic remnant from the past, a storehouse of super-stitious nonsense plaguing humanity. None of it is to be taken very seriously, except, perhaps, in order to reject it unconditionally. On the other hand there are persons who take what they call "religion" very seriously. For them religion functions to define the members of their group as the "good ones" standing over against a world of evil enemies that must be vanquished. This kind of religion too often can encourage a kind of extremism ending in violence, for at its heart lies a violent rejection of anything perceived as foreign or different. Between these two extremes lie many of us. We recognize the value of science, willingly conceding that all natural phenomena must be explained naturalistically. The Enlightenment changed us; modernism and postmodernism changed us, and pre-Enlightenment religion is no longer a possibility for us. Yet we are loath to accept that this means that we must banish anything having transcendental significance from our lives. Still, we also recognize that religion can be dangerous. Religion is dangerous when it becomes absolutist and Manichean, that is, when it mistakes what always must be a finite and conditioned apprehension of the transcendent for the transcendent ground itself, and when it further bases its reactionary exclusion of what it perceives as other on this fundamental mistake. In such cases, religion degenerates into idolatry. Idolatry, however, is not only the stuff of fundamentalisms. It is a perennial danger tempting each of us, and it tempts in myriad ways. Authentic religion requires a certain kind of openness, and a willingness to live with uncertainty. It requires the recognition of our finitude and of the conditioned character of all our knowledge; it requires a willingness to depend on what to us must remain, in fundamental ways, unknown. These attitudes are very difficult to achieve in practice.

How, then, are we to think about religion such that we can both answer its naturalistic critics and provide a program for the avoidance of idolatry? A serious engagement with the character of human finitude is necessary to deal with the latter. The problem that scientific naturalism poses to religion is yet more complex. Any attempt to mediate between science and religion, however, must come to terms with the question of human consciousness, for it is human consciousness that is, after all, our window to the world, however we may conceive it. It thus appears that the key to mediating between both a scientific naturalism that denies any possibility of transcendent meaning and a reactionary fundamentalism claiming possession of absolute truth lies in an investigation of the nature of the subject, its relation to the world, and the possibility of its relation to a ground transcending both self and world. This investigation is one that cannot be constrained by a certain naturalistic bias at the outset. Such a bias would be in place if the knowing and willing subject were to be conceived as simply yet another object in the world, that is, as a bit of brain matter in motion on which supervene certain strange states of consciousness. In such a case, the phenomenon of consciousness is merely objectified and made an object *in* the world. Here the more difficult questions of the nature of subjectivity *as such*, as that which supplies the primordial window upon the world, are completely bypassed.

It was first and foremost the groundbreaking philosophy of Immanuel Kant (1724–1804) that brought to light the fact that all knowledge is the product of a fundamental *activity* of consciousness. For Kant, an investigation of the possibility of objective knowledge led back to an investigation of the conditions of the knowing subject. The nature of the subject and the character of its fundamental activity, that is, the transcendental conditions of knowledge, were thereby placed at the forefront of philosophical inquiry. Kant's Copernican revolution in philosophy fueled a corresponding revolution in theology. Friedrich Daniel Ernst

Schleiermacher (1768–1834) is often referred to as the father of modern theology. Influenced by Kant, he placed the subject at the forefront of theology: it is through consciousness that God relates to the world. The meaning of theological utterances was to be traced back to the subject's religious experience, an experience whose transcendental conditions could themselves be investigated. This experience is one having both cognitive and volitional components; both components were understood by Schleiermacher as fundamentally interrelated and as stemming from the depths of consciousness. The self experiences the absolute through the immediate self-consciousness; the way the self apprehends its relation to the absolute in turn conditions the way that world is apprehended, valued, and felt. In *The Christian Faith* Schleiermacher says of the individual that has undergone a religious transformation: "now all his activities are differently determined...and even all impressions are differently received—which means that the personal self-consciousness, too, becomes different" (*CF* §100.2; *KGA* I.13,2 107; 427). Insofar as the personal self-consciousness has been transformed, the actions that arise from it, too, will be different from those of the former self. However, Schleiermacher was also aware of an inverse relation: how the self relates to others conditions the way that the self is conscious of its absolute dependence. The two poles are inherently related. As such, central to Schleiermacher's outlook was his ethical theory. It is in the sphere of ethics that religion has its ultimate meaning, for the fruit of all true religion lies in its transformative power over the self.

Here lies the significance of Schleiermacher's achievement. His focus on religious experience and the transcendental conditions of subjectivity allowed him to provide an account of religion that was neither reductionistic nor dogmatic.[1] Religious experience has its

[1] Notable recent European treatments of Schleiermacher's work dealing with his analysis of transcendental subjectivity and human finitude are: Peter Grove, *Deutungen des Subjekts: Schleiermachers Philosophie der Religion* and Sarah Schmidt, *Die Konstruktion des Endlichen*. In *Deutungen des Subjekts* Grove details Schleiermacher's analysis of subjectivity, paying particular attention to his transcendental analysis of self-consciousness and how it relates to his philosophy of religion. Schmidt's study focuses on Schleiermacher's *Dialectic* as an analysis of the conditions of the possibility of knowledge given the character of our finite subjectivity. Another excellent treatment of Schleiermacher's ethics is Peter Berner, *La Philosophie de Schleiermacher:*

origins in the transcendental conditions of subjectivity itself, and can therefore not be reduced to or explained in naturalistic terms alone;[2] it is grounded in an absolute that transcends the self. On the other hand Schleiermacher emphasized this fact, that the absolute *transcends* consciousness; as such, the self only experiences the effects of the absolute on consciousness.[3] As Schleiermacher argued in the *Dialectic*, the transcendental unity of the self is merely *analogous* to the unity of the absolute.[4] Moreover, the knowing subject is finite and situated, and as such can offer only a partial perspective on the world. This means that all action, if it is to be truly ethical and capable of refracting the divine love, must proceed from the awareness of the limited and perspectival character of the self's standpoint. It must be acknowledged that in all human knowing there is no "view from nowhere;" all acts of knowledge are conditioned by the inherently particular and subjective standpoint from which they first originate. This does not imply imprisonment in a solipsistic world, but it does mean that the construction of knowledge is first and foremost an *inter-subjective* enterprise that occurs through dialogue, and that in this enterprise "beginning in the middle is unavoidable" (Dial *KGA* II 10/1, 186, §62).

Behind Schleiermacher's theological achievement lay a rigorous grappling with fundamental metaphysical problems. As such his theology cannot be adequately understood aside from his philosophy.

Herméneutique, Dialectique, Ethique. Berner's study emphasizes the relation between Schleiermacher's ethics, his theory of knowledge, and his hermeneutics.

[2] Andrew Dole is certainly mistaken when he reads Schleiermacher as a determinist who believed religion could be thoroughly explained naturalistically. See Andrew Dole, "Schleiermacher and Otto on Religion." This reading completely ignores the significance of Schleiermacher's transcendental analysis of self-consciousness.

[3] Robert Adams correctly notes that Schleiermacher's theological method "is connected with a long tradition of theologians (such as Maimonides and Aquinas) who have been reluctant to claim positive knowledge of the divine nature as it is in itself.... Schleiermacher insists on the preeminence of the way of causality (*CF*, 1830, § 50.3). Indeed, it is hard to think of a theologian who has adhered more rigorously or more exclusively than he to the way of causality." "Faith and Religious Knowledge," 44.

[4] Peter Grove's analysis of central passages of the *Dialectic* is certainly correct: "Der entscheidende Schritt besteht darin, daß *diese Einheit der Subjecktivität* als *Analogie des übersubjektiven Grundes* erklärt wird. Der zweite Satz lautet ohne Weglassungen: 'In diesem also haben wir die Analogie mit dem transcendentalen Grunde, nämlich die aufhebende Verknüpfung der relativen Gegensäze' (*KGA* II/10.1, 266). *Deutungen des Subjekts,* 509.

Moreover, his philosophy is of interest in its own right. This is especially true of his philosophical ethics, which has as its presupposition his account of personal identity and the nature of self-consciousness. Hans-Joachim Birkner has noted: "without a doubt, Schleiermacher's philosophical ethics represents his most important achievement, and in the history of ethics constitutes a completely original project."[5] More recently, Gunter Scholz has claimed that Schleiermacher's ethics "has a far greater significance" than his other achievements; "it tackles the more important problems, has a much wider perspective, and can lay claim to greater originality."[6] And in the *Cambridge Companion to Friedrich Schleiermacher,* Frederick Beiser concludes his piece on Schleiermacher's ethics with the following:

If it [Schleiermacher's ethics] is not recognized as one of the fundamental areas of his philosophical achievement, the problem lies with the public rather than the author. Schleiermacher's comprehensive conception of ethics; his insistence that ethics broaden its horizons, that it investigate such important phenomena such as love, free sociability and friendship; his demand for the restoration of the highest good; his critique of the fact-norm distinction; and his insistence that our ethics ultimately depend upon our general metaphysical view of the world – all these remain a challenge to ethics today. If the subject is as dreary in 2002 as it was in 1802 it is because we have failed to listen to powerful voices like his own.[7]

Because Schleiermacher's philosophical ethics are inherently bound up with his metaphysics of the absolute and philosophy of religion, his ethics is especially relevant to the question of how to conceive of the relation between religion and ethics. Schleiermacher presents the two as integrally related. Contra Kant, who sought to make religious conviction rational by portraying it as the consequence of moral commitment, he grounds virtuous character in the self's relation to the transcendent. In this he is much closer to Plato. His philosophy thereby offers an original understanding of how ethics can be grounded in religion, one that avoids the pitfalls plaguing a

---

[5] Hans-Joachim Birkner, *Schleiermachers Christliche Sittenlehre im Zusammenhang seines philosophisch-theologischen Systems,* 37.

[6] Gunter Scholz, *Ethik und Hermeneutik: Schleiermachers Grundlegung des Geisteswissenshaften,* 7.

[7] Frederick Beiser, "Schleiermacher's Ethics," 79.

divine command theory of ethics, namely, heteronomy. The religious
self does not act morally because a source *external* to it commands
it; rather, the self in whom the God-consciousness is dominant is
infused with the divine love. Because the motive for such a person
to act morally is found in the depths of the self as informed by the
divine love, heteronomy is avoided.

By focusing on the transcendental conditions of subjectivity,
Schleiermacher was able to argue that the self's relation to the divine
has a direct effect on the self's relation to others. The self stands in
relation to the *whence* of all existence through the immediate self-
consciousness, the point from which all self-consciousness originates.
God can never be an object *for* consciousness. Representation of
God as such an object is always "a corruption," "for anything that is
outwardly given must be given as an object exposed to our counter-
influence, however slight this may be" (*CF* §4.4). Rather, God affects
self-consciousness more in the way of a *formal* cause infusing a person
with the divine love; this in turn has effects on how the individual
relates to others. This partially grounds Schleiermacher's original
claim that the relation to God and the relation to the neighbor are
so intrinsically tied to one another that both are identical: "in this
Kingdom of God . . . the establishment and maintenance of the fellowship of each individual with God, and the maintenance and direction
of the fellowship of all members with one another are not separate
achievements but the same" (*CF* §102).

Schleiermacher's focus on the transcendental ground of character
allowed him to combine the advantages of an ethic of virtue with an
ethic that also affirms the significance of duty. Through his development of the idea that the immediate self-consciousness lies at the root
of both spontaneity and receptivity, Schleiermacher offered a coherent account of how feelings and inclinations, and indeed the whole of
a person's receptivity, could be morally transformed through reason.
He thereby developed the underpinnings of an insightful moral psychology having the resources to deal with theoretical problems plaguing Kantian ethics. Whereas a good part of Kant's theory of virtue
rests on the moral autocracy of practical reason over the inclinations,
that is, moral strength of will over recalcitrant desires, Schleiermacher
was able to account for how feelings and desires rooted in the conative
side of human nature could play an important role in the ethical

expression of the self. His transcendental turn in ethics also allowed him to affirm both genuine freedom and the *unity* of an agent's character throughout the process of moral transformation.

One of Schleiermacher's most original contributions to ethics lies in his analysis of the importance of *individuality* for ethical life. Individuals are the primary building blocks of community; the building of community is the purpose of ethical life. But community can only be built through an appreciation of the fact that all human knowing and doing orients itself from a particular and finite standpoint. To be sure, the standpoint of the individual is one that must be continually transcended through human communication. But the new perspective achieved through communication itself still remains a finite and conditioned one that must itself be transcended through the building of ever widening circles of community. Schleiermacher's ethics begins with an understanding of individuals as particular, *embodied* beings having the capacity for communication. The foundations of his ethical system allow him to acknowledge the ultimate value of the individual *qua* individual, that is, the individual in all of his or her particularity. The individual is irreplaceable; his or her perspective is unique, non-transposable and indispensable to the ethical community. As such, the situation of each individual calls for a particular range of responses appropriate to it in all of its particularity. Furthermore, the body is the outward sign of the individual's perpective, the medium through which he or she communicates, and as such can become the organ of the spirit.

Schleiermacher's insights are bolstered by a rigorous metaethical analysis of the nature of (a) the individual's relation to the divine or the absolute; (b) the character of self-consciousness and personal identity; (c) the relation of the self to others and its effect on self-consciousness; and (d) the specific character of *individuality* and its relation to the formation of the ethical community. This metaethical analysis ultimately has as its goal Schleiermacher's attempt to understand the role of Christ as the founder of the Christian ethical community. His philosophical and ethical analysis has a theological goal: to make intelligible the life of the Christian community in Christ. Schleiermacher's ethics, however, has much to offer both Christians and non-Christians alike. For in his attempt to make intelligible the life of the Christian community in Christ, he also developed an ethics and philosophy of religion whose starting point is an appreciation of the role that subjectivity and finitude plays in all human life and in the building up of communities.

It took many years for Schleiermacher to arrive at the contours of his own system. Crucial to his philosophical development was his encounter with Spinoza, Kant, Leibniz, Jacobi, and Fichte. Kant's influence was the most decisive; even as he moved beyond him to develop his own original system, the ideas he took from Kant continued to shape his philosophical outlook. Any attempt to understand Schleiermacher's mature thought must take into account his encounter with these thinkers. The goal of the present study is to provide an exposition and analysis of the key metaphysical concepts undergirding Schleiermacher's mature ethical system. Because these ideas were developed over time and in relation to the philosophy of other figures, an exposition of Schleiermacher's philosophical ethics requires an engagement with Schleiermacher's philosophical development. As a result, two goals drive the organization of the present study: first, an exposition of Schleiermacher's metaphysics, especially as this metaphysics touches upon the problem of the nature of self-consciousness and personal identity, and second, an analysis of the development of his thought.

In the first chapter, "The Philosopher's Stone," I examine several fundamental philosophical problems regarding the conditions of the possibility of moral transformation preoccupying the early Schleiermacher, especially as he struggled to come to terms with Kant's practical philosophy. Included in this set of issues is the problem of transcendental freedom and how it relates to an agent's character, as well as the problem of the relation of the faculty of representation (knowing) to the faculty of desire (doing). Both questions have to do with how we are to conceive of the unity of the self throughout its changing states. The principle focus of the chapter is Schleiermacher's early essay *On Freedom* (1790–2), although I also look at Schleiermacher's notes on Kant's second *Critique* (1789), the third of his *Dialogues on Freedom* (1789), and his critical review of Kant's *Anthropology from a Pragmatic Point of View* (1799). In these early pieces Schleiermacher argued against Kant's idea of transcendental freedom and for a compatabilist view of freedom allowing us to affirm the continuity of an agent's character. However, he also takes note of the significant difficulties that such a compatibilist understanding of human freedom poses with regard to understanding the individual as the *initiator* of an action. Moreover, he struggles with an essential problem posed by Kant's fundamental division of the sources of human knowledge into spontaneity and receptivity. If the two are fundamentally distinct, how then is it possible to relate knowing to doing? Knowing has to do with our spontaneity, while doing is dependent on a moment of desire that spurs action, and desire, Kant believed (for good reasons), has to do with our passivity or receptivity. How, then, is it possible that desire can relate to our spontaneity (e.g., the moral law itself, which is generated by practical reason), so that we can recognize the *worth* of the moral law? Both Schleiermacher's concern with the problem of the continuity of an agent's character throughout change, as well as his early treatment of the problem of the relation of the faculty of representation (knowing) to the faculty of desire (doing) sheds light on his later, mature analysis of self-consciousness as grounded in a transcendental moment (the immediate self-consciousness). This transcendental moment not only makes possible the transition between knowing and doing, but also grounds the unity of a person's character.

In the second and third chapters I provide an in-depth analysis of two of Schleiermacher's early pieces on Spinoza, *Spinozism* and the *Short Presentation of the Spinozistic System*, both from about 1793–4. The position put forward in these essays is fully consonant with Schleiermacher's earlier determinism. My second chapter, "The Principle of Individuation," examines the grounds for Schleiermacher's claim that there are no genuine individuals. Schleiermacher adopts Kant's distinction between noumena and phenomena; while individuals may *appear* at the phenomenal level, we cannot identify a noumenal principle of individuation guaranteeing the identity of a thing. An analysis of appearances reveals that each appearance fully depends for its existence on what is different and outside of it. As such, there are no real, noumenal agents; everything about the self is fully determined by what precedes its existence and lies outside of it. Yet all of these arguments are made in the context of his adoption of Kant's transcendental idealism. The adoption of this standpoint, I argue, proves decisive for Schleiermacher's later thought.

While Schleiermacher gives up his Spinozism, Kant's analysis of transcendental subjectivity remains a fundamental feature of his philosophical and theological system.[8] It is this focus on the transcendental conditions of subjectivity that allow him to affirm later that the self is transcendentally *free* in relation to the world; the self is not a mere turnspit mechanistically determined by this-worldly forces. Rather, the immediate self-consciousness is the principle locus wherein the divine causality is immediately operative as a formal and *in-forming* cause in the deepest recesses of the self.

My third chapter, "Personal Identity," continues the analysis of *Spinozism*. In it I focus on Schleiermacher's long discussion of personal identity. This discussion is extremely significant for Schleiermacher's later understanding of reflective self-consciousness. In it Schleiermacher reveals himself to be intimately acquainted with both Kant's transcendental deduction as well as Kant's chapter on the Paralogisms in the *Critique of Pure Reason*. Most significantly, Schleiermacher argues, in agreement with Kant, that we have no access to a substantial noumenal self. Rather, identity of the subject is cognizable only in and through the synthesis of the manifold of intuition. The only reflective access we have to the self is through the *products* of its transcendental activity; the transcendental activity itself, however, cannot become an object *for* consciousness but is only given in immediacy. The philosophical position Schleiermacher develops here is key to an understanding of the position he develops in the *Monologen,* which is more representative of his mature thought.

In "The World is the Mirror of the Self," I discuss Schleiermacher's *Monologen* in the context of his 1797–8 study of Leibniz's philosophy. It is during this period that Schleiermacher had his first *direct* contact with Leibniz, reading the original sources. Prior to this period his knowledge of Leibniz was second hand. Here we find a more positive reception of Leibniz's thought, one that remains decisive for Schleiermacher's mature system. I argue, however, that this positive reception of Leibniz is mediated through Schleiermacher's adoption of Kant's understanding of transcendental subjectivity.

---

[8] On this crucial point my reading diverges from that of Julia Lamm in *The Living God: Schleiermacher's Theological Appropriation of Spinoza,* who does not recognize a fundamental change in Schleiermacher's later thought on this foundational issue.

Schleiermacher also agrees with Kant, over against Leibniz, that individuals stand in genuine interaction with one another. It is here that we find Schleiermacher affirming both a qualified monadic individualism as well as transcendental freedom. Both affirmations go hand in hand. The actions of the self are not merely the products of a series of inter-worldly causes. Schleiermacher recognized, along with Leibniz and Kant, that the categories of substance and intelligible freedom mutually imply one another; something is a substance if its mode of action is grounded in its intrinsic properties. Furthermore, the self, in its fundamental transcendental unity and activity, is not an object that can stand in a causal relation to other objects in the world. Through the immediate self-consciousness the self stands in *direct* relation to the absolute; this is a relation unmediated by objects in the world given *to* consciousness. It is through this relation that the self is free in relation to the world. In the *Monologen* Schleiermacher presents his vision of the transcendentally free being who expresses him- or herself into the world. The self has no reflexive access to itself aside from the way that it unites its representations and constructs its world; in a play on Leibniz's idea of the self as the mirror of the world, Schleiermacher affirms that "the world is spirit's most beautiful work, its self-created mirror." Here Schleiermacher is well on his way to one of the fundamental ideas behind the *Dialectic* and *The Christian Faith,* namely, that the rule through which a person connects representations and thereby represents the world to herself is seamlessly integrated with her desires, and hence with her actions. All are elements of the person's self-expression, itself the product of the transcendental activity of the self. The self knows itself through this expressive activity, which is received and reflected back to it through the activity of others.

Chapter 5, "The Highest Good," begins an analysis of Schleiermacher's *Notes on Ethics* from 1805/06. This is an outline of Schleiermacher's mature ethical system. In this chapter I examine Schleiermacher's understanding of the highest good, the final goal of all ethical action. In the *Notes on Ethics* Schleiermacher describes the highest good as the "ensouling of human nature by reason." His exposition of the highest good reveals his eschatological conviction that the *natural* world will be perfected. The goal of moral action does not lie beyond this world; it is the perfection of this one.

Consequently, Schleiermacher's conception of the highest good stands in sharp contrast to Kant's. The first part of the chapter examines Schleiermacher's early critique of Kant's understanding of the highest good. This analysis sheds light on his later critique of Kant, especially as Schleiermacher developed it in his *Outline of a Critique of Previous Ethical Theories* (1803). Whereas a fundamental bifurcation between reason and nature pervades all of Kant's philosophy, Schleiermacher held that if human nature as it appears in this world is to be ensouled, it must be possible for the sensuously conditioned desires to be infused with ethical content.

In Chapter 6 "Individual and Community," I outline Schleiermacher's vision of how human nature is to be ensouled through reason. Here I focus on Schleiermacher's positive conception and valuation of embodied, finite individuality as the fundamental building block of community. I provide an analysis of Schleiermacher's understanding of embodied individuality, the finite and perspectival character of all human knowledge that issues from such a standpoint, and the character of community, established through dialogue, as that through which finite standpoints can be enlarged to include the perspective of others and of other groups. For Schleiermacher it is through the establishment of community that human nature is ensouled.

The way that a person's relation to one historical individual and the community founded by him can be the occasion for the transformation of the self through the mediation of the divine love is the subject of Chapter 7, "Transforming the Self through Christ." Schleiermacher's claim that it is through the work of Christ in transforming ethical outlooks that the God-consciousness is freed is certainly a theological one. Nevertheless, bolstering the claim are fundamental presuppositions regarding the nature of Christ's God-consciousness, as well as an understanding of how the self-consciousness of one individual can transform the self-consciousness of others, a view rooted in Schleiermacher's ethical theory. This chapter offers an examination of a claim central to Schleiermacher's Christian philosophy and theology, namely that Christ's activity is a *person forming* activity through which selves are ethically transformed.

My last chapter, "Outpourings of the Inner Fire," explores the significance of Schleiermacher's understanding of the moral transformation of the self in regard to a contemporary problem in the philosophy of religion, namely, that of religious pluralism. Through an analysis of arguments found in *On Religion* (especially the third edition of 1821) as well as in the *Christian Faith* (second edition 1830–1), I first argue that Schleiermacher's theory of religion offers a generally coherent account of how it is possible that differing religious traditions are all based on the same experience of the absolute. A significant problem facing the religious pluralist, however, is how to distinguish between genuine and illusory religious experience. I show how Schleiermacher's theory offers clear criteria for making such judgments. Since the immediate self-consciousness, the locus of the self's relation to the divine, also stands in relation to the moments of the sensuous self consciousness, it is the character of this relation between the immediate, transcendental self-consciousness and the moments of the sensuous self consciousness that determines how the world is understood, valued, and felt. Consequently for Schleiermacher the test of true piety lies not in the orthodox character of a person's beliefs, but in how the person views and values the world and others around him or her, and in the actions that issue from these ways of taking the world. While it may be impossible to achieve a universal theology, we may yet come to a consensus regarding a *universal practice* and the experience that attends it.

Despite the importance of Schleiermacher's ethical theory, it has received little attention in the English-speaking world.[9] Richard R. Niebuhr's *Schleiermacher on Christ and Religion: A New Introduction*[10] called attention to Schleiermacher's understanding of the *person-forming* activity of Christ. However, the book is more concerned with Schleiermacher's theology and does not offer a systematic analysis of the relation of Schleiermacher's philosophy of religion and

---

[9] This is partly due to the fact that many of Schleiermacher's most significant writings on ethics have only recently been translated into English, or are yet to be translated. His *Outline of a Critique of Previous Ethical Systems* remains untranslated. Furthermore, Brent Sockness has called attention to the "unfinished and initially unpublished character of Schleiermacher's mature work in the philosophical disciplines." He notes that "aside from the Academy addresses, which were printed in a relatively obscure organ of the Prussian Academy of Sciences, the *Grundlinien einer Kritik der bisherigen Sittenlehre* was the only major philosophical work of Schleiermacher to be published during his lifetime. Consequently, his initial philosophical impact occurred almost exclusively via his lectures at the university"; Sockness, "The Forgotten Moralist: Friedrich Schleiermacher and the Science of Spirit," 326.

[10] Richard R. Niebuhr, *Schleiermacher on Christ and Religion: A New Introduction*.

theology to his ethics. Another book concerned with Schleiermacher's ethics is Albert Blackwell's *Schleiermacher's Early Philosophy of Life: Determinism, Freedom, Phantasy.*[11] This book focuses on the early Schleiermacher, but does not offer an account of how his early ethics relate to his more mature views, or how these hook up with his philosophy and theology. Other English speaking treatments are limited to journal articles.[12] My own book is intended as a corrective to this neglect; it is my hope that both philosophers and theologians will come to recognize the importance of Schleiermacher's oeuvre.

---

[11] Albert Blackwell, *Schleiermacher's Early Philosophy of Life: Determinism, Freedom, Phantasy.*

[12] Three of the most significant treatments in journal articles are by Brent Sockness and have appeared quite recently. These are: "Was Schleiermacher a Virtue Ethicist? *Tugend* and *Bildung* in the Early Ethical Writings" and "The Forgotten Moralist: Friedrich Schleiermacher and the Science of Spirit." In the latter essay Sockness details the reception of Schleiermacher's ethics in both Germany and in the English-speaking world. In his article "Schleiermacher and the Ethics of Authenticity," Sockness argues that Schleiermacher is not successful in fusing his transcendental turn with his ethics of authenticity. This study will show that Schleiermacher was in fact quite successful in uniting both themes, especially when his ethics are understood in relation to his philosophy of religion. An excellent description of the development of Schleiermacher's ethics is Frederick Beiser's "Schleiermacher's Ethics," in the *Cambridge Companion to Schleiermacher*. Other significant English language treatments of Schleiermacher's ethics appearing in journal articles include Julia Lamm, "The Early Philosophical Roots of Schleiermacher's Notion of Gefühl, 1788–1794," and a series of essays by John Crossley, including his "Schleiermacher's Christian Ethics in Relation to his Philosophical Ethics."

1

The Philosopher's Stone

In this chapter I will focus on the development of the early Schleiermacher's ethical theory. At this early stage, we find Schleiermacher working on issues closely related to a problem that would continually preoccupy him throughout his life, namely, the question of the ground of the unity of the personality. As I demonstrate in this study, Schleiermacher's answer to the question evolved over the years. By the time he had produced the first edition of the *Christian Faith* appearing in 1821–2, it had already achieved its definitive contours. But Schleiermacher arrived at the position that he did through a sustained reflection on foundational metaethical issues. He did so by engaging the philosophies of figures such as Spinoza, Leibniz, Kant, Jacobi, Schelling, and Fichte. Two of the greatest influences on Schleiermacher's thought, I will argue, are Kant and Leibniz.[1] In this chapter I discuss how Schleiermacher's early ethics were shaped by his attempt to deal with the problems raised by Kant's understanding of transcendental freedom. In particular, we here find Schleiermacher concerned with the problems that positing transcendental freedom poses to the unity of the personality.

In his ethics Kant distinguishes between the moral principle of discrimination (*principium diiudicationis*) and the moral principle of execution (*principium executionis*). The former has to do with ethical judgment—how we decide that an action is right or wrong, and the latter with what *moves* us to do the right thing. It is a fundamental

---

[1] In his February 2, 1790 letter to Brinkman, Schleiermacher writes that his "belief in this [Kant's] philosophy increases day by day, and this all the more, the more I compare it with that of Leibniz" (*KGA* V.1, no. 134, 191). While Kant is certainly a leading influence, so is Leibniz. As I will show later in the book, Schleiermacher's mature position is one that imposes a Kantian turn on Leibnizian ideas.

feature of Kant's critical ethics that he considered the two to be intrinsically intertwined: the moral principle of discrimination, i.e. the categorical imperative, can only be valid if we are transcendentally free. As a *rational*, and thereby a universal and *a priori* practical principle, its bindingness cannot depend on any empirically given desires. This, however, implies that a purely rational principle can be an incentive for the will. Kant himself was deeply perplexed about how this could be possible, calling the difficulties occasioned by such an idea "the philosopher's stone."

The early Schleiermacher, on the other hand, while sympathetic to Kant's project, became increasingly dissatisfied with some of the deep philosophical problems posed by the notion of transcendental freedom. How do we connect a transcendentally free act with the nature of the subject? Insofar as the act is transcendentally free, it cannot be understood in terms of causes, and this means that it cannot be connected with the previous state of the individual before he or she engaged in the act. Insofar as this is the case, the act is given *ex nihilo* and cannot be connected with an agent's character. Given the intractability of this problem, Schleiermacher wanted to preserve Kant's understanding of the moral principle of discrimination as a rational principle while denying that the moral principle of execution is not connected with feeling and with the character of the agent. Hence the ground of an action must be found in the totality of an agent's representations, that is, how a person understands a situation is a crucial factor in the determination of how that person will act. Since a person's character is intricately involved with how a person assesses a situation, this move allows Schleiermacher to connect the ground of an action with character.

In this chapter, I work through these ideas by taking a thorough look at some of Schleiermacher's early essays and reviews. My main focus will be Schleiermacher's early essay *On Freedom*, written between 1790–2. I will, however, also be taking a look at Schleiermacher's notes on Kant's second *Critique* (1789), the third of his *Dialogues on Freedom* (1789) and his critical review of Kant's *Anthropology from a Pragmatic Point of View* (1799). While other treatments have detailed Schleiermacher's arguments and disagreements with Kant as set out in these works, they have not paid sufficient attention to the *development* of Schleiermacher's views regarding these questions. Whereas many of Schleiermacher's contemporary commentators understand *On Freedom* as standing in fundamental continuity with his earlier treatments of Kant's moral philosophy[2] I will argue that Schleiermacher's *On Freedom* is not only the most mature, but also the most Kantian of Schleiermacher's early ethical writings. Reflection on many of the issues regarding freedom and morality led him to reject empiricism as a foundation for morals, thereby bringing him closer to Kant. It is no doubt true that significant differences between Kant's theory and his own still remained. However, it is important to locate precisely at what point it is that Schleiermacher disagreed with Kant in *On Freedom*. His disagreement with Kant at this point is a different and more subtle one than that expressed in his earlier writings; for one, by this time the philosophy of moral sense no longer had the same influence that it once had on Schleiermacher's thought.[3] Rather, here we find Schleiermacher

[2] In his book *Deterministische Ethik und kritische Theologie*, Günter Meckenstock notes that Schleiermacher's intention is to make Kant's practical philosophy more consistent (50). However, after detailing the deep differences between Kant's practical philosophy and the variety of moral sense philosophy espoused by Schleiermacher in the *Freiheitsgespräch*, he goes on to note that Schleiermacher's task in *On Freedom* is to fill out the outlines of the theory sketched in the "Notes on Kant" and in the *Freiheitsgespräch* (51). In her article "The Early Philosophical Roots of Schleiermacher's Notion of Gefühl, 1788–1794" Julia A. Lamm reads *On Freedom* as continuing the "trajectory begun in *On the Highest Good*" (82), interpreting it as developing an understanding of *Gefühl* in which it is presented as "the faculty that not only harmonizes the moral sentiments but also enables us to transcend certain sentiments in order to attain higher ones" (89); I have not found evidence for this reading in the text. Albert Blackwell's book *Schleiermacher's Early Philosophy of Life: Determinism, Freedom and Phantasy,* presents Schleiermacher as denying the possibility of the *direct* influence of reason on the will in *On Freedom* (44), thereby understanding the essay as standing in direct continuity with his earlier works. Another fine essay in which *On Freedom* is discussed at some length is John P. Crossley's "The Ethical Impulse in Schleiermacher's Early Ethics," although the specific issue with which I am concerned is not addressed in it.

[3] As pointed out by John Wallhauser in his article "Schleiermacher's Critique of Ethical Reason: Toward a Systematic Ethic," by the time Schleiermacher writes his *Outlines of a Critique of Previous Ethical Theories* (published 1803), he clearly rejects the more recent English and French moral philosophy as belonging to traditions of feeling (29). The problem with this tradition, as with other eudaimonistic theories, is "its failure to draw a clear line between the ethical and the natural (reason and nature); it tends to collapse the ethical into a description of natural impulses rather than positing a distinct sphere and power of its own (reason/spirit)" (30).

performing a subtle about face concerning the issue of whether reason can influence the will, one that will lead him notably closer to Kant's views.

The chapter will be divided into three parts. In the first part, I will discuss why Kant asserts that reason can, in fact, pose as an incentive to the will as well as the nature of the deep philosophical problems that this idea has posed. In the second part I will discuss Schleiermacher's attempt to circumvent some of these difficulties. Here I discuss both of his earlier, more naive treatments of the problem dating from 1789, as well as his rather sophisticated attempt to provide us with what seems, at first blush, to be a more palatable, compatibilist account of freedom, one which nonetheless seems to cohere with the main outlines of a Kantian ethic found in his more mature treatise *On Freedom*. The third section will provide a philosophical assessment of Kant's and Schleiermacher's respective positions, analyzing both their strengths and weaknesses.

THE STUMBLING BLOCK [*STEIN DES ANSTOßES*] OF ALL EMPIRICISTS

It is a well-known fact that in his fully critical ethics Kant came to the conclusion that a moral law binding all rational agents implies transcendental freedom. This is a "thick" concept of freedom that must be understood in a strictly incompatibilist or indeterminist sense. It implies "a power of absolutely beginning a state, and therefore also of absolutely beginning a series of consequences of that state."[4] An "absolute beginning" is one that is not preceded by another temporal state that *determines* it and is as such independent from all determining causes. Kant himself was aware of many of the difficulties that such a conception posed and called it "the stumbling block [*Stein des Anstoßes*] of all empiricists but the key to the most sublime practical

---

[4] Immanuel Kant, *Critique of Pure Reason*. References to the *Critique of Pure Reason* are to the standard A and B paginations of the first and second editions and will henceforth be included in the body of the chapter preceded by *KRV*. In this case the reference would appear as *KRV* A445/B473.

principles for critical moralists"[5] In his notes on Kant's second *Critique* as well as in his essay *On Freedom*, Schleiermacher details many of these difficulties and tries to offer an alternative account of how a rationalistic ethic can co-exist with a compatibilist account of freedom. Before we can understand both the difficulties and the ingenuity of Schleiermacher's attempts at a solution, however, it is important to understand the depth of the problem as Kant himself did.

While the semi-critical Kant believed that the principle of discrimination through which the moral law is determined is purely intellectual and *a priori*, at this stage he did not think that such an intellectual principle could pose as a moral incentive [*Triebfeder*] to the will. In his *Lectures on Ethics*, dating from 1775 to 1780, Kant noted that

Moral feeling is the capacity to be affected by a moral judgment. My understanding may judge that an action is morally good, but it need not follow that I shall do that action which I judge morally good: from understanding to performance is still a far cry ... The understanding, obviously, can judge, but to give to this judgment of the understanding a compelling force, to make it an incentive that can move the will to perform the action—this is the philosopher's stone.[6]

A little later Kant notes, "Man is not so delicately made that he can be moved by objective grounds."[7]

In his critical ethics, however, Kant came to the conclusion that the possibility of being moved by objective grounds (the moral law) carries with it the implication of transcendental freedom. The critical Kant came to this conclusion because the very idea of a moral principle that is *necessarily* binding implies that its bindingness cannot depend on any empirically given desires. The validity of a hypothetical imperative lies in a preceding desire for an object, that is, *only* given a particular desire to achieve a certain goal is the will

---

[5] Immanuel Kant, *Critique of Practical Reason*. All future references to Kant's second *Critique* will be cited in the body of the text itself. They will be indicated by *KprV*, followed by the Berlin Academy Edition volume number and pagination; reference to Beck's English translation will follow a semicolon. In this case the references would appear as *KprV* 5:7; 8.

[6] Immanuel Kant, *Lectures on Ethics*, 45.   [7] Ibid. 68.

necessitated to perform certain actions in order to accomplish it. The rule given through such an imperative is only hypothetically necessary, and this implies that any kind of rule for the will based on a preceding desire cannot necessitate the will categorically. This means, however, that the *bindingness* of a categorical imperative cannot depend on any empirically given desires. According to Kant, this in turn implies transcendental freedom, for the moral law can only be binding upon us if it can move us to action, but insofar as it is *categorical* it can bind us only insofar as a previously existing desire *is not* the ground of the incentive. The incentive must, rather, be grounded in reason, and insofar as reason is itself a product of our spontaneity, such an incentive is intricately involved with the power of absolutely beginning a series of actions, and hence with transcendental freedom.

The two most profound difficulties raised by Kant's scheme have to do with a) how a purely intellectual principle can motivate the will and with b) the problem of transcendental freedom. Kant recognized both the intractable nature of the two problems, as well as their intrinsic connection when he noted, "how a law in itself can be the direct motive of the will (which is the essence of morality) is an insoluble problem for the human reason. It is identical with the problem of how a free will is possible" (*KprV* 5: 72; 75). Schleiermacher's notes on Kant's second *Critique* are principally directed to coming to terms with precisely these two difficulties. We should keep in mind that these notes are Schleiermacher's earliest attempt to come to grips with these issues, and are subsequently beset with incongruities overcome in his later reflections.

In his notes on Kant's second *Critique* Schleiermacher expresses dissatisfaction with Kant's account of respect for the moral law, the locus of Kant's discussion of how a purely intellectual principle can motivate the will. In his second *Critique* Kant had explained that the moral law checks self love and *strikes* down self conceit (*KprV* 5: 73; 76); furthermore, respect "weakens the hindering influence of the inclinations through humiliating self-conceit; consequently, we must see it as a subjective ground of activity, as an incentive for obedience to the law" (*KprV* 5: 38; 40). Schleiermacher complains that Kant's account still fails to provide an explanation for the *genesis* of the feeling connected to the influence of the moral law: "Only a negative feeling originates directly from the relation of practical reason to self-conceit, and if one says everything that one possibly can about an inhibition of the causality of a pathologically driven feeling...it is still, however, not an incentive."[8] Furthermore, Schleiermacher adds that

> it seems to me that he [Kant] did not achieve this either [clarifying the genesis of a feeling *a priori*], for even if I understand that practical reason must occasion an effect on feeling, all that I can understand by this "a priori"...is first only an indirect effect in that certain ideas, which would otherwise encourage the feeling, are destroyed; second, only negative in that what was otherwise present in feeling through those ideas is annulled; third, no particular distinct feeling...How the positive can be understood *a priori* is still left as empty as before, as is the claim that this feeling distinguishes itself from all other.[9]

Schleiermacher is correct to note that Kant's account provides for only an indirect influence of the moral law on feeling: in checking self love and striking down self conceit it blocks the effect of these pathologically motivated feelings and thereby strengthens the moral incentive. These are, however, already *effects* of the moral law on previously existing feelings, and while an explanation of these effects on these pre-existing feelings may help to illuminate certain psychological processes, it still affords us insight neither into the nature of the incentive directly connected with the moral law nor into how such an incentive is possible. In other words, while Kant may have provided us with an account of the *effect* that the moral law has on an individual when s/he recognizes its absolute worth, he still has not explained how a person can recognize such absolute worth in the moral law to begin with. The explanation of how practical reason occasions an effect on feeling is left just as obscure as before, and no

---

[8] "Notizen zu Kant: *KpV*" in *Schleiermacher Kritische Gesamtausgabe, Jugend-schriften 1787–1796*, 132; henceforward *KGA* I.1. All English excerpts from Schleiermacher's notes on Kant's second *Critique*, as well as Schleiermacher's "Note on the Knowledge of Freedom" and his "Review of Kant's *Anthropology from a Practical Point of View*" are my own translations. The translated texts can be found in their entirety in my "A Critical-Interpretive Analysis of Some Early Writings by Schleiermacher on Kant's Views of Human Nature and Freedom (1789–1799) with Translated Texts."

[9] *KGA* I.1, 133.

real explanation is given as to how we can understand the genesis of a feeling *a priori*.

It is important to grasp the deep structure of the difficulty concerning how a purely intellectual principle can become a motivating ground of the will. In order for the moral law to motivate us it must affect the faculty of desire in some way, and this involves feeling.[10] The problem becomes particularly acute since feeling has to do with our sensuous nature, and thereby with our receptivity, that is, our capacity for being affected from without. The understanding, on the other hand, is spontaneous. Spontaneity and receptivity are, according to Kant, two distinct faculties of human nature. How can feeling be affected by the moral law (a purely intellectual principle)? In order for it to be so affected there must be some capacity in our very faculty of *receptivity* that already allows that faculty to *recognize* the *unconditioned* worth of the moral law, but this already involves a judgment of the understanding. This would imply that the faculty of *receptivity* is itself somehow capable of true judgment, which is impossible. The problem thereby seems to be intractable. It can be understood from yet another angle. The judgment of the unconditioned worth of the moral law presupposed by such an incentive has

---

[10] In his book *Schleiermacher's Early Philosophy of Life: Determinism, Freedom and Phantasy*, Albert Blackwell represents Kant's understanding of the moral incentive as follows: "Incentives involve feelings, and yet, if moral obligation is not to be undermined, the means of influence of the moral law cannot involve feeling 'of any kind whatsoever' " (29). Later on he notes "unlike Kant and Reinhold, Schleiermacher never speaks of the influence of reason on the will as being 'direct.' The influence of reason upon our intentions is by means of incentives, and the incentives of reason, like all other incentives, involve feelings"(44). This is a somewhat misleading presentation, both of Kant and of Schleiermacher's understanding of him, since Kant never asserts that reason cannot influence feeling; in fact, the whole section entitled "On the Drives of Pure Practical Reason" in the second *Critique* concerns precisely how reason does influence feeling. For instance, Kant notes "Whatever checks all inclinations in self-love necessarily has, by that fact, an influence on feeling. Thus we conceive how it is possible to understand a priori that the moral law can exercise an effect on feeling since it blocks the inclinations ... " *KprV* 5: 75; 78. When Kant speaks of the influence of reason on the will as being direct, he does not mean that it does not have an influence on our affective nature; in fact, it must, if reason is to be an incentive. What Kant does mean is that no pre-existing feeling can be the ground or the basis of the validity of the moral law; if it were, the law would be reduced to a hypothetical imperative. As can be seen from my discussion of Schleiermacher's *On Freedom*, below, by the time that Schleiermacher writes this treatise he is fully in agreement with Kant's reasoning regarding this issue.

two components. Insofar as we stress the *absolute and unconditioned* worth of the moral law, we must rely on reason for the judgment of its unconditioned character. However, insofar as we stress the *worth* of the moral law, we are concerned with a question of value, and hence with the subject and his or her attitudes or feelings, since the assignment of worth cannot be defined in purely logical or rational terms. Hence the question becomes: how can the rational principle itself be the *ground* of the absolute *worth* that the moral subject must assign to it? [11]

In the "Notes" we find Schleiermacher attempting to come to grips with this problem. While he agrees with Kant that the moral law cannot be empirically grounded, he questions whether making feeling indispensable to the determination of the faculty of desire necessarily results in an empirically grounded practical principle. He believes that he can show that the implication is not an inevitable one, arguing that the ethical principle of discrimination (*principium diiudicationis*) can be separated from the ground of moral motivation (*principium executionis*). The key here, according to Schleiermacher, is not to equate the determination of the faculty of desire with the giving of rules for the will, two elements closely connected in Kant's practical philosophy. Schleiermacher does not consider Kant justified in having linked the two: he complains that Kant has shown neither that they are analytically nor synthetically combined.

It is here that Schleiermacher's analysis of the inadequacy of Kant's theory of non-moral motivation comes in. This theory specifies that the faculty of desire is empirically determined when pleasure is what *marks* an object as worthy of desire. Yet if *pleasure* is that which marks an object as worthy of desire, the pleasure gotten from the realization of the object, and not the object itself, is the final goal

---

[11] Much the same is noted by Dieter Henrich in his article, "Das Problem der Grundlegung der Ethik bei Kant und in Spekulativen Idealismus." There he notes that "Die Vernunft für sich allein hat keine Kraft 'eine Handlung zu exekutieren'. Selbst die Billigung (*complacentia*), die wir dem Guten zollen, ist kein in der Logik zu definierender Akt. Sie ist wie jene emotionaler Natur. So scheint eine *Antinomie* zu bestehen, die zu lösen den Stein des Weisen ausgraben heißt: Entweder die Ethik wahrt den rationalen Charakter der sittlichen Forderung; dann sind die Triebfeder des sittlichen Willens nicht verständlich zu machen. Oder sie geht von der Sittlichkeit als einer Kraft zu handeln aus; dann is der Vernunftcharakter des Guten nicht zu wahren." 369.

of non-morally motivated action. But Schleiermacher remarks that there is something wrong in thinking that pleasure, rather than the realization of a desired *object*, is the goal of non-moral motivation. The correct understanding of the relation between satisfaction and desire is that the realization of an object brings satisfaction *because* it is desired.

Schleiermacher thereby argues that Kant could only have shown that the determination of the faculty of desire was synthetically combined with the giving of rules for the will on the presupposition that "the feeling, which is necessary in order to set the faculty of desire in motion is also the only possible end to which the desire itself could be directed."[12] He reasons that if the feeling of pleasure is not the end to which an empirically given desire is directed, then feeling can motivate without at the same time determining the rules of action for the will. At this point it is important to recall the Kantian analysis of the lower faculty of desire and its relation to heteronomous action. An object is desired because its realization will bring pleasure, and reason figures out the means for the realization of the object. However, because it is desire that marks out the object to be realized in the first place, desire is the ground of the rule for the will; reason is only instrumental in providing the rule through which the object of desire can be achieved. Schleiermacher concludes that if pleasure is not the final goal of non-moral action, the lower faculty of desire cannot be the ground of any rules for the will. Kant's linkage between the principle of execution and that of discrimination has been thereby effectively severed.

What Schleiermacher has accomplished here, however, remains rather questionable. Given this account, Schleiermacher is still faced with the task of providing an account of how an *object* of desire relates to the emotional character of the agent, that is, of how it is that the object of desire comes to be desired. More importantly, his argument here seems to be at cross-purposes with his initial goal, which was to ground the moral incentive in feeling or moral sense. Such a theory holds that the worth that the moral law has for us is based on the satisfaction that is associated with acting on it, on the one hand, and the pangs of conscience linked with failing to live

---

[12] "Notizen zu Kant: *KpV*" *KGA* I.1, 131.

up to it, on the other. But if, as Schleiermacher seems to want to be arguing here, an object is not desired in virtue of the pleasure it will bring, presumably then acting morally cannot be attractive to us because of the satisfaction that is associated with acting on the moral law, either.

SCHLEIERMACHER'S COMPATIBILIST PROPOSAL

In the third of his *Dialogues on Freedom* (1789) Schleiermacher attempts to forge a middle position between Kant's understanding of respect for the moral law and a theory of moral sensibility. The dialogue involves three friends, the Kantian Kritias, Sophron, whose position represents Schleiermacher's, and Kleon. Towards the latter part of the dialogue Sophron reminds Kleon that their intention in discussing these matters was to determine the extent to which reason influences our actions, and concludes that "we have found nothing but that such an influence can nowhere take place, and that moreover all our actions flow from the feeling of pleasure and the attempt to get it."[13] He proceeds to outline a theory of moral sensibility wherein experience is a key component in allowing us to determine which actions will bring us pleasure and which will bring us pain. It is experience that "acquaints us with the different powers of our soul; it is that which informs us of the nature of our pleasure and that it is only harmony and perfection that can delight us" (*KGA* I.1, 155). The imagination works with this data, thereby giving us a foretaste of virtue.

Sophron later qualifies his original statement that the influence of reason on our actions can nowhere take place: insofar as we find pleasure in virtue, reason *can* influence the will. Hence he notes that "the capacity to act according to rational grounds means nothing other than the capacity to be determined by a feeling of pleasure that works through the moral ideas of reason" (*KGA* I.1, 160). He continues by noting that this "pleasure is completely sensory; it has a

---

[13] "Freiheitsgespräch," *KGA* I.1, 153; future references to the text will be included in the body of the chapter. All excerpts are my own translations.

sensory magnitude and a sensory effectiveness, although it is caused by an object in which nothing sensory is to be found, namely the eternal and unchangeable laws of reason" (*KGA* I.1, 160). Despite the fact that Schleiermacher here concedes that reason can have an influence on the will, the crux of the matter is that it can have such an influence in virtue of a pre-existing disposition to find pleasure in the moral law. At this point Schleiermacher has not grasped the intrinsic interconnections between the principle of discrimination and that of execution discovered by the critical Kant: if the latter is empirically grounded, that is, is dependent on a given condition or susceptibility of the subject, then so is the former. It is impossible to be moved by a practical principle in virtue of pre-existing susceptibilities to find pleasure in such a principle, and to at one and the same time identify the underlying maxim on which one is acting with eternal and unchanging laws of reason. This is because if one is moved to act in accordance with a practical principle because it brings one pleasure, the maxim underlying one's action to act on the practical principle is that of maximizing one's own happiness or pleasure, a merely subjective principle which could never qualify as a universal law.

Another significant feature of Schleiermacher's account in the third of the dialogues is his attempt to provide a detailed analysis of the psychological conditions of the possibility of moral motivation. Thus he makes the observation that while reason does play a role in moral motivation, it is not the only factor involved. He notes that

we therefore cannot maintain that this feeling is determined by pure reason alone (which indeed is always unaltered and the same) but must affirm rather that it is determined by the receptivity of the faculty of sensation [*des Empfindungsvermögens*] to being affected by the representation of the moral law. This receptivity is dependent upon other conditions each time.[14]

(*KGA* I.1, 163)

Insofar as feeling is involved, it depends on the receptivity of the faculty of sensation. This receptivity is not, however, a given constant, and is not always affected in the same way by the moral law.

---

[14] Quoted from Albert Blackwell's introduction to Schleiermacher's *On Freedom*, xv.

How it is affected by the moral law depends upon at least two factors: (1) the strength with which the moral law is represented and (2) other factors, such as previously existing emotions, wants, wishes and desires, which may interfere with or enhance the impact that the moral law has on the faculty of sensation. For example, if an individual is overly preoccupied with professional advancement, and is considering acting on an immoral maxim, this preoccupation may be so strong that it overpowers the effect that the moral law has on feeling. The effect of his/her prior preoccupation on feeling may be so strong that it overtakes that faculty altogether, leaving little possibility for it to be affected by the moral law. The moral law may thereby fail to be an incentive for the will.

The story Schleiermacher offers here has some similarities to the one he will offer in his longer treatise *On Freedom*. Both are intended to show how an account of moral motivation can be fully integrated with an account of a person's character. There are, however, some significant differences between the story offered in the third dialogue and the one offered in *On Freedom*; the former seems almost primitive compared to the more robust theory offered in the latter treatise. The *Freiheitsgespräch* portrays an individual's desires as having an effect on his/her total emotive constitution; this prior determination of feeling limits the effect that a given representation can have on feeling and thereby serves to determine the person's future desires. For example, my desire for more money may be connected with a particular dissatisfaction concerning my present state as well as with a feeling of heady excitement given the prospect of a viable get-rich-quick scheme. These pre-existing feelings may in turn determine how much I will dwell upon other representations, for instance the idea of enjoying my present situation and time with my husband. I may be so overwhelmed with dissatisfaction that I am not a millionaire, and so dizzy with the emotion that the idea of a future possibility of wealth evokes in me that I cannot dwell upon the idea of enjoying what is presently within my grasp. Given my prior emotional state, the representation of what is presently enjoyable cannot make a deep enough impression on me, for it simply cannot hold my interest, nor can it change my present feelings. Note that this amounts to a strict determination of action by desire, or a strict determination of future desires by past desires.

In contrast, Schleiermacher's account of moral motivation in *On Freedom* is much more sophisticated. In fact, a reader of the first part of the treatise would be struck by its almost thoroughly Kantian character. How far Schleiermacher's views have swung in a Kantian direction in the first section of *On Freedom*, particularly as compared with the position espoused in the notes on Kant's second *Critique* as well as in the *Freiheitsgespräch*, can be gauged by his avowal that the principle of discrimination cannot be effectively separated from the principle of execution. He notes that "reason becomes practical only through the idea of obligation to its laws,"[15] that is, "reason's dictums must be able to become objects of an impulse" (*KGA* I.1: 233; 18). He reasons further that

this must be true not simply to the extent that what reason commands happens to be in accord with some inclination, that is insofar as reason's dictums relate mediately to a sensible object, but rather precisely insofar as the dictums relate immediately to the law. That is, even if in some particular case the law's will should become actual through an accidental relation, the law has no influence on the faculty of desire, and so this relation cannot establish the idea that it is possible in every case to realize the command of reason. This involves a feeling, and thereby an impulse, which relates immediately and exclusively to practical reason and at the same time represents practical reason in the faculty of desire.   (*KGA* I.1: 233; 18)

In other words, the moral law must itself be a motive for the will.[16] His argument for the claim accords with Kant's: if the moral law were not able to pose as an incentive to the will, the coincidence of one's maxims with the moral law would be merely accidental. Furthermore, under such a scenario, whatever one's practical principle, it cannot

---

[15] *On Freedom*, trans. by Albert L. Blackwell. The German can be found in *KGA* I.1, 219–356. Future references to the text will be included in the body of the chapter. I first provide the KGA pagination; reference to Blackwell's English translation will follow a semicolon. In this case the reference would appear as *KGA* I.1 232; 17.

[16] Note that Schleiermacher's claim regarding the need for the immediacy of the relation of practical principles or "dictums" to the moral law is in principle equivalent to Kant's claim that "what is essential in the moral worth of actions is that the moral law should determine the will directly" *KprV* 5: 71; 75. This is in fact the opposite of the position he espoused in *On the Highest Good*, where he noted that "the law of reason can never determine our will immediately" ("Über das höchste Gut," in *KGA* I.1, 123). Blackwell is mistaken when he claims that one of Schleiermacher's main points in *On Freedom* is to criticize Kant's idea that an *a priori* practical principle can directly influence the will. Blackwell, 29ff.

be a categorical imperative. What would really be driving an action would be some presupposed end, and this means that moral requirements would be treated as hypothetical imperatives instead of as intrinsically obligatory.[17] In such a situation a categorical imperative *as such* would have no influence on the will, and while one's maxims might accord with legality they would not be *moral*. In order for the categorical imperative to be the principle that is in fact guiding one's will it must in fact be chosen as such. In order for it to be chosen, however, it must be able to be deemed a principle *worth* acting on, and as such it must be able to pose as an incentive to the will.

What makes this work more sophisticated than the third of his *Dialogues on Freedom*, however, is Schleiermacher's distinction between *choice* and *instinct*, and what he does with it. In the first part of the treatise Schleiermacher tells us that "insofar as impulse to some particular activity can be determined by a single object alone, the faculty of desire is called *instinct*, but insofar as it arrives at some particular activity solely by comparing several objects it is called *choice*" (*KGA* I.1: 224; 8). Key here is the idea that in instinct a being's desire is "hard-wired" to a particular object or group of objects. There is no complex mechanism internal to the subject that allows for variation in desire. Thus Schleiermacher lists the following two characteristics of instinct: (1) "an action persists only until the determining object itself ceases, and (2) ... where instinct is present, desire follows immediately upon the appearance of the object, and the tendency toward action follows immediately upon desire" (*KGA* I.1: 224; 9). In such a case the organism is so constituted that the very appearance of the object elicits desire. Later on he notes that if external objects "were to include not only the basis for our being affected ... but also the basis for the preponderance necessary to every act of choice, then with every external object there would have to be given not only a general influence on the faculty of desire but also a determinate quality and quantity of this influence, not alterable by any inner characteristic of the subject" (*KGA* I.1: 235; 20). In contrast, choice involves a complexity of processes *internal* to the subject. The individual

---

[17] Henry Allison provides an insightful analysis of Kant's arguments regarding the issue in *Kant's Theory of Freedom*, 99–106.

that has choice is not hard-wired to desire any given thing; further, such a being can find value in several different things and compare their relative strengths. As such, the attraction that any given object effects upon the faculty of desire does not immediately occasion *desire* per se, but rather, "the object appears and the faculty of desire *craves*...the complete determination of impulse still remains suspended by consciousness of the necessity to take into account several determining grounds, and only when this has occurred does it *desire*" (*KGA* I.1: 226; 10). Hence the determinative feature of choice is the ability of the individual to postpone action and to weigh alternative options. This ability is possible because while an object may no doubt affect the will, it is yet not, of itself, sufficient to determine the will to action.[18]

The idea of choice, involving as it does several possible objects of desire, naturally elicits the question of what is going to ground the final determination of the faculty of desire one way or another. Schleiermacher carefully distinguishes the idea of *choice* from the idea that given *several objects of choice* the will is determined to act through the outcome of the *balance* of attractive and repulsive forces elicited by these objects. He notes that

if several simultaneously affecting objects partially annul their influence reciprocally, we could regard what remains as itself an object (since with respect to its influence it would be determined in only one way). This object's impression would be unalterable, and the faculty of desire would be absolutely determined to it.   (*KGA* I.1: 235–6; 20)

It is important to note that the "balance of forces" view that Schleiermacher rejects is more sophisticated than the naive notion that an agent simply acts on its strongest desire, since if action on one's strongest desire precludes a whole host of other options, the cumulative attraction of these other options may serve to outweigh the strength of one's strongest desire. Schleiermacher rejects this more sophisticated view because it presents the subject as simply being affected from without. In it *external* influences, whether

---

[18] So Schleiermacher: "Whenever our faculty of desire is affected from without, we are conscious that this is not yet sufficient to determine it, and every determination of impulse appears to us within the realm between craving and desiring" (*KGA* I.1: 227; 11).

they be the influence of a single object, or the influence of a balance of attractive and repulsive forces elicited by several objects, are represented as the ultimate determining ground of an individual's choice.

Given his observations on choice and instinct, Schleiermacher concludes that while the moral law can motivate, it cannot of itself be *sufficient* to determine the will. He arrives at this conclusion by first noting that a "natural undeterminedness of the will is necessary if that relation of the law to the faculty of desire entailed by the idea of obligation is to be possible" (*KGA* I.1: 233; 17), in other words the idea of obligation is inapplicable to a will that *necessarily* acts in accordance to the moral law.[19] Moreover, if acting in accordance with the moral law is truly to involve choice, the law cannot be sufficient to determine the will to action. The impulse or incentive provided by the moral law "must have exactly the same relation to the faculty of desire as every other"[20] (*KGA* I.1: 233; 18), and this means that just as other objects can be viewed as desirable without their desirability being a sufficient condition of their initiating action, so it is the same with the moral law. We must, in fact, hold this to be the case in order to make sense of how it is possible that persons can stand under an intrinsic moral obligation and yet fail to meet its demands.

Schleiermacher concludes that "no single object of our faculty of desire, whether internal or external . . . has a determinative influence,

[19] On this point he stands in fundamental agreement with Kant; see *Groundwork for the Metaphysics of Morals*, where Kant notes that "if reason for itself alone does not sufficiently determine the will, if the will is still subject to subjective conditions (to certain incentives) which do not always agree with the objective conditions, in a word, if the will is not *in itself* fully in accord with reason (as it actually is with human beings), then the actions which are objectively recognized as necessary are subjectively contingent, and the determination of such a will, in accord with objective laws, is *necessitation* . . . The representation of an objective principle, insofar as it is necessitating for a will, is called a 'command' (of reason), and the formula of the command is called an *imperative*"(*KGS* 4: 413; Wood, 29–30).

[20] My interpretation of what is going on is fundamentally at odds with that of Julia Lamm, who in her book *The Living God: Schleiermacher's Theological Appropriation of Spinoza*, argues that this idea "marks Schleiermacher's most rebellious stance against Kant" 45. To the contrary, as my discussion below of Kant's incorporation thesis will demonstrate, Schleiermacher is at this point in his argument still in fundamental agreement with Kant. It is only much later in his argument that the two positions will diverge.

invariable in all cases, either upon the faculty of desire in general or upon its particulars, so that the preponderance of impression requisite for any complete action of the faculty of desire cannot be grounded in such objects" (*KGA* I.1: 236; 21). If this is true, we are still confronted with Schleiermacher's question "Wherein must the origination of the preponderance of one portion of the determining ground of choice over other portions be grounded in each case?" (*KGA* I.1: 234; 19). In other words, Schleiermacher asks, if the attraction or repulsion that an object or its realization holds for us is not of itself sufficient to determine the will, then what, ultimately, is the ground of the will's acting on one desire rather than another? Schleiermacher answers that this ground must be found in our subjectivity; more precisely, the effect that an object of desire can have upon the will is determined by the way in which that object is *represented*. Hence Schleiermacher notes that "Even if in some particular case the preponderance of one impulse over others is based in such accidental determinations of the faculty of desire as have been produced through its preceding activities, these in turn have their first ground in the state of the faculty of representation ... " (*KGA* I.1: 237; 22). Note that this position is the exact opposite of the one espoused by Schleiermacher in his earlier third *Dialogue on Freedom;* there the impact made by a representation was limited and determined by preceding activities of the faculty of desire. Here the reverse is true; just how attractive a course of action is depends on how it is represented:

the preponderance in which every comparison of choice must end in order to pass over into a complete action of the faculty of desire must in every case be grounded in the totality of present representations and in the state and interrelations of all the soul's faculties that have been produced in the progression of representations in our soul.   (*KGA* I.1: 237–8; 22)

Which ideas will be associated with an external object, and which desires, in turn, will be connected with these ideas depends on our faculty of representation. For instance, our desire for an object may vary with what we know of it. Put before a hungry individual a sumptuous feast and she will of course desire it, but let her find out that it is poisoned and her desire will surely wane. Further, the desirability of an object is tied with how prominently it stands before consciousness. In some cases an individual may enable himself to forego a temptation by putting the offending object out of mind and concerning himself with other things. On the other hand, it is no doubt true that desire is often heightened by dwelling upon a coveted thing.

These and other related examples lead Schleiermacher to conclude that no object is itself the ground of its desirability or attractiveness to the will; rather it is desirable only insofar as it is represented as such, and this means that desire is always intrinsically connected with the representing activity of the subject. Because it is, there is "no degree of impulse, however great [that] can be conceived to which an impulse of higher degree cannot be juxtaposed" (*KGA* I.1: 239; 25). This is what Schleiermacher calls "the boundlessness of impulse" (*KGA* I.1: 239; 25). By this he means that since the attraction an option holds for us is always a function of how it is represented, no matter how great the inducement to do one thing, it is still possible to be moved to do the opposite. This is because the degree of attraction of the opposite course of action also rests upon how it is represented. Hence it is always in principle possible to follow the dictates of morality, no matter how great the temptation to do otherwise: even if some "sensible feeling is unduly elevated by my representations" yet "a series of representations is possible through which the feeling representing practical reason might be affected more strongly" (*KGA* I.1: 240; 25).

The similarities of Schleiermacher's argument to that of Kant's are deep and surprising. An important feature of Kant's practical philosophy is his claim that "freedom of the power of choice has the characteristic, entirely peculiar to it, that it cannot be determined to action through any incentive *except so far as the human being has incorporated it into his maxim*,"[21] that is, human freedom involves an activity of the subject through which an inclination or desire is deemed *worth* acting upon, or taken as a fitting ground of action. Henry Allison has dubbed this Kant's Incorporation Thesis and has rightly pointed to its pivotal place at the core of Kant's practical philosophy. A central implication of this claim is that an incentive

[21] Immanuel Kant, *Religion Within the Boundaries of Mere Reason*, (*KGS* 6: 24; Giovanni and Wood, 73).

or desire of itself is not a reason for action, and this means further that the adoption of a practical principle or a maxim is never a causal consequence of a person's being in a state of desire.[22] Schleiermacher's understanding of choice, involving as it does the assertion that while objects of desire may affect the will, they are not sufficient grounds for the determination of action, carries with it some of the same implications.

There are, however, some significant differences between Schleiermacher's position and Kant's. While Schleiermacher grounds the ultimate worth that a subject assigns to a particular course of action in the activity of the subject, and not in the causal consequences of one's being in a state of desire, he still wants to be able to link the subject's activity with its prior states. Noteworthy is the fact that Schleiermacher grounds the ultimate worth that a subject will assign to an object of desire in the faculty of representation, the present state of which can be connected with a subject's preceding states in a lawlike manner. The weight of the whole of Kant's incorporation thesis, on the other hand, rests on the *spontaneity* of the subject. Because a spontaneous action cannot be subjected to the principles of causal determination, the action cannot be grounded in the agent's prior states.[23]

It is at this point, then, that Kant and Schleiermacher part company. In positioning the sufficient ground of an action in a subject's representations, Schleiermacher has, through one and the same argument, come as close as he possibly could to Kant's practical philosophy while at the same time having laid the groundwork for his own psychological determinism. He thereby seems to have provided a "compatibilist" version of a Kantian practical philosophy and overcome the stumbling block of all empiricists.

---

[22] On this aspect of Kant's practical philosophy, see Allison's *Kant's Theory of Freedom*, especially 39–40, although the whole book is an extended argument concerning the importance of the incorporation thesis for Kant's theory of freedom.

[23] It is, however, significant that according to Kant in the *Religion*, the ground of an agent's actions can be traced to the fundamental disposition. We can thus connect the agent's action with his/her character, but *which* fundamental disposition the agent has chosen is still a matter of transcendental freedom.

KANT OR SCHLEIERMACHER?

Schleiermacher's compatibilist account of freedom and moral motivation has much to recommend it. For one, it allows us to understand our psychological processes in such a way that we can learn to steer the course of our desires. He notes that "if we must seek the basis for particular activities of the faculty of desire elsewhere than in the state and other activities of the soul, then the inquiries concerning our soul so natural to each of us are cut off at the root—inquiries concerning laws of the soul's various faculties . . . premises that would have been requisite to come to some certain result, and the result that certain premises would have produced" (*KGA* I.1: 240; 24–5). Later on he notes that "without this idea we could in no way justify our efforts to affect wills . . . " (*KGA* I.1: 242; 28). The validity of the idea that our present state is connected in a law-like manner with what precedes it, and that further, it is the ground of our future states, is connected with a certain practical interest: it allows for the care of the soul, that is, the nurturing of dispositions that in the future will bear moral fruit. On the other hand, the doctrine of the freedom of the will, through which one comes to think of oneself as instantly capable of realizing a moral goal without this involving a long and arduous training of one's character and dispositions is, according to Schleiermacher, self deceptive. The feeling of freedom hides from us the fact that "everything that yet lies between the present moment and the anticipated one, as a means or preceding links in the chain, really belongs to the attainment of that state" (*KGA* I.1: 294; 79). The idea that there is no ground determining our ability to reach a moral goal other than our very intention of realizing it (transcendental freedom) only lulls us into unconcern through the false certainty that such an intention is all that is required to achieve the proposed end. Such a certainty "always does its utmost to make us miss our goal" (*KGA* I.1: 294; 79). On the other hand the doctrine of necessity, through which we can connect previous states of the soul with future ones, allows us to understand how we may affect ourselves and others in such a way as to bring us closer to moral perfection; it allows for us to undertake a "therapy of desire." Key to such self-affection is the strengthening of the ethical impulse: whether it will be strong enough to overcome the opposing inclinations all depends upon the preceding period in which it was forged. Schleiermacher asks: " ... will the ethical impulse ... be strong enough to prevail over opposing inclinations?" and answers that necessity presents this as "depending upon the content of the intervening period—upon the strengthening or weakening of ethical feeling contained therein, upon the increasing or diminishing power therein of ethical impulse through action, both generally and in the particular respect under consideration" (*KGA* I.1: 295; 80). Necessity teaches that because prior moral states affect future ones, "You would have become so less (morally good) than perhaps you will, had you not so vitally desired it in advance" (*KGA* I.1: 295; 80).

Note all of this stands in agreement with a compatibilist understanding of freedom, according to which a person could have done otherwise, and is hence free, provided that he or she had had different sorts of desires. This understanding allows Schleiermacher to distinguish his own brand of determinism from fatalism. The idea behind the fatalism of Greek tragedy is that a given result will necessarily occur regardless of causal antecedents; Schleiermacher's determinism, on the other hand, propounds that given certain causal antecedents, a given result will necessarily follow. While the former principle is of no use to an investigation of the mechanism of desire and its consequences, the latter is indispensable to any kind of psychological insight, and hence to a therapy of desire.

Connected with Schleiermacher's practical criticisms of the idea of transcendental freedom is the fact that the conditions under which an act may be attributed to an agent give rise to a certain "antinomy of agency." This antinomy is closely related to Kant's third antinomy, developed in the first *Critique*.[24] Recall that the third antinomy concerns the possibility of appealing to another mode of causality beside that developed in the second analogy (causality in accordance with the laws of nature). The kind of causality in question is transcendental freedom, understood as "the power [Vermögen] of beginning a state spontaneously [von Selbst]" (*KRV* A533/B561). Since Schleiermacher's arguments take the side of the antithesis of this

---

[24] The connection of the antinomy of agency with the cosmological conflict is noted by Allison in *Kant's Theory of Freedom*, 28.

antinomy, let me begin with a short exposition of it as it is presented by Kant in the first *Critique* and later discuss its relevance to an understanding of the antinomy of agency.

The antithesis of the third antinomy is relatively straightforward. According to it, if we assume transcendental freedom (defined as "a power of absolutely beginning a state, and therefore absolutely beginning a series of the consequences of that state" [*KRV* A445/B473]), then the unity of experience would be rendered impossible. This is because every action "presupposes a state of the not-yet acting cause" (*KRV* A445/B473), that is, we must assume the existence of an agent before it initiates an action, and furthermore, this agent must exist in some given state. However, insofar as an action is transcendentally free, it would be an absolute beginning and as such in no wise grounded in the prior state of the agent. This means that the two states, that of an agent before the initiation of an action and that of the agent initiating the action could not be connected in a lawlike manner.

As Allison notes, while the recognizably Leibnizian argument of the antithesis concludes that if transcendental freedom were to be assumed the unity of experience would be annulled, it also supports the familiar compatibilist account of freedom also connected with Leibniz. Leibniz had argued that an action must have a sufficient reason grounded in the prior states of an agent; to deny this is to deny the conditions under which the act could intelligibly be attributed to that agent. The same point had already been made by Hume and other compatibilists, and Schleiermacher argues along the same lines in *On Freedom*. A condition of act attribution is that we should be able to relate an action to an agent and his or her character, that is, we must be able to understand how it flows from that character. If transcendental freedom is assumed, however, no such connection between the action and the character of the agent is possible. Schleiermacher asks, "How can I be accountable for an action when we cannot determine the extent to which it belongs to my soul?" (*KGA* I.1: 316; 100–1). Our ability to attribute the motive for an action to an agent depends on that action's being explicable in terms of an agent's character. Failing such a condition, the actions "have no ground at all, not even immediately, and are based on chance" (*KGA* I.1: 316; 101), which means they have nothing to do with the condition of the agent, that is, his or her psychological states and disposition. Schleiermacher concludes that this idea of "complete chance ... certainly annuls morality more than anything else" (*KGA* I.1: 317; 101).

The thesis of the third antinomy is also significant in that it relates in important ways to the conditions of the possibility of act attribution. The thesis of the antinomy stipulates that it is necessary to appeal to transcendental freedom, since without it mere causality in accordance with the laws of nature would be subject to two contradictory demands. These are, first, the principle that every event must have a cause and second, the principle of sufficient reason. The latter requirement is understood in the manner developed by Leibniz in his polemic with Clarke: every occurrence must have a sufficient reason both in the sense that it have antecedent causal conditions and in the sense that it have a complete explanation. As Allison puts it, it is understood as both a "logical principle requiring adequate grounds for any conclusion and as a real or causal principle requiring sufficient preconditions for every occurrence."[25] According to Kant, the law of nature itself demands that "nothing takes place without a cause sufficiently determined a priori" (*KRV* A446/B474). If, however, this very same law of nature requires us to understand every event as itself having a cause, then the requirement that a cause be sufficiently determined a priori cannot be met. Since each event will have its ground in a cause preceding it that is also an event and that is, as such, subject to the same requirement that it also be grounded in a preceding event, completeness in the series of grounds determining an event can never be given.

Now the problem encountered in the thesis of the third antinomy becomes relevant to the question of act attribution in that if the causality of nature is universally applied to actions, we would be unable to find a sufficiently determined ground of an action that is attributable to an agent per se. Instead, the grounds for each action can eventually be traced to events pre-existing the agent and so having nothing to do with him or her. Schleiermacher is at the very least aware of these difficulties when he puts the

---

[25] *Kant's Theory of Freedom*, 17.

following argument in the mouth of the opponents of his doctrine of necessity:

This resonance of the soul is in turn a product of preceding and occasioning impressions, and so, resist as we may, all is at last dissolved in external impressions. So, of all that belongs to the action, what can we then assign to the agent? Do we see the agent in some way? We can think of the agent only as suffering! Or where is the power that is active? It dissolves into infinitely many infinitesimally small external forces that leave us with nothing to think of as firmly active in the subject.   (*KGA* I.1: 257; 42–3)

The difficulty is a profound one: if we assume that all events are subject to causal law, it becomes hard to distinguish actions from events. Committing suicide by jumping off a ten-story window would be little different from being pushed by someone from behind in the significant sense that in both cases a pre-existing chain of events led to the disaster with inexorable necessity; in both cases the individual simply suffers what occurs to her. As Schleiermacher acutely notes, in such a scheme the individual functions as a mere placeholder for a given causal chain: s/he flashes "all the colors, but merely according to the laws of refraction. Of all that you see in the person's actions, nothing belongs to the person" (*KGA* I.1: 257; 43). Since the person does not initiate any action but is merely the locus in which a certain causal chain occurs, we cannot attribute the actions to her.

To summarize: the antinomy of agency suggests that act attribution is subject to two conflicting requirements. The first is that an act be explicable in terms of an agent's character; the second is that an agent should be the initiator of an act if it is to be attributed to him or her. While Schleiermacher obviously tries to meet the first requirement, it is unlikely that he succeeds in meeting the second. A simplistic understanding of the differences between Kant and Schleiermacher might suggest that while Schleiermacher decided to go with the first requirement and to accept his losses regarding the second, Kant did just the opposite. Kant's position is, however, much more complicated than this. He wants to hold that *both* the thesis and antithesis of the third antinomy are compatible, since transcendental idealism creates a logical space for the idea of transcendental freedom. It is important to realize that Kant's transcendental idealism is a way of—as Allen Wood puts it—demonstrating the "compatibility of compatibilism and incompatibilism."[26] Kant finds his way around this seemingly intractable antinomy through his affirmation that both points of view, i.e. the transcendental standpoint (corresponding to freedom) and the empirical standpoint (corresponding to determinism) are legitimate. Both freedom and determinism, however, can be attributed to the same subject only when in each case the attribution is made from a different standpoint.[27] Insofar as the subject is considered as appearance, determinism applies; insofar as the subject is considered in itself, freedom applies.

In his review of Kant's *Anthropology from a Pragmatic Point of View*, Schleiermacher raised serious questions about the viability of such an option, especially as regards the possibility of a pragmatic anthropology. How is one to affect oneself, to engage in any kind of therapy of desire or care of the soul if transcendental freedom is presupposed? If we speak of that which affects the mind, in the way that Kant does in his *Anthropology*, do we not then begin to treat the self as an appearance?[28] What then of freedom? From a practical perspective, Kant's two points of view are very difficult to keep separate. We often assume freedom when we think of ourselves as resolving to make a radical change in our lives, but it is often the case that in order for such a change to become a reality we must nurse our subsequent desires in certain directions, we must be equipped with certain psychological insights about ourselves that will facilitate change in these desires, and we must suffer

---

[26] Allen W. Wood, "Kant's Compatibilism," see especially 99–101.

[27] In the *Critique of Practical Reason*, Kant notes: "The union of causality as freedom with causality as the mechanism of nature, the first being given through the moral law and the latter through natural law, and both as related to the same subject, man, is impossible unless man is conceived by pure consciousness as a being in itself in relation to the former, but by empirical reason as appearance in relation to the latter. Otherwise the self-contradiction of reason is unavoidable" (*KprV* 5: 6; 6).

[28] In his review of Kant's *Anthropology*, Schleiermacher notes: "This gives rise to the question: where do the 'observations about what hinders or promotes a mental faculty' come from, and how are these observations to be used for the mind's expansion, if there are not physical ways to consider and treat this expansion in terms of the idea that all free choice is at the same time nature?" [*KGA* I.2, 365–9]. Here he has in mind Kant's assertion in the *Anthropology* that so long as observations respecting that which hinders or stimulates a faculty such as memory are used practically, they belong in a pragmatic anthropology, one that presupposes freedom.

through all the stages that are involved in such a change. All of this involves some form of determinism. The question then remains whether Kant was justified in requiring transcendental freedom from a moral point of view. Cannot the concept be dispatched with altogether in the way that Schleiermacher does? Does Schleiermacher succeed in showing that the reality of the moral law as a motivating principle is consistent with a strictly compatibilist account of freedom?

Despite the ingenuity of Schleiermacher's discussion, I believe the answer to the question whether the concept of transcendental freedom can be dispatched with is no on two counts. First, Schleiermacher ultimately fails to show how, assuming determinism, an action can be understood as having been initiated by an agent, rather than the agent being a mere locus wherein a predetermined event takes place. There are hints in parts of *On Freedom* regarding how this implication might be avoided, but they are undeveloped. Were they developed, however, I believe they would ultimately imply transcendental freedom at some level.[29]

Second, and more importantly, Schleiermacher's account of moral motivation ultimately fails to satisfy important conditions that are necessary if the moral law is to be conceived as a rational practical principle obligating all rational agents. The problem in Schleiermacher's analysis is the following. If we can provide a deterministic account concerning why an individual chooses to do x, while we may have provided an exhaustive *causal* account regarding why x was chosen, we still would not have shown that the agent had sufficient *reasons* for doing x, that is, we would not have shown why the agent *ought* to have done x. An agent who does x because s/he was causally necessitated to do so cannot rationally justify her actions on these grounds. We need carefully to distinguish rational necessity

---

[29] For instance, in the middle of *On Freedom*, Schleiermacher notes: "We do not want to feel a freeing from all necessity, because this exhibits itself in no case whatsoever, and our pretense would also be a vain attempt, but only a freeing from the compulsion of the object, and this will occur whenever we determine our faculty of desire through an idea that relates to pure self-consciousness" (72). As Crossley notes in his article "The Ethical Impulse in Schleiermacher's Early Ethics," "This view of accountability must mean, however, that a person has the power to alter his or her character, even if particular actions are determined by the state of a person's character at any particular time" (14).

grounded in objective laws of reason from causal necessity stemming from antecedent conditions, a distinction that Schleiermacher fails to make. While the *incentive* of the moral law is not sufficient to determine the will to action from a causal standpoint, the objective validity of the moral law itself provides sufficient reasons for action in accordance with it, and in this sense the moral law is rationally necessary. While Schleiermacher ultimately recognizes that if reason is to be the source of moral laws it must be possible that pure practical principles can have an influence on feeling, he yet wants to give an account of how the extent of this influence is determined by antecedent conditions in the subject, thereby once more reducing his account to deterministic principles. However, Schleiermacher's move, as ingenious as it is, only pushes the problem he recognized in *On Freedom* one step further back. There, it will be recalled, he noted that there must be an "impulse" that relates exclusively to practical reason, otherwise actions could only accidentally be in accordance with the moral law. However, in order for an agent to have *sufficient* reasons for action it is not enough to say that the moral law provides an incentive for action in the same way that other empirically conditioned desires have an influence on the will. The agent must also in principle be able to provide an account of why all these impulses are not on a par with one another, for instance, we must be able to give an account of why the impulse to be moral is *superior* to, or has more value than, the desire to kill when one feels like it. Unless the agent acts in accordance with the moral law *because* she recognizes that her impulse to be moral has more *worth* than her other non-moral desires, such action would be in accordance with the moral law only *accidentally*. The recognition of such a worth, required in order for her action not to be merely accidentally in accordance with the moral law would, however, imply transcendental freedom. Were the recognition of the worth of such a principle to be grounded in pre-existing susceptibilities of the agent, the principle could not be one that is universally and categorically binding, since the ability to act in accordance with it would thereby depend on the existing conditions of the agent.

2

The Principle of Individuation

In Schleiermacher's *Spinozism* as well as in his *Short Presentation of the Spinozistic System,* both from around 1793–94, he continues his preoccupation with the question of personal identity. In *On Freedom* Schleiermacher was unable to provide an account that made sense of the idea that an *agent* is the initiator of an action. In that essay he realized that in denying transcendental freedom and espousing determinism, the agency of the agent disappears, since the causal grounds for each action ultimately can be traced back to events pre-existing the agent. Each representation and desire that arises in the psyche is itself causally necessitated by a prior mental state of the agent, and the first mental state of an agent would itself be the product of efficient causes that preceded the existence of the agent in time. On this view the "agency" of the agent "dissolves into infinitely many infinitesimally small external forces that leave us with nothing to think of as firmly active in the subject" (*KGA* I.1, 257; 42–3). In *Spinozism* and in *The Short Presentation,* Schleiermacher embraces a position fully consonant with this result. Specifically, he argues that there are no genuine individuals, and hence no real (noumenal) agents. As such, there is no way to make sense of the notion that an agent is the initiator of an action. In *Spinozism* he argues for three principle claims. First, there are no justifiable criteria for making judgments concerning the identity of things. Second, there are no justifiable criteria for making judgments regarding the identity of persons. And third, there are no individuals. Because there are no individuals, there must be only one substance in which everything inheres. Only it has complete reality. His position is developed in relation to the views of Spinoza, Leibniz, Kant, and Jacobi. He rejects Leibniz's views, defends

Spinoza against many of Jacobi's charges, and adopts Kant's critical, transcendental idealism as his own.[1] He argues that Kant's critical principles, if thought through to their logical conclusion, ultimately lead to a qualified Spinozism.

This chapter, as well as the following one, will be devoted principally to a careful examination of the arguments Schleiermacher proffers in *Spinozism*; the material in the *Short Presentation* will be addressed as well, but mostly insofar as it sheds light on the former essay. In this chapter, I will focus on Schleiermacher's argument, directed principally against Leibniz and the Leibnizians, that there is no such a thing as a principle of individuation. In defending this claim, Schleiermacher provides two major arguments, one epistemological in nature, and another that is metaphysical. First, I very briefly discuss the historical context of Schleiermacher's two pieces on Spinoza, and then proceed to provide an analysis of Schleiermacher's epistemological and metaphysical arguments against the principle of individuation.

---

[1] In her book *The Living God: Schleiermacher's Theological Appropropriation of Spinoza*, Julia Lamm calls Schleiermacher's position a "post-Kantian Spinozism." Lamm identifies four themes she believes Schleiermacher develops here and carries through into his later material: monism, determinism, realism, and non-anthropomorphism. The interpretation I offer in this book differs significantly from Lamm's. While the first chapter of Lamm's book, devoted to the Spinoza essays, provides a good overview of the themes that Schleiermacher treats in the essays, it does not sufficiently emphasize that Schleiermacher's principle concern in *Spinozism* is to argue that there are no genuine individuals and to counter some of the Leibnizian positions adopted by Jacobi. Schleiermacher, however, continued his preoccupation with the question of the individual in the *Monologen*, revising the position taken in *Spinozism* in significant ways. As has been recently argued by George di Giovanni in *Freedom and Religion in Kant and His Immediate Successors*, the problems of freedom and the individual stood at the heart of philosophical disputes in Germany in the late eighteenth century. Di Giovanni takes account of the "set of problems that drove popular philosophy—notably the problem of how to reconcile individual identity with the mechanism of nature" (54). In this and the following chapters I argue that one of Schleiermacher's main goals is to understand the relation of the individual to both the world and to the absolute, both in theoretical and practical terms. This is a dominant theme continued in the *Speeches* and the *Monologen,* and is significantly echoed in *The Christian Faith* as well. Significantly, it was Jacobi who had sounded the alarm regarding the question of the individual. Although he disagreed with him on fundamental points, Schleiermacher held Jacobi in high regard and had even hoped to dedicate the first edition of *The Christian Faith* to him. It is no surprise that Schleiermacher, too, dedicated significant energies to understanding the place of the individual in light of the attraction that Spinoza's insight held for him.

THE BACKGROUND

Schleiermacher begins *Spinozism* by copying forty-four of F. H. Jacobi's paragraphs in which Jacobi had attempted to present "Spinoza's system in its true form *and according to the intrinsic coherence of its parts.*"[2] These forty-four paragraphs represent the second, and longest, exposition of Spinozism and its spirit presented by Jacobi in his *On Spinoza's Doctrine in Letters to Moses Mendelssohn.*[3] Jacobi had argued, famously, that all systematic philosophy leads to fatalism and atheism, and that the philosophy of Spinoza was the clearest and most consistently developed position that results from taking rational thinking to its logical conclusion. Left to its own devices, human reason would end up affirming pantheism. Spinoza is a "consistent rationalist,"[4] and "Spinozism is atheism." Furthermore, "all ways of demonstration end in fatalism."[5] As a defender of orthodox theism and freedom of the will, Jacobi argued that these dangerous and fatalistic views could only be refuted through a "*salto mortale,*" or leap of faith.

On Spinoza's Doctrine in Letters to Moses Mendelssohn had appeared in 1785, the same year as Mendelssohn's *Morgenstunden,* and contains Jacobi's correspondence with Mendelssohn, in which the question of Gotthold Ephraim Lessing's Spinozism was discussed at length. Lessing had died on February 15, 1781. When Jacobi had heard through Elise Reimarus that Mendelssohn planned to write something on Lessing, he became rather anxious. He did not want Lessing to be used as a witness in favor of the theism of the German Enlightenment, and he feared that Lessing's real views would be suppressed. Confident that Elise would relay the message to Mendelssohn, he wrote to Elise,

---

[2] Gérard Vallée, *The Spinoza Conversations between Lessing and Jacobi,* 118. Vallée's book contains translations of important parts of Mendelssohn's *Morgenstunden* and *An die Freunde Lessing',* as well as of F. H. Jacobi's *Über die Lehre des Spinoza's* and *Wider Mendelssohns Beschuldigungen.* The material is translated from Heinrich Scholz's *Die Hauptschriften zum Pantheismusstreit zwischen Jacobi und Mendelssohn.*

[3] The forty four paragraphs are in Jacobi's April 1785 letter to Mendelssohn. Cf. Scholz, *Hauptschriften,* 141–65. These are, unfortunately, left out of Vallée's translation. A complete English translation of *Concerning the Doctrine of Spinoza in Letters to Herr Moses Mendelssohn* can be found in *F. H. Jacobi: The Main Philosophical Writings and the Novel Allwill,* translated and edited by George di Giovanni.

[4] Vallée, *The Spinoza Conversations,* 12.   [5] Ibid. 123.

You know perhaps, and if you do not know I confide it to you here *sub rosa*, that Lessing in his final days was a firm Spinozist. It is conceivable that Lessing may have expressed this view to others; in that case it would be necessary for Mendelssohn, in the memorial he intends to dedicate to him, either to avoid certain matters totally or at least to treat them with the utmost caution.[6]

Mendelssohn took the bait, and asked for more information. In November of 1783, Jacobi sent Mendelssohn a long report of his conversation with Lessing. Jacobi reports that Lessing told him that "the orthodox concepts of divinity are no longer for me; I cannot stand them. *Hen kai Pan!* I know nought else." And to top it off, Lessing claimed, "If I am to call myself by anybody's name, then I know none better" [than the name of Spinoza].[7] A long correspondence between Jacobi and Mendelssohn ensued, finally published by Jacobi in *Über die Lehre des Spinoza*. Among other things, the book contains Jacobi's understanding of the "spirit of Spinozism," as well as his arguments that Spinozism is equivalent to atheism, and that all rationalism, including that of Leibniz, eventually dissolved into Spinozism.[8]

In understanding *Spinozism,* it is important to remember that Schleiermacher is directly responding to Jacobi, and that Jacobi espoused versions of key Leibnizian doctrines. Jacobi understood Leibniz as having thought of the monads as *vinculum compositionis,*[9]

---

[6] Vallée, *The Spinoza Conversations*, 5.   [7] Ibid. 9–10.

[8] For a more in-depth discussion of the Pantheism Controversy, see Frederick C. Beiser, *The Fate of Reason: German Philosophy from Kant to Fichte,* as well as George di Giovanni, *Freedom and Religion in Kant and His Immediate Successors,* especially pp. 137–51. Paul Franks also provides an excellent discussion of Jacobi's influence and the question of post-Kantian Spinozism in *All or Nothing,* 84–145.

[9] In his February 1712 letter to Des Bosses, Leibniz notes the following regarding the *vinculum substantiale:* "If the *vinculum substantiale* of monads did not exist, all bodies, together with all of their qualities, would be nothing but well-founded phenomena, like a rainbow or an image in a mirror, in a word, continual dreams perfectly in agreement with one another, and in this alone would consist the reality of those phenomena." G. W. Leibniz, *Philosophical Essays,* 198–9. For Leibniz, the *vinculum* explains the underlying nature and per se unity of corporeal substance. The best, most nuanced discussion of the role of this idea in Leibniz's philosophy can be found in Robert M. Adams, *Leibniz: Determinist, Theist, Idealist,* 299–307. Adams, however, concludes that Leibniz "never had a deep personal commitment to the view that there are corporeal substances, one per se" (307). Jacobi, on the other hand, understood the *vinculum* as guaranteeing both the principle of individuality and of personhood: it is the principle of the indivisibility of the unity of the manifold, and he determined this

that is, the monads supply a principle of the indivisible unity of the manifold. Jacobi called this principle the "I." This I "distinguishes itself from all experiences and representations" and provides unity to the manifold given through consciousness of the world. According to Jacobi "all truly real things are individuals or single things, and as such are (a) living essences, principles (b) perceptive and (c) active, and they are outside one another."[10] He stressed the active character of these living principles, that is, their freedom, and he conceives of the individuals as *spontaneously* reacting to one another. At the same time, Jacobi stressed the community of all individuals: all the individuals reciprocally determine one another.[11] Because of their nature, "the concepts of unity and plurality, of activity and passivity, of extension and succession" are innate in individuals.[12] Jacobi also adopted the Leibnizian notion of the pre-established harmony.[13]

THE EPISTEMOLOGICAL PROBLEM

In the following passage cited by Schleiermacher, Jacobi comments upon both Leibniz and Spinoza:

Nevertheless, Bourget believed he had discovered a furthering of Spinozism, or rather of its spirit, in even this new system. Leibniz answered him: I do not see how you want to bring out Spinozism here. On the contrary, it is precisely through the monads that Spinozism is overcome. For so many monads, so many real substances or indestructible, and at once living mirrors of the universe, or concentric worlds, exist. Contrary to this, according to Spinoza, there can be only one single substance. Were there no monads, then Spinoza would be correct. All outside of God would be ignored, and would disappear as an accidental attribute, for the things would be lacking their

---

principle as the "I." On this point see Eilert Herms, *Herkunft, Entfaltung, und erste Gestalt des Systems der Wissenschaften bei Schleiermacher,* 129.

[10] F. H. Jacobi, *Werke,* Volume II, 261. All translations from Jacobi's *Werke* are my own.

[11] Jacobi, *Werke,* IV₁ 225ff.   [12] Jacobi, *Werke,* II, 261.

[13] George di Giovanni provides an excellent discussion of Jacobi's philosophy in "The Unfinished Philosophy of Friedrich Heinrich Jacobi," the introductory chapter to *F. H. Jacobi: The Main Philosophical Writings and the Novel* Allwill. He also discusses Jacobi's philosophy in *Freedom and Religion.*

own ground of endurance or substance, which is given through the monads. This is completely right. Spinozism can only be grasped with success from the point of view of its individuation, in which case then it must be replaced by either Leibniz's monads or the Eleatic acatalepsy. In his (Spinoza's) system the *individua*, or individual things, are yet so little as the Godhead itself, which brings forth the infinite from the infinite in an absolutely necessary way. But he gives no justification of the inner possibility of such individual things in the absolute continuum. He gives no account of their division and of the community of their effects, and this on account of an astonishing war of all against all bringing with it a fleeting individuality that unites, in a tangled way, all unity in and with the infinite.[14]   (*KGA* I.1, 547)

In both *Spinozism* and the *Short Presentation*, Schleiermacher pro-ceeds to defend Spinoza, and argues that Leibniz's philosophy is not an improvement over that of Spinoza. The principal question at issue, according to Schleiermacher, is whether we have grounds for thinking that there exist individuals having their own ground of endurance or subsistence *in themselves*.[15] Schleiermacher adopts the Kantian distinction between phenomena and noumena, and he does not deny that individuals appear as phenomena. What he denies is that there exist objects that *in themselves* are individuals and that have *within* them their own ground of endurance. He marshals several arguments for why we do not have good grounds for thinking that there are discrete individuals. In what follows I will discuss each of these.

---

[14] All translations from *Spinozism* and the *Short Presentation*, which can be found in *KGA* I.1, are my own. All future references to these two pieces will be indicated by *KGA* I.1 with page numbers following, and will be internal to the text.

[15] Adams identifies another, related problem in assessing the relation of Leibniz to Spinoza. The question is whether "the world is something external or additional to God" (126). In his book *Leibniz: Determinist, Theist, Idealist,* Adams provides an account that is historically sensitive to Leibniz's changing views. The earlier Leibniz, writing in 1676, "flatly affirms the Spinozistic idea that finite things are only modes" (129). By 1688 Leibniz has, however, changed his views. In his paper "On the Abstract and the Concrete" (*c.*1688) Leibniz argues that there must be a genuine distinction between God and creatures, for God's reality is infinite, that of creatures is finite. Because the powers are distinct (one is infinite, the other finite), there must be two subjects to which these powers can be ascribed. As Adams notes: "We are left, I think, with the following answer to the question whether Leibniz's conception of God as *ens perfectissimum* has, inescapably, Spinozistic implications: it does not. The relation of the limited attributes of creatures to the absolute attributes of God is not the relation of mode to attribute, since they exclude each other from any one subject, by virtue of the negation involved in the creaturely attributes" (134).

He first notes that two questions must be distinguished: first whether individual finite things *have* substance, and second, whether they *are* substances. He admits that all finite things have substance, but denies that they are substances (*KGA* I.1, 547). A thing may *have* substance insofar as the one substance grounding everything is its ground, or insofar as it is made up of a part of the universal substance. This however, does not mean that *it* is a substance. For something to be a genuine substance, it must have its own principle of endurance or subsistence separating it from other substances, that is, it must have its own principle of individuation. The first question, that of whether things have substance, has nothing to do with the principle of individuation itself, "for if it is granted that a thing A has something substantial in itself, it does not thereby follow, that, and to what degree, it is to be considered as a separate thing" (*KGA* I.1, 547–8). Schleiermacher contrasts Spinoza's understanding of how things possess substance with that of Leibniz: "the latter says: yes, the finite (extended) things have something substantial in them, namely the monads. The former says: yes, what is substantial in them is the being which is a part of the universal substance" (*KGA* I.1, 548). Schleiermacher argues that the problem with Leibniz's position, however, is that it provides us with no way of identifying the principle of individuation. Leibniz's idea of monads does not clarify "how that which I recognize through pure reason as substance is unified" (*KGA*, I.1, 548). In other words he fails to provide adequate criteria through which we can determine that something is an independent substance.

Schleiermacher assumes a thoroughly Kantian standpoint when he poses his question to Leibniz concerning the principle of individuation. Our continuously changing perceptions are "given to us as sensation and change of sensation" (*KGA* I.1, 549); moreover, the "whole world of sense is there in and through you" (*KGA* I.1, 550), that is, the world of sense is given to us in and through modifications of the mind. The question then becomes how the continual flux of perceptions can generate our everyday objective experience of tables and chairs. Leibniz's principles do not make clear to him "how and why I consider the objects given to me in outer experience as separate from one another, how I thereby come to combine into an objective unity its manifold, and on what it depends that I connect exactly this many and exactly this manifold?" (*KGA* I.1, 548). Although Leibniz has shown "how and that many substances are possible" (*KGA* I.1, 548) his positing of the monads remains a mere hypothesis. Schleiermacher asks,

> But tell us something about how and why you distinguish the phenomena as separate objects. Does this distinction have to do with the one combination, so that you would know you have grasped precisely that which results from a monad connection through your representation? How might you know this? Or does it have to do with this: that just what you see as your object belongs to a common central monad? How do you know this then, and how have you achieved this knowledge of monads through which to separate the individuals from one another?   (*KGA* I.1, 548)

In other words, Schleiermacher asks, how do we know that the activity of the understanding, in producing phenomenally distinct objects such as tables and chairs, actually hooks up with what are metaphysically real individuals, that is, individuals in themselves? Leibniz believed that we are in contact with God alone and that our knowledge of all other things derived from our relation to God. In §28 of his *Discourse on Metaphysics* Leibniz notes that, "there is no external cause acting on us except God alone, and he alone communicates himself to us immediately in virtue of our continual dependence ... It can then be said that God is our immediate external object and that we see all things by him."[16] Leibniz explains our ability to know other monads through God's conservation of the ideas of such monads in us. It is likely this idea that Schleiermacher has in mind when he notes "just what you see as your object belongs to a common central monad." According to Leibniz, we know of other individuals and their states in virtue of the pre-established harmony: "But in simple substances the influence of one monad over another can only be ideal, and can only produce its effect through God's intervention, when in the ideas of God a monad rightly demands that God take it into account in regulating the others from the beginning of things" (*Monadology*, §51).[17] From the very

---

[16] Leibniz, *Philosophical Essays*, 59. On Schleiermacher's access to this text as well as to these ideas, see note 3, chapter 4, "The World is the Mirror of the Self." As I note in the introduction, it is only in 1797–8 that Schleiermacher comes to study the original Leibnizian texts.

[17] Leibniz, *Philosophical Essays*, 219.

beginning God harmonizes all monads and their states with one another, and it is through this harmony that our knowledge of other individuals is guaranteed. Schleiermacher complains that this way of understanding the matter, however, remains a mere hypothesis. If we begin with the fact of the continual flux of perceptions in inner sense, there is no way to know that the phenomenal individuals we experience map onto individual things in themselves. The "*vinculum* of the monads is something so completely unknown and undetermined" (*KGA* I.1, 548–9). Hence Schleiermacher concludes, "The most that one can admit is that, objectively, Leibniz solved the problem through a hypothesis, namely, of how individual things could be possible in the continuum of extension and of consciousness." However, Schleiermacher claims, Leibniz did not touch upon the corresponding subjective question: "through which effects of these things on us are we constrained to make this distinction in experience as well?" (*KGA* I.1, 548).

Schleiermacher takes what he understands as Kant's account of the "subjective ground of individuation"[18] as decisive, and notes that is something "of which we will all be in agreement, for hereafter no one can ground it validly to the exclusion of his system" (*KGA* I.1, 550). Schleiermacher thereby explains how we come to have the phenomenal experience of individuals that we do in terms of Kant's analogies of experience. These analogies provide an account of how and why the continuous change of perceptions given in inner sense must be interpreted in such a way that we think of phenomenal substances as (a) enduring, (b) changing in accordance with natural laws, and (c) existing simultaneously and in thoroughgoing interaction, or community, with one another. Schleiermacher notes that "According to your currently reigning mode of thinking, you say, in fact, that the application of the laws of the understanding makes experience out of these perceptions, and particularly the analogies of experience constrain you not only to combine the idea of a necessary connection between an earlier state and a later state with each change, but also to think of something real and persisting as grounding

---

[18] When Schleiermacher speaks of the "subjective ground of individuation," he is referring to the phenomenal individuation of Kant's appearances. He takes this ground to be "subjective" insofar as phenomena are the result of the operations of the synthesis of the imagination.

each sensation" (*KGA* I.1, 549). Kant's first analogy of experience stipulated that time determination requires us to posit the existence of a persisting substance underlying the changes of appearance.[19] According to the second analogy, time determination also requires that we be able to provide an *objective* account of the succession of changes in an appearance. Such an account of the order of changes must be distinguishable from the order given in the apprehension of successive representations. Kant argues that in order for such an objective account to be possible, we must think of all alterations as occurring in accordance with the law of cause and effect. Lastly, Kant's third analogy stipulates that in order for us to be able to think that the sequence of our perceptions is grounded in an object, we must think of substances as in space and in thoroughgoing interaction, or community with one another. These three analogies, having to do with persistence, succession, and simultaneity, must be assumed if objective experience is to be possible, that is, if we are to be able to distinguish between our subjective apprehension of perceptions and the appearances as objects of experience.

Schleiermacher's point is that these analogies only give an account of *phenomenal* reality, that is, of how we must connect the representations given to us in sensation in order to arrive at objective experience. The analogies in no way guarantee that this phenomenal reality hooks up with the way things are in themselves. Hence he notes,

You may not claim that the ground of the plurality of substances in space lies in the plurality of substances in themselves, for this claim would contradict your remaining doctrine. Even less may you give this reason for your

---

[19] This is because (a) we are aware of time only in and through the relation of the representations given in inner sense to one another; as such time cannot be perceived. (b) The representations given to inner sense are continuously changing and do not endure. (c) However, only through that which persists does duration acquire a magnitude. (d) Time itself cannot be that which endures, that is, time cannot be the changing thing underlying the changes since it is that through which the changes are to be measured. (e) What persists must therefore be the object itself, that is, the substance. (f) Hence, everything that changes can belong only to the *way* in which this substance or substances exist. (g) This further implies that because substance is the substratum of everything real and always remains the same, its quantity in nature can be neither increased nor destroyed. I provide a detailed analysis of Kant's first analogy and its relation to his refutation of idealism in my chapter "On Some Presumed Gaps in Kant's Refutation of Idealism" in Rameil (ed.), *Metaphysik und Kritik*.

subjective perceptions of the plurality of finite substances (phenomena), since the whole world of sense is in and through you. How then does it come about that you reduce your perceptions to determinate objects, individuals? You answer that this stems from the original synthesis of the imagination, which gives unity to the manifold. Since by itself it does not brand each individual sensation as an individual, and yet also does not collect them all together under a single unity, what then is the ground of your operation? What justifies their separation? Thus, if for Leibniz individuation is explained only through a shaky hypothesis, and is thereby also not something solid and completely true, then for you it is something completely arbitrary, and yet belongs to that which you alone call real and certain.

(KGA I. 1, 549–50)

Schleiermacher here seems to be directly taking issue with Jacobi. He claims Jacobi cannot consistently affirm that the plurality of substances in space is grounded in the plurality of things in themselves, "for this claim would contradict your remaining doctrine." Jacobi did believe that phenomena were grounded in things in themselves. He did not, however, hold to the Kantian-like views Schleiermacher seems to be attributing to him, and which would pose difficulties for such a view.

To judge from what he says in *Spinozism*, it is unclear whether Schleiermacher was fully acquainted with Jacobi's doctrines at this point, or whether he misrepresents Jacobi's position as a rhetorical strategy. For example, he assumes that Jacobi agrees with him concerning how we arrive at the "subjective principle of individuation." In invoking the analogies to support this "subjective principle," it is clear that Schleiermacher has Kant's doctrine in mind, and Schleiermacher proceeds as if Jacobi must agree with Kant's critical idealism as Schleiermacher understands it.[20] However, Jacobi's own doctrines were quite different from Kant's. Specifically, Jacobi adhered to a direct, unmediated realism. He denied that we arrived at the conclusion that things exist through any deductive process; he claimed there is an immediate connection between our conviction of the existence of things and our representations. This unmediated conviction of existence extends to both our own existence and to the existence of

---

[20] Schleiermacher's discussion of the analogies as supporting the *subjective* principle of individuation is misleading, since for Kant the analogies of experience are conditions of the possibility of *objective* experience.

things outside of us. We become aware of things outside of us "with the same certainly with which we become aware of ourselves."[21] Not only do we arrive at the conviction of the existence of ourselves and of things outside of us in the same way, that is, without any mediation, we also arrive at both convictions simultaneously. According to Jacobi, we become aware of both our self-consciousness and things "in the same instant, in the same indivisible moment, without before or after, without any operation of the understanding, yes, without the conviction of the concept of cause and effect even remotely beginning in them."[22] In 1787 Jacobi wrote,

The thing brings just so much to the awareness of consciousness, as consciousness does to the awareness of the thing. I experience that I am, and that something is outside of me, in the same indivisible instant: and in this instant my soul is no more affected by the thing as it is by itself. No representation, no conclusion mediates this double revelation. Nothing enters the soul between the awareness of the real outside of it. Representations do not yet exist; they first appear afterwards in reflection, as shadows of things that were present. We can also always lead them back to the real from which they are taken and which they presuppose. We must thereby go back to the real each time if we wish to know whether they are true.[23]

Jacobi, then, rejects Kant's analogies of experience, for these clearly involve the activity of the understanding. Moreover, Kant's refutation of idealism, coming as it does after the analogies in the second edition of the first *Critique,* presupposes the analogies. In his refutation of idealism Kant sought to show that awareness of the time determination of inner experience presupposes outer experience, that is, experience of things outside the self. Both Kant and Jacobi are in agreement that awareness of the self is intrinsically tied up with awareness of things outside the self. They disagree, however, on *how* this comes about. According to Kant, the activity of the understanding is required in order to distinguish objective experience from my merely subjective apprehensions. Self-consciousness and the distinction between self and world thereby depend upon the activity of the understanding. According to Jacobi, on the other hand,

---

[21] Jacobi, *Werke,* II, 143; IV₁ 211.   [22] Jacobi, *Werke,* II, 176.
[23] Ibid. 175.

we have a direct, *unmediated* awareness of both self and world. No representations and no activity of the understanding mediate this awareness.[24] Representations are themselves mere shadows of this immediate, direct awareness.[25]

Schleiermacher's argumentative strategy is to assume that Jacobi must agree that what we have to work with is a manifold of sensations on which the understanding must operate in order for objective

---

[24] In *Freedom and Religion*, di Giovanni provides a useful discussion of Jacobi's attempt to discover "the right formula for representing how an experiencing subject, in becoming aware of himself, equally becomes conscious of the presence of an external world." At the heart of this formula is Jacobi's insight that fundamental awareness of the self is given in *action*. The self knows itself immediately in the *feeling* of power that the subject has of itself when it acts. As such, Jacobi analyzes a fundamental, existential dimension of human being in the world. His formula representing how experience is possible, found in his 1787 book entitled *David Hume on Faith, or Idealism and Realism, a Dialogue* is summarized by di Giovanni as follows: "(1) Self-awareness originates in a subject's feeling of power. (2) This feeling immediately implicates the presence for the subject of an external something that exists in itself and interferes with the felt power, but at the same time provides the feeling with a reality check. (3) Representation is called into play as the reflective attempt on the part of the subject to sort out the difference between his own self and the external things resisting his power" (83).

[25] Schleiermacher's notes on Jacobi's work, from about the same period—1793–4—show that he is aware of Jacobi's direct realism and his arguments for it. Schleiermacher copied the following from Jacobi's *David Hume über den Glauben oder Idealismus und Realismus* (1787):"Therefore, however, as a realist I must say: all knowledge could come completely from belief alone, since things must be given to me before I am in a position to recognize relations" (*KGA* I.1, 595). Schleiermacher also copies Jacobi's arguments that certainty of outer things must be an unmediated certainty. The Kantian philosophers, according to Jacobi, are merely "empirical realists" but they are not "genuine realists." And he continues: "The validity of empirical evidence is just that which is in question. That things appear to us as outside of us requires no proof. That, however, these things are thereby not pure appearances in us, not mere determinations of our own self and thereby nothing as representations of something outside us, but rather that they are representations in us that relate to beings outside us really existing in themselves and that are taken from them—against this not only can doubts arise, but it is often the case that the strongest understanding cannot overcome these doubts through rational grounds. Your unmediated certainty of outer things would thereby be a blind certainty according to the analogy of my belief" (*KGA* I.1, 596). In *Spinozism* Schleiermacher makes no mention of this stance, namely of the possibility of a direct, unmediated realism, and of Jacobi's claim that we have this direct access to things through *belief*. If he had been aware of this at this point, one would expect that he would have dealt with it when he asked the question of how it is possible to distinguish between inner sense and outer appearances. It therefore seems to me that he must have written *Spinozism* before he began to think about Jacobi's direct realism.

experience to be possible. Schleiermacher's question to Jacobi, "How then does it come about that you reduce your perceptions to determinate objects, individuals?" (*KGA* I.1, 550) only makes sense on the assumption that Jacobi had adopted key elements of Kant's transcendental idealism. It is clear, however, that Jacobi rejected most of the critical philosophy. In its place was his direct realism. Hence the question of how we can be certain that our phenomenal experience of individuals is grounded in things as they are in themselves is not really an issue for him. This is because according to Jacobi's system, we never really begin with phenomenal experience. We begin with a direct awareness of the things as they are in themselves. Just like our representations, phenomena are mere shadows of that which we already directly apprehend. The question of how we can move from our phenomenal awareness of individuals to individuals as they are in themselves does not, then, cut against his system.

Contra Jacobi's position, Schleiermacher affirms "our whole manner of separating things into individuals is in no way an effect of this whole from the outside, but is rather an inner action. It is thereby either determined in accordance with our necessary laws grounded in representations, or is a wholly blind instinct. Leibniz must thereby throw his lot in with Kant . . . " (*KGA* I.1, 552). Schleiermacher affirms that the manifold of sensation that comes to us from the outside does not bring with it its own interpretation. What is given to us through the senses is "sensation and change of sensation." This explains why our "perceptions are not continuous" (*KGA* I.1, 549), that is, the sensations we experience are continuously in flux. Moreover, since we first begin with our subjective *apprehension* of these sensations, Schleiermacher asks the Kantian question "how would you have arrived at the distinction between inner sense and outer intuitions?" (*KGA* I.1, 552). Kant's answer to this question is the analogies of experience. As we have noted above, Schleiermacher refers to these as well and is in agreement with Kant on this point.

How is the distinction between self and outer objects possible? Given that our "perceptions are not continuous," we never have direct access to that which underlies the continually changing determinations of the appearance, for we do not have a continuous perception of the underlying substrate. We merely infer it. For that matter, we have no access to a permanent representation of the self that endures throughout the change in *its* representations (considered as its determinations). And this inference to substance as that which underlies the changing determinations of the thing is a result of the application of the necessary laws of the understanding to what is given in sensation. It is therefore the result of our own activity and is not merely *given* to us from the outside. In all objective knowledge of the appearances, the synthesis of the imagination is continuously at work. For example, how the visual field is integrated with the auditory and tactile fields is the work of this synthesis. The perceptions that come to us from the visual field do not, in themselves, contain those of the auditory or tactile fields. Schleiermacher notes, "You separate the thing, viewed as chaos, in several objects in accordance with the different modes of perception. It is at least difficult to grasp how the imagination should thereby come to connect that into a unity which does not allow itself to be taken together, because it does not grasp it [viz., the visual field] in another [viz., the tactile field], and they cannot be made to follow one another" (*KGA* I.1, 553). What Schleiermacher calls chaos is the uninterpreted manifold of perception. Moreover, he argues, not only are the perceptual fields, insofar as they are purely given, not integrated with one another, but the data from each field also require the activity of the understanding in order for this data to make sense. Schleiermacher affirms, "the eye in itself is not skilled to distinguish objects. It shows the unpracticed seer everything on a single plane and distinguishes only colors. And if we now need it principally for this [distinguishing objects] this then happens, so to speak, only through a shortened kind of calculation, the rules of which we could only have come by through long practice. Even so little touch. It distinguishes only degrees of hardness and fluidity" (*KGA* I.1, 553). The upshot of all of this is that, contrary to Jacobi's views, Schleiermacher believes we have no unmediated access to things. We have immediate access to our perceptual states, and only given the activity of the synthesis of the imagination on the manifold of sense do we come to the ordinary world of tables and chairs. But if this is the case, what guarantee do we have that the phenomenal world of tables and chairs actually maps onto things in themselves?

Schleiermacher's next argument has to do with the nature of phenomenal individuals. He argues that whatever understanding we come to have of such individuals is only an approximate,

probable concept. From the phenomenal point of view, individuals are determinate masses. He defines a determinate mass as "the
point of unity of several of these modifications at each moment."
The modifications he has in mind are those of "movement and rest,
representation and desire" (*KGA* I.1, 551; cf. 574). It is because we
believe we can identify such a point of unity of these modifications
that we call something an individual. But can such a point of unity
really be identified? The problem is that of the continuous change in
state of the appearances. He tells us, "no particle can remain completely the same throughout because of continuous change. Rather,
in part the same mass takes on different determinations, and in part
the same determinations pass over into a different mass. Yes, I cannot
even determine which mass is to be regarded as an individual, for
this mass is also divisible in thought" (*KGA* I.1, 551). The way that
Schleiermacher is thinking of "mass" is in terms of a kind of substrate,
that is, mass seems to be an extended kind of stuff that is the bearer
of the properties, or determinations of a thing. However, we never
have a continuous perception of such a mass. We perceive only its
changing states. But this means that the substratum, shorn of all of
its properties, is not continuously identifiable. It is therefore unclear
how Schleiermacher can assert that different determinations pass over
into the *same* mass, and that the same determinations pass over into
different masses. How could we possibly know that something is the
same mass, or is a different mass apart from its determinations? If
however, the substratum is thought of as extended, then what remains
continuously identifiable are particular portions of space.

This way of thinking echoes the theory Plato puts forward in the
Timaeus, and Schleiermacher is very likely referring to it here through
his reference to Plato. In the *Timaeus* Plato had asked, "Do all these
things of which we always say that each of them is something 'by
itself' really exist?" Plato tells us that that which is perceived by the
senses is "constantly borne along, now coming to be in a certain
place and then perishing out of it." Space, one the other hand, "exists
always and cannot be destroyed. It provides a fixed state for all things
that come to be."[26] On this theory, space is the only continuously
identifiable substrate, and all coming to be and perishing are its

---

[26] Plato, *Timaeus*, translated by Donald J. Zeyl, in *Plato: Complete Works* 1255.

determinations. Space is, as such, the receptacle that "receives into itself" all becoming. Plato calls belief in the existence of things "by themselves" the subject matter of true opinion. It is significant that that is exactly what Schleiermacher calls these here—he tells us that "Alone, as is said, the practical use confirms that the concept [of the individual] has no other validity than that of an approximate, probable concept, and that everything that touches upon it can only be, as Plato says, a δόξαν ἀληθην" (*KGA* I.1, 551). On such a view, the only real individual is the extended, material substrate; in itself it is indeterminate and one. It is the receptacle for all becoming.[27] In the *Short Presentation of the Spinozistic System*, Schleiermacher claims that it is the continual coming into being and perishing of things, that is, their continual flux, that led Spinoza to posit the unity and eternity of the one substance (*KGA* I.1, 564, 567). At this juncture Schleiermacher seems to be reading Spinoza in light of Plato.

The extended character of this material substrate means that it is divisible. As noted above, he argues that "Yes, I cannot even determine which mass is to be regarded as an individual, for this mass is also divisible in thought." Given its divisibility, and given the fact that all the smaller particles out of which such a mass is composed "are not perfectly homogenous with the whole, . . . this [whole] will therefore

---

[27] In *A Study of Spinoza's Ethics*, Jonathan Bennet interprets Spinoza as putting forward a similar theory. He notes ". . . at Spinoza's most basic metaphysical level there are no occupants, but only space, its different regions altering in orderly ways." In *Behind the Geometrical Method*, Edwin Curley characterizes this theory, which he rejects as a proper interpretation of Spinoza, in the following way: "We might argue, for example, that for Spinoza, as for Descartes, ordinary physical objects are best viewed as larger or smaller portions of one continuous physical object, portions distinguishable from their neighbors only because they happen for a time to be qualitatively different. Ultimately there is just one extended thing, the whole of the physical universe (Descartes's "body in general"). The existence of lesser extended things just consists in the one extended thing's being qualified in certain ways at certain times and places. To say that the piece of wax is a mode of the one substance is to say that the one extended thing has certain properties at certain places and times . . . " (31–2). It is important to note, however, that Schleiermacher did not ultimately read Spinoza in this way. He recognized the significance of the fact that for Spinoza extension and thought are mere modes, or expressions of the one substance. As such, while space is the only continuously identifiable substrate that takes on changing determinations, it by no means follows that it, and the things that come to be and pass away in it, are to be completely identified with the absolute. They are, rather, merely an *expression* of it.

not be the point of unification for all [the particles] in the same way"
(*KGA* I.1, 551).[28] An extended thing that we think of as an individual
may be composed of different particles that are themselves the "points
of unification" of different forces. Schleiermacher seems to be asking,
why then should we call these composites individuals? Are such composites really individuals, or merely aggregates? On what grounds do
we distinguish individuals from mere aggregates? This is the upshot
of Schleiermacher's argument when he writes:

You call your body an individual although many parts are completely foreign
to it and do not have any part in its nature. You attribute an identity to it
even though its mass, as well as its character, change almost hourly. You
do not call the air in the room an individual, even though, on account of
its local connectedness, it undergoes a completely different series of changes
than what is separate from it, which then at the moment of separation already
ceases to be homogeneous with it. For example, you do not call several pieces
of wood on a heap an individual, even though they are completely one with
one another in relation to motion and rest. For the most part, you thereby
apply the concept only in a one-sided way and think that you are right. Yet
you must necessarily be aware that the concept is imperfect.

(*KGA* I.1, 551–2)

Moreover, Schleiermacher argues, things undergo constant change.
If so, then which determinations are we to think of as essential in
order for a thing to preserve its identity? Just how many changes
in determinations can a thing undergo before it loses its identity?
In the end, the whole concept of the individual "falls apart little by
little into those parts to which, together, a proper series of changes
can be attributed. This is thereby the sole canon according to which
your idea of individuals—mediated in part through sight, mediated
in part through touch—realizes itself" (*KGA* I.1, 553–4). In other
words, what we think of as an individual amounts to a series of
extended parts that together undergo a "proper" series of changes.
But just how do we identify this "proper" series of changes? How are
we to grasp the concept that allows us to unite these parts and their

---

[28] The *Short Presentation* contains a related argument. He claims that "the plurality
of phenomena" cannot relate to a plurality of noumena. This is because "we can divide
a physical individual in many parts. Were each individual in the world of sense to
correspond to one in the intelligible world, then we must be in a position to increase
the number of things in themselves" (*KGA* I.1, 574).

changes such that we think of them as an individual? Such a concept, Schleiermacher argues, can only be an approximate, probable concept. Even in its "practical use" it is not a "self-contained and perfectly delimited concept."

THE METAPHYSICAL PROBLEM

So far, we have examined Schleiermacher's epistemological objection to the positing of individuals: we have no access to the *vinculum* of the monads—that in virtue each monad has its *per se* unity, and in virtue of which we can distinguish one from another. We have access only to phenomena. As such we have no way of knowing what constitutes genuine individuals; this was the principle flaw in Leibniz's system. Leibniz's positing of individuals remained a mere hypothesis. A long, remarkable passage towards the beginning of *Spinozismus* provides insight into Schleiermacher's metaphysics and why he does not believe that there are substantial individuals. Jacobi had written: "What we call sequence or duration is at bottom pure illusion. For since the real effect is given at once with its complete real cause, it is differentiated from it only through the representation [*der Vorstellung nach*]. Hence sequence and duration must be, in truth, only a certain form and manner of viewing the manifold in the infinite" (*KGA* I.1, 526). In response to this Schleiermacher comments:

These words only first lead me to a certain materialistic view, in which the Spinozistic relation of the noumenon to the phenomenon almost fuses with the Kantian. This view can also be attributed to the Leibnizian. Let us suppose a common noumenon lies at the ground of each succession of appearances, through which we believe we hold an individual in view. If one also wants to assume only some agreement with the appearance of the thing, then this noumenon, considered in itself, must contain not only everything essential that the appearances in the series have in common with each other, but also that through which each member distinguishes itself from the others. Therefore, a being that should represent or view this thing in itself as one, without duration and succession, must therein at once perceive the preformed seed of all those appearances, the ground of all those relations of things to others from which the appearances develop themselves for us. Naturally, however, such a being must have a faculty of representation different from our own. It need not be bound to such a limited unity in the connection of the manifold. This is because, since it [the manifold] contains parts that we cannot think of in one [representation], this unity would not be in that representation. For instance, a noumenon lies at the ground of the seed and all its development up to the maturity of the tree. Such a being would already see in the seed the whole tree and everything that lay in between, and all that would be one to it. Because it must relate to one being, we could think of all that is coincidentally different, which opposes itself because of its relation to a concept, not as within one another, but outside one another, [yet] in accordance with each other. In this way the whole expresses itself to us only in a series of appearances, in which all is together, which may be together only for our faculty of representation, and all is separate, which must be separate as a consequence of the same. I believe that in this presentation nothing is contained that contradicts the Kantian view of things … If a noumenon should be the ground of the whole series of appearances from seed to tree, then this series may not end here, it must extend itself to all previous trees and seeds and those that follow, and because the mechanical and chemical changes in the thing, and the ground of their relation to others, must be just so well preformed as the organic, which are so precisely interconnected with it, then this series must extend throughout the whole world of sense, and we thereby come once more to the Spinozistic relation. (*KGA* I.1, 526–7)

Here Schleiermacher makes use of two different ways in which noumena, or things in themselves, function in Kant's philosophy. For Kant, appearances result from the application of the categories, or concepts of the understanding, to the manifold of sensible intuition. This has two implications regarding the relation between appearances and things in themselves that stand in tension with one another. First, the concept of an appearance implies the idea of a thing in itself. In the A edition of the *Critique of Pure Reason*, Kant noted, "appearance can be nothing for itself and outside our mode of representation. Thus, if there is not to be a constant circle, the word 'appearance' must already indicate a relation to something the immediate representation of which is, to be sure, sensible, but which in itself, without this constitution of our sensibility (on which the form of intuition is grounded), must be something, i.e. an object independent of sensibility" (*KRV* A251–2). An appearance implies something *that* appears. The appearance and the thing in itself are not two *things*, but are, rather, the same thing considered in different ways in transcendental reflection. The thing in itself just *is* that which appears when we attempt to think the latter in abstraction from how it must appear to us given our constitution. The appearance just *is* the thing in itself insofar as the latter presents itself to us, given "the constitution of our sensibility." In other words, the appearance and the thing in itself are the same thing considered from two points of view.

Nevertheless, Kant also spoke of appearances as being grounded in, or having their basis in, things in themselves. After all, they are given to us in sensation, and it is through sensation that we are affected by an "unknown something." In the *Prolegomena* Kant claims, "And we indeed, rightly considering objects of sense as mere appearances, confess thereby that they are based upon a thing in itself, though we know not this thing as it is in itself but only know its appearances, namely, the way in which our senses are affected by this unknown something. The understanding, therefore, by assuming appearances, grants the existence of things in themselves also..."[29] This is the second way in which we can think of the relation between the appearances and things in themselves. However, this way of understanding this relation tempts us to think that things in themselves and appearances are two distinct things. We can be led to think of the former as the cause or ground of the appearances, and of the appearances as their effects, where ground and effect somehow stand "outside" one another. Clearly, there are tensions between both ways of understanding the thing in itself. Both are indisputably found in Kant's text.[30] And Schleiermacher refers to both in his analysis.

The beginning of the passage clearly begins with the second view of this relation: "a common noumenon lies at the ground of each succession of appearances." However, Schleiermacher's argument depends in large part on his analysis of the distinct character of our mode of representation through which appearances are given to us. Appearances are given to us successively. For instance, when I view any object, such as a house, I first grasp one aspect of it, let us say the front, and then as I circle around it I apprehend the side and the back. I grasp the object through successive apprehensions. Through

[29] Immanuel Kant, *Prolegomena to any Future Metaphysics,* [314–15].
[30] For a discussion of the problem of the relation of things in themselves to appearances, see Henry E. Allison, *Kant's Transcendental Idealism: An Interpretation and Defense,* in particular the chapter "The Thing in Itself and the Problem of Affection."

them different aspects of the thing are revealed to me. The whole object is not given to me all at once. Furthermore, our very thinking is discursive; we first think one representation and then another. Hence what we are given through our successive apprehensions is a series of successive appearances. That we think of things as enduring (duration) throughout the states of their changes (succession) is a consequence of this mode of representation, together with the possibility of objective experience. As a result of our mode of apprehending what is given to us in sensation, the manifold of intuition contains parts that cannot be given all at once in a single representation. In other words, those things that are "coincidentally different" in our apprehension of the manifold are given "not as within one another, but outside one another." As such, given our mode of representation, "the whole expresses itself to us only in a series of appearances, in which all is together which may only be together for our faculty of representation, and all is separate, which must be separate as a consequence of the same." Were we to abstract from our mode of representation, we might imagine how another being without our limitations would think what we must apprehend successively. Such a being would "have a faculty of representation different from our own." A being that can represent the thing in itself would view it as "one, without duration and succession," that is, it would represent all of it at once, in a single intellectual intuition. As such it would view "the preformed seed of all those appearances, the ground of all those relations of things to others from which the appearances develop themselves."

This passage from *Spinozism* can easily lead us to conclude that Schleiermacher understands the noumena and the appearances to be one and the same thing, viewed from two points of view. Schleiermacher does not speak of the noumenon as something *different* from the appearances. There are not two *things* or two *worlds*, the world of noumena and the world of phenomena. The noumenon does not *stand outside* the appearances, acting as their cause. It is true that Schleiermacher speaks of the noumenon as the *ground* of the appearances. But such talk of the noumenon as ground need not commit him to thinking of the two as constituting two worlds. The noumenon grounds phenomena only in the sense that, were we to be capable of an intellectual intuition, we would see that everything that appears phenomenally is already contained in the noumenon. God, as "ground" of the world does not stand outside of the appearances. This, of course, rules out the theistic vision in which God is understood as different from the world, as existing independently of it, and creating it "out of nothing." Schleiermacher's reading of Spinoza also seems to rule out panentheism. In panentheism, there is a distinction between God and world, but the world is "in" God. Still, on this view God is yet more than the world. What Schleiermacher seems to espouse here, however, is more pantheistic in nature. Insofar as Schleiermacher puts forward a double aspect view of the relation of noumena to phenomena, the view coheres with a thoroughgoing identification of God and world.

Spinoza's philosophy contains a related point, and no doubt this is one of the main reasons that Schleiermacher believed that the two philosophers were saying essentially the same thing. In proposition 18 of the *Ethics*, Spinoza claims, "God is the immanent, not the transitive cause of all things." A transitive cause stands outside of its effect, that is, the effect lies beyond the cause. Not so with an immanent cause. The effect of an immanent cause cannot even be conceived apart from it. As Spinoza notes in demonstrating this proposition, "Everything that is, is in God, and must be conceived through God." Moreover, Spinoza claims, "outside of God there can be no substance, that is, a thing which is in itself outside God."[31] Insofar as God is an "immanent" cause there is an important sense in which God cannot be distinguished from the world, that is, nature is not a substance independent of God. The demonstration of Spinoza's Proposition 28, reproduced in its entirety in Jacobi's text and copied by Schleiermacher, contains similar claims. Its concluding lines affirm, "But all things that are, are in God, and so depend on God that they can neither be nor be conceived without him."[32] Schleiermacher adopts this understanding of the way that God relates to the world. He notes, "The infinite thing does not bring forth finite things and what belongs to them in a transitive way, not insofar as one is destroyed by the other, but rather only insofar as all belong to the eternal, unchangeable being" (*KGA* I.1, 529). The question, of course, still

---

[31] Benedict de Spinoza, *A Spinoza Reader: the Ethics and Other Works*, 100.
[32] Ibid. 104; cf. *KGA* I.1, 514.

remains whether God completely exhausts God-self in nature, so that God and nature can be completely identified.[33] Jacobi certainly understood Spinoza in this way, as is attested by the sixth paragraph of his forty-four paragraphs describing Spinoza's system. There he notes that "Therefore, the finite is in the infinite, so that the embodiment of all finite things is one and the same with the infinite thing, as in each moment it encompasses the whole of eternity, past and future in the same way" (*KGA* I.1, 514–15). Schleiermacher is working with this interpretation of Spinoza. And in light of this interpretation, it makes eminent sense to think of God and world as identical, only viewed from two different points of view.[34]

Schleiermacher argues that the view he puts forward here "can also be attributed to the Leibnizian" (*KGA* I.1, 526). What can he possibly mean here? He later notes, in agreement with Jacobi, that the Leibnizian position—when understood correctly—must ultimately dissolve into Spinozism. There he claims, "Now admittedly this personal God is not the cause of the world, and I have, after all, clearly shown that Leibniz, too, must arrive at such an idea of the deity" (*KGA* I.1, 532). In other words, he argues that given Leibniz's presuppositions, Leibniz cannot consistently hold to a *creatio ex nihilo*, and Leibniz's position is ultimately non-theistic. In §36 of the *Monadology* Leibniz had noted "there is an infinity of past and present shapes and motions that enter into the efficient cause of my present writing, and there is an infinity of small inclinations and dispositions of my soul, present and past, that enter into its final cause."[35] This means that the

---

[33] Curley, in particular, questions whether a careful reading of Spinoza warrants an identification of the one substance with the whole of nature. He refers to Letter 43, and notes "Spinoza is in fact contending, against Velthuysen, that his having said that all things emanate necessarily from the nature of God does not commit him to holding that the universe is God. I take this letter to be a clear rejection of that kind of pantheism." *Behind the Geometrical Method*, pp. 36ff, 149, n. 52.

[34] Paul Franks characterizes this move as one common to the German Idealists: "When they reject Kant's Two Essences view, the German idealists adopt what is in effect a Two Aspects view: the empirical aspect of a thing corresponds to the way in which a thing's being as it is, is ground in its relations to other things within the totality; the transcendental aspect of a thing corresponds to the way in which a thing's being as it is, is grounded in its relation to the totality and ultimately to the totality's absolute first principle. On this view, there is one world, understandable in two ways, or from two standpoints" Paul W. Franks, *All or Nothing*, 145.

[35] Leibniz, *Philosophical Essays*, 217.

ultimate ground of the state of any thing is completely determined by causes lying outside of it, causes that go back to infinity. However, Leibniz argues, if such efficient causes go back into infinity, we cannot give a sufficient reason for the state of anything unless we look outside the infinite series of conditioned beings. In §37 he claims, "It must be the case that the sufficient or ultimate reason is outside the sequence or *series* of this multiplicity of contingencies, however infinite it may be."[36] And in §38, Leibniz continues, "And this is why the ultimate reason of things must be in a necessary substance in which the diversity of changes is only eminent, as in its source."[37] The sufficient reason for the infinite series of conditioned beings lies eminently in God.

Why does Schleiermacher believe this leads to Spinozism? There are two reasons, both intimately related. First, if the state of each thing depends upon an infinite series of efficient causes, and if, moreover, this state itself determines all future states onto infinity, then there is a sense in which this state of the thing cannot be conceived through itself, since it stands in interdependence with all other elements in the series that lie outside of it. It can only be completely conceived through the whole world system, the elements of which mutually determine each other, and which thereby determine it. But since this system is infinite, it can only find its sufficient reason in God, who stands outside the series and contains all determinations of what occurs in the world only eminently. As such, the state of a thing cannot be conceived through itself; it can ultimately only be completely grasped (in terms of its sufficient reason) in relation to the infinite series of all finite things and in relation to the One that contains this series eminently. Second, given the fact that things are continuously coming into being and passing away (and changing into one another), what is the principle of individuation through which we are to mark off the beginning of one individual and the end of another? There is only one continuously identifiable substrate that takes on changing determinations, namely extension itself, which Schleiermacher conceives of in an organic sense. Hence, Schleiermacher notes, given the "alternating bringing forth and destruction of the organic parts of its

---

[36] Ibid. 218.   [37] Ibid.

extent [the extent of the world soul]," "finite individuals...are not absolute." We therefore have, "once again, Spinozism."

A similar kind of reasoning lies behind Schleiermacher's claim that "If a noumenon should be the ground of the whole series of appearances from seed to tree, then this series may not end here, it must extend itself to all previous trees and seeds and those that follow...This series must extend throughout the whole world of sense, and we thereby come once more to the Spinozistic relation." If the tree stands in complete interdependence with the series of events that lie outside of it, on what grounds do I mark off the noumenal ground *of the tree* from the noumenal grounds of all other things that I think are different from the tree, but upon which the coming to be of the tree depended? Moreover, in thinking of the noumenal ground of this tree, I must think of the whole series and its relation to God, which contains this series eminently. But I must think of the same series and its relation to God when I try to give a sufficient reason for *another* tree. The sufficient reason, and hence the noumenal ground of both trees, is the same. If the same noumenon grounds this tree and a future tree, on what grounds can I provide a noumenal distinction between the two trees? It is these kinds of considerations that lead Schleiermacher to affirm the Spinozistic idea that there is only one substance.[38]

Whereas in *Spinozism* Schleiermacher attempts to work out a view consistent with both Kant and Spinoza, in his *Short Presentation* Schleiermacher focuses on the differences between the two. He notes, "It cannot be claimed straight out, that the infinite thing relates to the

---

[38] For an excellent discussion of similar and related problems and how they drive post-Kantian Spinozism, see Franks, *All or Nothing*, in particular chapter two. Franks identifies what he calls Holistic Monism, a version of German Idealism that he argues is incompatible with one of Kant's fundamental commitments (namely that there are many noumenal agents). Two important characteristics of philosophical systems that embody holistic monism are the following: First, "the Holistic requirement is that, in an adequate philosophical system, empirical items must be such that all their properties are determinable only within the context of a totality composed of other items and their properties." Second, "the Monistic requirement is that, in an adequate philosophical system, the absolute first principle must be immanent within the aforementioned totality, as its principle of unity" (85). Both requirements follow from Spinoza's understanding of substance as that which can be conceived through itself, that is, that which requires nothing outside of itself for its intelligibility.

finite in the same way in Spinoza as in Kant. For otherwise Spinoza would have had to discover the critical philosophy before Kant" (*KGA* I.1, 573). Moreover, he grants that from the standpoint of the critical philosophy, nothing can be said about things in themselves. Critical idealism could not "presume to go further" and to attribute to the noumenon "a positive unity and infinity." Of this "it could know nothing" (*KGA* I.1, 574). He is aware of the critical distinction between logical grounds and real grounds, and defends Spinoza from the accusation that he has mixed up the two (*KGA* I.1, 564–5). He notes that he himself had been tempted to think that Spinoza had made this mistake. He concludes, however, that Spinoza came to the conclusion that "there must be an infinite thing, in which everything finite exists," because all things are in flux, and no existence can be attributed to such things when they are considered in themselves (*KGA* I.1, 564–5); he thereby claims that Spinoza does not conclude to the existence of an infinite thing through a confusion of logical and real grounds. How Schleiermacher arrives at this conclusion remains unclear.

Schleiermacher's own argument concerning the noumenal ground of the tree, discussed above, does seem to ignore the distinction between logical and real grounds. As Kant had noted, it is "evident beyond all possibility of doubt, that if the conditioned is given, a regress in the series of all its conditions is set as a task". One must, however, distinguish between logical and real grounds. A logical ground has to do with propositions. It requires that if a given proposition is posited, we must also assume that all its conditions or premises are presupposed. This is "simply the logical requirement that we should have adequate premises for any given conclusion" (*KRV* A500/B529). In the case of states of affairs, however, we move from some actual, conditioned state of affairs, to another state of affairs that conditions it. According to Kant, however, this search for conditions is an "empirical synthesis." In an empirical synthesis, the conditions are only accessible through the activity of the synthesis itself. Given that what is given in empirical intuition must conform to the forms of intuition, space and time, and that what can be given through these are *mere relations*,[39] it is impossible for the

---

[39] *Critique of Pure Reason,* B66–7.

unconditioned (itself not conditioned by its relation to anything else) to be given in intuition. Moreover, the contribution of the subject in the activity of this synthesis cannot be ignored.[40] This means that the imperative to search for the conditions for any given conditioned is only set as a regulative task. Since the elements of the synthesis must always be given to us successively through the forms of intuition, we cannot assume that once the conditioned is posited, all of the conditions are given along with it. Schleiermacher's argument regarding the noumenal ground of the tree, however, seems to ignore just this distinction. He assumes that we can inquire into the sufficient ground of each appearance, and thereby concludes that such a ground can only be grasped completely in terms of the whole series of appearances (the whole of the world) as well as in terms of what contains this series eminently. Hence he believes that once the conditioned appearance is given, we must assume that all of its conditions (the world as a whole, and God as its ground) is also given. Only in this way can he move beyond Kant's affirmation of the unknowable character of things in themselves and affirm that because the same ground conditions all appearances, there can be only one noumenon.

Significantly, Kant had recognized that if space and time are thought of as features of things in themselves, Spinozism results. In the *Critique of Practical Reason* he argued that

if this ideality of time and space is not assumed, only Spinozism remains, in which space and time are essential determinations of the original being itself, while the things dependent upon it (ourselves, therefore, included) are not substances but merely accidents inhering in it. For if these things exist only as its effects in time, which would then be the condition of their existence itself, the actions of these beings would have to be merely *its* actions, which it performs anywhere and at any time. Spinozism, therefore, in spite of the absurdity of its basic idea, argues far more cogently than the creation theory can ... (*KprV* 5:101–2)

What is given in intuition is always conditioned; it always stands in relation to something else and cannot be grasped outside of

---

[40] On this point, see Henry Allison's discussion in *Kant's Transcendental Idealism*, 53ff. See also Michelle Grier, *Kant's Doctrine of Transcendental Illusion*, in particular chapters three and four.

this relation. If we are transcendental realists and think that space and time are features of things in themselves, then we must also assume that things in themselves can be completely described in terms of these spatial and temporal features, which, however, only exhibit things as they stand in *relation* to one another. If things in themselves are spatial and temporal, their properties, too, are intrinsically relational. But if all we have are things whose properties are all intrinsically relational (such that each thing and its properties cannot be grasped outside of its relation to other things), there can then be no plurality of genuine *substances*, each of which must contain the principle of its own activity *within itself* if it is to be a substance. Instead, the action of all phenomenal beings must be thought of as the temporal effects of a single, unconditioned being, and hence we come back to the Spinozistic relation. While Schleiermacher adopts the Kantian view of the ideality of space and time, in *Spinozism* he does not address why Kant believed that transcendental idealism blocks the Spinozistic conclusion. He demonstrates more awareness of this in the *Short Presentation* where he notes that while "Spinoza likewise proceeds from the universal problem, to find the unconditioned from the conditioned ... Kant at least allows the thought of an unconditioned outside of the series of appearances. Spinoza thought no other unconditioned is possible than the complete totality of the conditioned" (*KGA* I.1, 574).

Schleiermacher's preferred argument for the claim that there is only one thing that really exists has to do with the constant flux of appearances. In a remarkable passage in *Spinozism* Schleiermacher affirms:

My sensualization is not taken from the object of space, but from time. However, the application is easy and natural. The actual true and real in the soul is the feeling of Being, the immediate concept, as Spinoza calls it. This, however, can never be perceived. Only individual concepts and expressions of the will can be perceived, and apart from these, there exists nothing else in the soul at any moment of time. Can one for this reason say that individual concepts have their distinct, individual being? No, nothing actually exists except the feeling of Being: the immediate concept. Individual concepts are only its revelations. Can one say that the immediate concept exists only as thinking in another? By no means. The immediate concept is the actual, essential ground of the soul. All those individual concepts inhere in its modes (understanding and will). Yet admittedly, one must not go on from this to say that the immediate concept is the sum of the individual concepts.

(*KGA* I.1, 535)

Schleiermacher does not proceed from the problem of the constant flux of appearances in space (as does Plato), but rather from the successive character of the apprehensions given to the understanding. Hence he notes that his own argument is "not taken from the object of space, but from time." Schleiermacher affirms, along with Kant, that time is the form of inner sense, that is, it is given in and through the way that the self successively apprehends the manifold.[41] And it is from the successive and fleeting character of these apprehensions that Schleiermacher proceeds to build his argument. These are what consciousness perceives, although they have no genuine subsistence in themselves, and hence have no real existence. What *is* real is "the feeling of Being, the immediate concept." The successive moments in the river of the soul's life—representations and desires— "are only its revelations."

A passage from the *Short Presentation* sheds light on what Schleiermacher means here. The passage in question is one in which Schleiermacher argues against the idea of an extramundane cause of the world. If the "infinite Monad" creates the world in such a way that it relates *to* a world that exists outside of it, "with what right does the infinite Monad not belong to the world?" For example, if we think of God as a kind of first cause, then we are thinking of God as standing in the same series of causes as all intra-mundane causes, and we cannot adequately distinguish God from the world. He notes, "It is, after all, the same in kind as the finite ones that make up the world, and between the two there is no other difference than that of degree, and this is not sufficient." Moreover the difference between the infinite Monad and the world cannot be the "immediacy," with which the infinite Monad represents the world. Such an idea is "inde-fensible, since representation cannot in any way be thought without a medium." Therefore, either the infinite Monad has

[41] "space and time make up what is characteristic of our form of representation" (*KGA* I.1, 575).

its own Monad-body, and is thereby a single individual, in the wretched sense in which the Godhead, according to Spinoza, is impossible, or the whole world is its body and thereby with it makes up only one thing. Were Leibnizianism to count on the possibility of thought without a medium, then at least it is easy to show that this cannot contain a single representation nor single determinations of the will. It is therefore something undetermined, which, after all, cannot be real without determinations, and so we would be once again back to Spinoza. (*KGA* I.1, 570)

If the infinite Monad has its own representations and determinations of the will that are distinct from the world, then it is an individual in the same way that all finite things are individuals, and there can only be a difference of degree between the finite and the infinite. This is the "wretched sense in which the Godhead is impossible" according to Spinoza, for then it would be one individual among others. Yet God cannot be counted among the number of individuals, for God does not stand under a common genus with things.[42] We can have no "general concept," of God, and as such, we cannot "give God the name of an individual;" in other words, God is not a thing among things, or an individual among individuals. But this is exactly how we think of God when we to try "distinguish God from the finite things," and think of God as "outside of them," that is, when we think of the world as different from God and God's determinations (*KGA* I.1, 569). If on the other hand, the infinite Monad is thought of as having no determinations, then it is nothing. The only other viable alternative, Schleiermacher argues, is to think of the world as God's determinations, and this brings us back to the Spinozistic relation.[43]

If God is not an individual among others, as Schleiermacher argues, then God can never be an object *for* consciousness. As Schleiermacher notes, the immediate concept—the feeling of Being, "can never be perceived." How then do we relate to it? It is given

---

[42] So Schleiermacher, "subsumption under numbers takes place only then, and in the things that one has brought under a common genus" (*KGA* I.1, 568–9).

[43] Lessing put forward a similar idea in his *On the Reality of Things Outside God*, where he argues that God does not reduplicate finite things such that they exist "outside" of God's ideas. Rather, finite things are identical with these ideas. See *Lessing: Philosophical and Theological Writings*, 32–33. For an analysis of Lessing's argument, see Henry E. Allison, *Lessing and the Enlightenment*, 70ff.

through the transcendental unity of apperception, in virtue of which all my representations are *mine*. Just like the immediate concept, this transcendental unity is not itself a representation. It is, rather, that function in virtue of which representations are brought to a unity. As such it is given immediately and never appears. It is the ground of all the self's representations, and not merely their sum.[44] By the time he gives his lectures on *Dialectic* (the first set of lectures was given in 1811), Schleiermacher provides a much more nuanced account of the way he conceives the transcendental unity of apperception to relate to the immediate concept. There he claims that "the transcendental," as that which both grounds and surpasses consciousness, "is also the idea of Being in itself under two kinds or forms and modes that are contrary and yet related to one another, namely, the ideal and the real, as conditions of the reality of knowledge."[45] Later on in the *Dialectic* he affirms that we can "completely abstract" from the distinction "between the transcendent and the transcendental."[46] The distinction is one coined by Kant: when we speak of the transcendental, we speak merely of the conditions of the possibility of experience, and hence too, of the activity of the transcendental subject in making

---

[44] As Sarah Schmidt notes in *Die Konstruktion des Endlichen*, "Das unmittelbare Selbstbewußtsein eint jedoch nicht nur die einzelnen Akte des Bewußtseins (ähnlich der Kantischen transzendentalen Apperception), sondern geht über das einzelne Subjekt oder Ich hinaus, indem es die Einheit des leidenden und handelnden Subjektes ist und als solche auch das Sein des Anderen einschließt, es ist 'gleichürprungliches Sein des Selbst und des anderen,' unser 'Für-uns-Selbst-Sein umfaßt unser gesamtes Sein für-anderes.' Da wir auch in unmittelbaren Selbstbewußtsein uns nicht als Stifter dieser Einheit erfahren, sondern sich uns vielmehr im Mangel ein Verweis auf etwas über uns Hinausgehendes zeigt, spricht Schleiermacher daher auch von einen "Abhängigkeitsgefühl" (159–60). Nevertheless, it is important to keep in mind, as I argue in the rest of the book, that a careful reading of the mature Schleiermacher shows that he does not simply identify the transcendent ground of consciousness with ultimate reality itself, but that rather, it is a rift in the immediate self-consciousness that signals the self's relation to ultimate reality. The idea is nicely captured by Manfred Frank in the introduction to his 2001 edition of Schleiermacher's *Dialectic*: "Das, was dem unmittelbaren Selbstbewußtsein [oder Gefühl] einleuchtet, wenn es zwischen dem einem und dem anderen Pol der Reflektions-Spaltung hin und herflackert, ist also nicht etwa die positive Fülle einer überreflexiven Identität, sondern vielmehr das *Negative von deren Mangel*" (92). See also Frank's chapter "Metaphysical foundations: A look at Schleiermacher's *Dialectic*" in *The Cambridge Companion to Friedrich Schleiermacher*, especially 26–33.

[45] *Dialektik: Aus Schleiermachers handscriftlichem Nachlasse*, edited by L. Jonas, Berlin: 1839, III. Abt. Bd. 4/2, 77.

[46] Ibid. 38.

experience possible. The transcendent, however, is that which lies beyond the limits of all possible experience.[47] Here the transcendent and the transcendental are identified in that the idea of Being, as the unity between the real and the ideal, must be assumed as a condition of the possibility of knowledge. Despite his familiarity with Kant's arguments against the possibility of knowledge of the transcendent, in *Spinozism* Schleiermacher had already come to the conclusion that it is through the transcendental activity of the self that the soul comes into contact with what is genuinely real. At this point, however, he does not believe that there is a genuine principle of individuation, or that the soul is a genuine substance. As such, there is no ground of personal identity. This is the subject of our next chapter.

---

[47] See *Critique of Pure Reason*, A295/B352.

3

Personal Identity

In the preceding chapter we have noted that in *Spinozism* and in the *Short Presentation of the Spinozistic System*, Schleiermacher adopted a thoroughly Kantian standpoint regarding the conditions of knowledge. We only have direct access to representations, the content of which is given to us in sensation. Furthermore, it is through the work of the understanding, in particular as exemplified in the analogies of experience, that we come to distinguish between inner and outer sense. However, Schleiermacher saw that given this starting point, we have no guarantee that what we perceive as phenomenal individuals have a noumenal ground. From an epistemic standpoint, we have no access to the *vinculum* of the monads. And from the standpoint of metaphysics, Schleiermacher argued, once we posit that phenomenal entities stand in thoroughgoing interdependence with one another, it becomes very difficult consistently to posit more than a single noumenal ground of all phenomenal reality. This, he believed, brings us back to the Spinozistic relation.

Schleiermacher's arguments in *Spinozism* move beyond the problem of the principle of individuation to the problem of personal identity. Of course, the two questions are inherently related. His protracted discussion of personal identity is significant for two reasons. First, it reveals the basic contours of Schleiermacher's understanding of subjectivity. This understanding is first and foremost a Kantian one. Even after Schleiermacher moves beyond the position he takes in *Spinozism* and in the *Short Presentation*, it remains a determinative influence on his thought and has significant consequences for his ethics. Given the discursive character of thought, the self is known only through its world; we have no access to the "inner" self, only to the "outer." Second, this discussion reveals the depth of Schleiermacher's grasp of what can be inferred from the Kantian theory of subjectivity regarding the metaphysical problem of the relation of self and world and the ground of both. His analysis proceeds from the question of what can be inferred from the unity of self-consciousness. It is heavily influenced by Kant's argument in the chapter on the paralogisms of the first *Critique*, where Kant argues that we cannot validly infer the noumenal substantiality of the self from the identity of self-consciousness. Schleiermacher argues, further, that even the conditions of the possibility of practical rationality do not warrant the inference that we are (a) noumenally real substantial beings and (b) that we are transcendentally free. This chapter continues the analysis of *Spinozism* begun in the last chapter. It is divided into two parts. In the first I discuss Schleiermacher's analysis of subjectivity along with his claim that the unity and identity of self-consciousness cannot ground metaphysical inferences to the noumenal reality of intelligible substances. In the second, I discuss his understanding of practical rationality and its relationship to determinism and the mechanism of nature.

PERSON, PERSONALITY, AND THE PRINCIPLE OF PERSONALITY

In a long passage in *Spinozism* Schleiermacher distinguishes between "person" and "personality," and claims that both concepts can be found in Kant and Jacobi.[1] Personality is "that property characteristic of a thing making it into a person." He will argue, however, that it is a necessary, but not a sufficient condition of "complete" personhood. Following Jacobi, he argues for a distinction between what he calls the "personality" and the "principle of personality," and defines these terms in the following way: "the personality is the characteristic property of a thing considered as a subject; the principle of personality is

[1] As Grove notes, another important source for Schleiermacher's discussion is the article on person and personality in Carl Christian Erhard Schmid's 1788 *Wörterbuch zum leichtern Gebrauch der Kantischen Schriften nebst einer Abhandlung* (Schmid, *Wörterbuch*, 276); Grove, *Deutungen des Subjekts*, 102.

the characteristic property of a thing as person if it is to be considered purely as object (*KGA* I.1, 539). The upshot of this distinction is the following: the principle of personality is *objective* and has to do with whether, objectively considered, a being has its own principle of individuation. This relates to our discussion in the previous chapter regarding the *vinculum* of the monads. Personality, however, is merely *subjective*. It concerns the relation between the merely logical, analytic unity supplied by the transcendental I in Kant's philosophy and its relation to self-consciousness. Does the relation of the transcendental I to self-consciousness ground valid inferences regarding the nature of the metaphysical self? The problem, as Kant had clearly noted in the paralogisms of the first *Critique*, is whether the analytic unity of consciousness—the transcendental I in virtue of which all my representations are mine—can be used as the basis for a rational psychology in which we attribute substantiality, simplicity, personal identity, and independence to the soul. In *Spinozism*, Schleiermacher clearly sides with Kant on this problem; his discussion is clearly informed by Kant's paralogisms.

Given the distinction between the personality and the principle of personality, Schleiermacher delineates three possibilities. He notes,

The foundational concept, namely, is overall identity with consciousness. a. If a thing is itself conscious of this identity, and also really possesses it, then it is a complete person, that is, a person in both respects, considered as subject and as object. b. If it is conscious of this identity, but does not really have it, then it is only subjectively a person but has no objective personality. c. If it really has this identity, but is not itself conscious of it, then it has objective personality but no subjective personality.   (*KGA* I.1, 539)

Only if some thing both has consciousness of its own identity and really possesses it can it be considered a "complete person." There are, however, two other possibilities. First, the fact that we are self-conscious does not allow us to make inferences concerning the noumenal reality of the self. It is therefore possible that a being have self-consciousness (personality) without it having any genuine substantiality grounding its consciousness of itself as an individual being (a principle of personality). This is what is being considered under option b. Second, what Schleiermacher describes under c.

concerns the possibility that animals, for example, which are not self-conscious, nevertheless possess a genuine principle of individuation. This may also be true of things having a principle of individuation, but which have no personality. All three options, a, b, and c, are genuine possibilities because personality and the principle of personality do not in any way imply or exclude one another. Each can exist with or without the other.

Schleiermacher remarks that he does not believe that from a purely theoretical standpoint "the second kind should be called a true person" and "even so little do I believe one can deny the third kind (the animals) would be a real person" (*KGA* I.1, 539). He thereby claims that the principle of personality (the principle of identity) is both necessary and sufficient for personhood. For our purposes, the most interesting claim is that the principle of personality (genuine *noumenal* substantial identity throughout change) is *necessary* for genuine personhood. We have already seen in the previous chapter that Schleiermacher denies that we have any epistemological access to the principle of identity of a thing. And from a metaphysical standpoint, he argues that we are led to conclude that there is only one noumenal ground of all phenomena. This excludes the idea of a plurality of noumenal agents.

The most significant aspect of Schleiermacher's long discussion of the relationship between the three concepts, person, personality, and the principle of personality is his claim that the consciousness of personality does not imply the substantiality of the noumenal self. In other words, the having of personality does not imply possession of a principle of personality. Moreover, Schleiermacher affirms that when we view a person objectively, from a third-person point of view, we can think of such an individual as an individual substance (that is, such an individual is phenomenally, as an object of experience, a substance). However, we cannot attribute unity and simplicity to the consciousness of such an individual. In making these claims, Schleiermacher clearly relies on the results of Kant's paralogisms. His argument here is worth quoting at length:

For Jacobi, the personality is what makes a being into a person of the second kind (for insofar as the thing thinks of itself as subject, and the unity of self-consciousness relates only to it as such, this cannot decide whether it possesses the personality of the first kind) and the principle of personality is what makes a being into a person of the third kind. However, then he should not say: each thing that possesses personality—and only this—is a person. If, therefore, the concept of the third kind were the actual foundational concept of a person, then the person of the second kind would be only an apparent person. A person of the first kind, however, would be a person with this consciousness, that she is a person. The question is whether a purely apparent person is possible. Jacobi admits the Kantian assertion that I can doubt whether my consciousness is continuous, more than he himself affirms it. This case of an apparent person thereby touches purely upon the possibility of doubt that consciousness can be continuous. In what sense can Jacobi admit this doubt? This must determine the point of comparison between his own doctrine and that of Kant's. Jacobi defined the personality as unity of self-consciousness and for him the person is a being that has consciousness of its identity. Since only the personality is technically the whole of what makes a being into a person, the consciousness of identity must thereby have to do with the unity of consciousness. There is no doubt about the latter. It is therefore empirically certain since I always refer one consciousness to a preceding one, and see many together as a joined series in which the representations that therein come to the fore are in fact different and outside one another. The different acts of consciousness, however, are related to one another through the identity of the subject through which the different representations are referred. There is therefore no doubt concerning the first expression (consciousness of identity), and no appearance of the same can take place in its stead insofar as merely the identity of self-consciousness of the transcendental unity of the I should be thereby understood. Alone the old school made a leap and said: where this transcendental unity is identical, there also its substratum, the substance, must be identical. If, then, this also were to be understood under the identity, the consciousness of which makes a being into a person, then in any case we find doubt and an appearance of the same instead. Namely, the thing [is] subjective if it does not proceed from itself and behaves itself as an object. Rather just as it considers itself in self-consciousness, it can never achieve the idea of the identity of a real substrate, for the consciousness, which is the sole *ratio cognoscendi* of self-consciousness, relates itself only to the outer of the thing, not to its inner, and the unity of this self-consciousness can thereby relate to the I and not to the substance. From an objective point of view, I then admittedly have a reason to attribute something that persists to a thing, to think the same thing as having consciousness, and to thereby ascribe a continuity of consciousness to it. In this way alone I cannot again attain the unity of self-consciousness, for I have no reason to arrive at the unity and inner connection of consciousness from its continuity. And if I also do this hypothetically, in that I attribute to consciousness a transcendental ground, then I may in no way identify this transcendental I with the real substrate or substance. Here thereby a double doubt, or moreover, uncertainty, is not only possible, but even necessary.

(*KGA* I.1, 539–41)

Briefly put, from the necessity of the transcendental unity of the I (worked out in Kant's transcendental deduction), we cannot conclude to the substantial unity of the self. Schleiermacher notes that the "consciousness of identity" has to do with the "unity of consciousness." In other words, the unity of consciousness is a necessary condition of the consciousness of identity. What does Schleiermacher mean by such a unity of consciousness? He tells us there is no doubt that there is such a unity. He calls it "empirically certain" in the sense that we know that we are aware of our own activity of bringing together representations that are "different and outside one another" in one consciousness. It is through the identity of the subject that the different representations are "bound with one another." What is the nature of this identity of which he speaks?

In §16 of Kant's *Critique of Pure Reason*, Kant begins his discussion of "that which itself contains the ground of the unity of different concepts in judgements, and hence of the possibility of the understanding, even in its logical use." His argument begins with the well known proposition that "the **I think** must **be able** to accompany all my representations; for otherwise something would be represented in me that could not be thought at all, which is as much to say that the representation would either be impossible or else would be nothing for me" (*KRV* B132). This "I think" is what Kant calls the transcendental unity of self-consciousness. It is the necessary condition for all combinations of representations. Since our consciousness is discursive, that is, we are conscious of representations that are "different and outside of one another," these can only be related to one another through the transcendental unity of consciousness. Such a transcendental unity is a necessary condition for our ability to form concepts, for it is through concepts that many representations are thought together under one representation. Hence the transcendental unity of consciousness relates to the analytic unity of the concept. But for any kind of combination to take place, a transcendental unity of consciousness through which different representations are grasped and then related to one another is presupposed. Since the representations, considered in themselves, are different and outside one another, the only way that they can be brought into relation with one another is through some third thing, to which both are related. This is the transcendental unity of consciousness itself, which first relates to representation x, and then to representation y, and relates x to y in and through the fact that they relate to it (the transcendental unity of consciousness).[2] This transcendental unity and its function is what Schleiermacher refers to when he notes that "I always refer one consciousness to a preceding one, and see many together as a joined series in which the representations that therein come to the fore are in fact different and outside one another. The different acts of consciousness, however, are related to one another through the identity of the subject through which the different representations are referred."[3] If the "I think" were not to accompany all my representations, that representation which the "I think" did not accompany could not be related to other representations, and hence could not be thought. The "I think" is as such the *ratio essendi* of the possibility of the combination of all representations, and hence of all thinking itself. The unity of consciousness to which Schleiermacher refers is just this transcendental unity. This is the "identity of self-consciousness of the transcendental unity of the I."

The *self*-consciousness of identity presupposes the unity of consciousness, that is, the transcendental unity of apperception. If I am to be *conscious* of myself as one and the same thinker of my representations, all my representations must be referable to a single "I think." I must, thereby, possess a unity of consciousness. This unity of consciousness, however, need not imply a consciousness of this unity, that is, self-consciousness. For instance, it is possible for animals to have consciousness without having self-consciousness.

---

[2] This analytic unity must be distinguished from the synthetic unity. The analytic unity allows us to infer that these representations all belong to the same subject, whereas the synthetic unity implies combination of representations in accordance with necessary laws making possible complex thoughts. As Henrich has noted, "the conditions constituting complex thoughts must surely be distinguished from the conditions of the mere co-presence of thoughts in one and the same subject." See Henrich, "Identity and Objectivity," 171.

[3] On this point, see also Grove's discussion in *Deutungen des Subjekts*, 101–11.

Schleiermacher does not bother to make this distinction here, as this problem is not his principle concern. His main concern, rather, is with whether the transcendental unity of apperception, and even the self-consciousness of this unity, implies the *substantial* unity and identity of the self. Schleiermacher mentions the "leap" made by the "old school", namely, the inference that "where this transcendental unity is identical, there also its substratum, the substance, must be identical." Is it possible to move from the "I" of apperception grounding the series of fleeting representations to the substantiality of the self? It is precisely this inference that Kant claimed is unwarranted, and his arguments for its lack of warrant can be found in his chapter on the paralogisms of pure reason. Kant there argues that substantive claims cannot be made about the transcendental subject, and that it is an error to attribute substantiality, simplicity, personal identity and independence to the soul. This is an error in judgment, which arises when we seek the unconditioned unity of apperception and think that it can be brought under the same concepts through which we think objects of experience.[4] Because the categories of the understanding cannot legitimately be applied to this unconditioned unity, we can have no concept of any object that corresponds to it (A339/B397).[5] The transcendental unity of apperception is a condition of thought that cannot itself be understood in terms of the conditions valid for the *objects* of thought, that is, this transcendental unity cannot itself be subsumed under the categories.

---

[4] In her book *Kant's Doctrine of Transcendental Illusion*, Michelle Grier convincingly demonstrates that the paralogisms are a specific instance of Kant's general theory of transcendental illusion in the Dialectic as a whole. Moreover, she notes the distinction between the inescapability of transcendental *illusion*, and the avoidability of the mistake in *judgment* that results from the application of the categories of the understanding to the transcendental unity of apperception, the supreme condition of all thought. Grier correctly claims: "in taking this illusion to be unavoidable, however, Kant is *not* claiming that we are necessarily deceived by it, as shown by his own distinction between the illusion and the deceptive inferences of rational psychology...the 'illusion' (here, in rational psychology) is said to *manifest itself* in a transcendental 'subreption,' referred to as the 'subreption of the hypostatized consciousness [*apperceptionis subtantiatae*]' (A402). However, Kant clearly wishes to distinguish the 'natural illusion' in rational psychology from the 'logical' error that characterizes the subsequent paralogistic *inferences*," 149.

[5] In his *Reflexion* 5553 Kant notes that the first paralogism mistakes the "unity of apperception, which is subjective," for the "unity of the subject as thing" (*Kants gesammelte Schriften*, 18:224).

In order to understand Schleiermacher's remarks, it is instructive to take an in-depth look at the Kantian arguments to which Schleier-macher refers. In his introductory remarks regarding the dialectical inferences of pure reason Kant characterizes the paralogisms in the following way: "from the transcendental concept of a subject that contains nothing manifold I infer the absolute unity of this subject itself, even though in this way I have no concept of it" (A340/B398). Kant's discussion of the problem of the paralogisms takes into consideration what was already noted by Hume in his *A Treatise of Human Nature*, namely, "When I turn my reflection upon myself, I can never perceive this *self* without one or more perceptions; nor can I ever perceive any thing but the perceptions. 'Tis the composition of these, therefore, that forms the self."[6] Hume's reflections on the problem led him to posit what is referred to, famously, as the "bundle" theory of consciousness, the identification of the self with the various thoughts, desires, and experiences that are the denizens of a person's psyche. Of course, Kant's own theory of mind is significantly different from Hume's. At the basis of Kant's understanding of mind is his positing of the transcendental I grounding all logical functions of judgment.[7] Nevertheless, Hume's observation is telling and plays a significant role in Kant's development of the paralogisms. When combined with Kant's understanding of the function of the transcendental unity, two things follow from Hume's observation regarding the fact that the self cannot be perceived. Both are inherently related. First, no perception of which I am aware can play the role of the transcendental unity of apperception grounding all functions of judgment. Any perception is itself an element that must be related to other elements of perception *through* the transcendental unity. Second, the *transcendental unity of the subject contains nothing manifold*. This is the *nervus probandi* of the paralogisms. It is *because* the transcendental unity can contain nothing manifold that one cannot have a perception of the self. Such a transcendental unity *cannot* contain anything manifold, for it is merely a logical function *through which* the manifold

---

[6] David Hume, *A Treatise of Human Nature*, 634.

[7] Paul Franks perceptively notes that the transcendental unity of apperception "expresses the finite character of a subject whose thought remains empty without data given to its receptive faculty." Franks, *All or Nothing*, 62.

is combined in accordance with the categories. Kant characterizes the I of apperception as an "empty representation ... of which one cannot even say that it is a concept, but a mere consciousness that accompanies every concept" (*KRV* B404/A346).

Kant develops the claim that the transcendental unity of the subject contains nothing manifold in the following passage concerning the first paralogism of substantiality from the A edition: "For the I is, to be sure, in all thoughts, but not the least intuition is bound up with this representation, which would distinguish it from all objects of intuition. Therefore one can, to be sure, perceive that this representation continually recurs with every thought, but not that it is a standing and abiding intuition, in which thoughts (as variable) would change" (*KRV* A350). The I of apperception is given with every thought. The problem, however, is that it is an *empty* representation. In other words, no abiding intuition is given with it, and hence it cannot be characterized in terms of any such intuition. Without such an intuition, *it cannot be distinguished* from other intuitions. And if it cannot be so distinguished, it cannot be picked out in such a way that it can be *related* to other intuitions. The self cannot, therefore, be thought of as a substance *in which* thoughts change. The categories of unity, simplicity, substantiality, and possibility are ultimately functions of unity for our representations. But without such an abiding intuition of the I that accompanies all my representations, there is no way to relate the transcendental self to other empirically given intuitions and to thereby unite them through a category. As such, the categories *cannot possibly* serve to unify the transcendental self with other intuitions, and hence the categories cannot be applied to it. To apply the categories in such a way would be to treat the transcendental self as if it were something empirically given, which it is not.

The application of the concept of simplicity to the "I think" is similarly problematic. Kant notes that "I am simple signifies no more than that this representation I encompasses not the least manifoldness within itself, and that it is an absolute (though merely logical unity)" (*KRV* A355). He continues:

so it is permitted to me to say, "I am a simple substance," i.e., a substance the representation of which never contains a synthesis of the manifold; but this concept, or even this proposition, teaches us not the least bit in regard to myself as an object of experience, because the concept of substance is used only as a function of synthesis, without any intuition being subsumed under it, hence without an object, and it is valid only of the condition of our cognition, but not of any particular object that is to be specified.

(*KRV* A356)

Whatever simplicity there is to the "I think" is not the simplicity that could be attributed to an intelligible substance. It is, rather, merely the logical requirement that all representations be related to the same "I think" if judgment is to be possible. Moreover, as noted above, the category of substance cannot be applied to the I in such a way as to make it into an object of experience: as Kant notes, here the notion of the I as substance can only be correctly applied as a function of synthesis, that is, the transcendental I *functions* in such a way as to allow my representations to be brought together through the functions of judgment.[8]

Kant's discussion of the substantiality and simplicity of the self ground his discussion of the third paralogism of transcendental psychology, namely that concerning personal identity. This problem is what is at issue when Schleiermacher notes, with regard to what he calls an "apparent person" (a being that is itself conscious of its identity, but to which *objective* substantiality cannot be attributed), that such a case "thereby touches purely upon the possibility of doubt that consciousness can be continuous." What does this doubt amount to? In an important passage introducing the third paralogism, Kant notes:

If I want to cognize through experience the numerical identity of an external object, then I will attend to what is persisting in its appearance, to which, as subject, everything else relates as a determination, and I will notice the identity of the former in the time in which the latter changes.

(*KRV* A362)

Kant affirms that a necessary condition of the attribution of identity to a thing involves the determination of some quality persisting in

---

[8] On the relation of the "I think" to the logical forms of judgment in Kant's thought, see Beatrice Longuenesse, *Kant and the Capacity to Judge*, especially 64–72.

appearance.[9] If Kant's analysis of this necessary condition for cognition of the numerical identity of an object is correct, then right off it can be seen that since the transcendental I contains nothing manifold, it cannot meet these conditions for the cognition of numerical identity. Since the I has no manifold, no part of it can persist in appearance. As such, I cannot continuously identify some quality of the I that endures throughout the changes in its representational states.

This is no doubt the argument that Schleiermacher has in mind in noting that when the self "considers itself in self-consciousness, it can never achieve the idea of the identity of a real substrate." What he says in what follows is elliptical, but of supreme importance for the understanding of the self that he will eventually adopt: "the consciousness, which is the sole *ratio cognoscendi* of self-consciousness, relates itself only to the outer of the thing, not to its inner, and the unity of this self-consciousness can thereby relate to the I and not to the substance." That consciousness relates only to the *outer* of the thing, and not to what is *inner*, concerns all objects of possible experience.[10]

---

[9] As Longuenesse notes, "For the concept of substance has no other meaning than that of being the referent of the term x to which all concepts of real determinations are attributed in judgment. Outside this relation to accidents, there is no substance, just as outside their relation to a substance there are no accidents" (Longueness, *Kant and the Capacity to Judge*, 331). She cites *Reflexion* 5861, in which Kant claims "Accidents are only the substance's manner of existing according to what is positive." She also cites the *Met. Volckmann*, "An absolute subject which would remain once we had abandoned all predicates cannot be thought and is thus impossible, because it is contrary to human nature, for we cognize everything discursively" (Ak. xxviii–1, 429–30). The point is that we can only know a substance through its determinations, but these must be given to us as the real in sensation. The problem for Kant then becomes, "How is it possible for 'realities' which are given to us only through the arbitrary and contingent interplay of our sensations, to be 'determined' in respect of the relation between subject and predicate in judgment?" Kant's answer to the question lies in the *synthesis speciosa*. As Longueness notes, "the schema of the relation between substance and accidents is the temporal relation between a real that is permanent and a real that changes" (332). But this means that in order to determine something as an empirical substance, we must be able to relate a determination of a thing that persists to changing determinations. Absent a real that persists and that can be related to continual change of representations in the self, we cannot attribute substantiality to the transcendental I. But since the I think has no manifold, with it there is given no reality that persists.

[10] The idea that we can know things only in relation to us, as well as their relations to one another only insofar as they stand in relation to us is firmly rooted in Kant's critical philosophy. This is what Schleiermacher means when he notes that we know only the "outer" and not the "inner" of a thing. In his first *Critique* Kant notes

This includes the self insofar as it is an object of experience, that is, the empirical self (the empirical self must be carefully distinguished from the transcendental self). In its consciousness of itself, the self can relate itself only to the manifold of its representations. However, all these representations go on to constitute the empirical world; they are all *relational* insofar as they represent the world in relation to the self. And insofar as some of these representations are of the self, they can only be of the empirical, embodied self in its relation and interactions with the world. As such, there is no representation of the *inner* self that contains some quality that appears; indeed there cannot be one, as the transcendental I does not itself contain a manifold. The *unity* and *identity* of self-consciousness is a feature of the transcendental I. This unity and identity, however, cannot be understood as a feature of the empirical self, that is, the self as substance in the empirical world. Hence the "unity of self-consciousness" can relate only "to the I and not to the substance."

In the *Critique of Pure Reason*, Kant frames the problem of personal identity in terms of ascertaining the identity of the self throughout its changing determinations, that is, in terms of the identity of consciousness throughout the continual change of its representations.

"Everything in our cognition that belongs to intuition . . . contains nothing but mere relations; of places in one intuition (extension), alteration of places (motion), and laws in accordance with which this alteration is determined (moving forces). But what is present in the place, or what it produces in the things themselves besides the alteration of place, is not given through these relations. Now through mere relations no thing in itself is cognized; it is therefore right to judge that since nothing is given to us through outer sense except mere representations of relation, outer sense can also contain in its representation only the relation of an object to the subject, and not that which is internal to the object in itself. It is exactly the same in the case of inner sense" (*KRV* B66–7); cf. *KRV* A283/B339, "a persistent appearance in space (impenetrable extension) contains mere relations and nothing absolutely internal," and *KRV* A285/B341, "whatever we can cognize only in matter is pure relations (that which we call their inner determinations is only comparatively internal)." For a discussion of the problem of the relation of a thing's monadic properties (properties that a thing has in abstraction from all relations) to its relational properties in Kant, see Franks *All or Nothing*, 36–51. What is important for our purposes here, however, is that both Kant and Schleiermacher clearly affirm that we have no access to the thing in itself, that is, the "inner" character of things independent of their relation to us. Hence, all we have access to is the outer, that is, things as they appear and stand in relation to us. We also only have access to the self as it appears, as it is given to us in inner intuition and as acting in the external world. Of the self we also know *only* the "outer" self.

Ultimately, the problem concerns the identity of the self through time. How is cognition of the identity of the self through time possible? Kant provides two answers, each stemming from a different point of view. From the point of view of the subject, time is *in* me. That is, insofar as time is that which orders *my* representations, and given that these representations are all mine, it goes without saying that it is the same *I* that relates first to one representation and then to another. Personal identity is unfailingly met with in *my own consciousness*. As Kant notes:

> Consequently, I relate each and every one of my successive determinations to the numerically identical Self in all time, i.e., in the form of inner intuition of my self. On this basis the personality of the soul must be regarded not as inferred but rather as a completely identical proposition of self-consciousness in time, and that is also the cause of its being valid *a priori*. For it really says no more than that in the whole time in which I am conscious of myself, I am conscious of this time as belonging to the unity of my Self, and it is all the same whether I say that this whole time is in Me, as an individual unity, or that I am to be found with numerical identity, in all of this time.
>
> The identity of person is therefore inevitably to be encountered in my own consciousness.   (*KRV* A362)

The story is quite different when the question concerns the empirical self, that is, the self as viewed from a third-person, "objective" point of view. When a person is viewed from such a point of view, one can, indeed, attribute substantiality to him or her in an objective sense, that is, I can think of him or her as something in the world interacting with other things in the world subject to all three of the analogies of experience. However, the kind of unity and identity of self-consciousness that I attribute to myself from a first-person point of view cannot be attributed to the self from a third-person point of view. As Kant notes:

> But if I consider myself from the standpoint of another (as an object of his outer intuition), then it is this external observer who originally considers **me** as **in time;** for in apperception **time** is represented only **in me.** Thus from the I that accompanies—and indeed with complete identity—all representations at every time in **my** consciousness, although he admits this I, he will still not infer the objective persistence of my Self. For just as the time in which

the observer posits me is not the time that is encountered in my sensibility but that which is encountered in his own, so the identity that is necessarily combined with my consciousness is not therefore combined with his consciousness, i.e., with the outer intuition of my subject.   (*KRV* A363)

In other words, the unity and identity of self-consciousness is available only from the first-person point of view. This unity and identity is merely the logical, or "formal condition of my thoughts and their connection" (*KRV* A363). This is a *functional* unity given through the activity of uniting all representations that are to constitute an experience in one consciousness. As such, it can only be apprehended in and through this *activity* of uniting representations, and can only be grasped from the first-person point of view. Moreover, when Kant notes that "time is in me," what he means is that from the point of view of the subject, time is generated through (a) my continuous apprehension of representations and (b) my connection of these representations in accordance with the analogies in such a way as to arrive at objective experience. Since the functional unity of the I is what apprehends and connects these representations, it must be logically identical throughout, that is, it is an *a priori* condition of the unity of experience from the first-person point of view. But when I observe another person, I do not have access to his or her activity of uniting representations, and hence to the unity and identity of that person's self-consciousness throughout the person's experiences. I therefore do not have access to the time in which the observer posits me, for it is "not the time that is encountered in my sensibility."

Kant further notes that the logical identity of the I does not warrant the supposition that there is an underlying identical substance serving as the substrate for the determinations of the self, i.e. its changing representations. This is because the functional identity of the I does not require the existence of a single substance for which the representations serve as determinations. In an important footnote in the third paralogism, Kant notes that it is entirely possible that such a functional unity co-exist with a state of affairs in which "representations, together with consciousness of them, flow from one [substance] to another." Hence "a whole series of these substances may be thought, of which the first would communicate its state, together with its consciousness, to the second, which would communicate its own state, together with that of the previous substance, to a third substance ... " He concludes that given such a scenario, the last substance would be conscious "of all the previously altered substances in its own states" (*KRV* A364). In other words, the functional unity, along with all the representations it unites, could be passed on baton-like from one substance to the next. Hence the functional identity would be preserved, including the content that it unites with it as well, without this having any implications concerning the identity of an underlying substance.

Schleiermacher most certainly has these arguments in mind. He notes that from a third-person, objective point of view I can think of another person or animal as something that persists throughout change and that stands in dynamic interaction with other changing substances. I think of such individuals as elements in my objective experience, in accordance with the analogies. From this third-person point of view I "have a reason to attribute something that persists to a thing," that is, I can think of such an individual as a substance that changes in dynamic interaction with other substances. Schleiermacher also claims, however, that I can "think this same thing as having consciousness," and that I can "thereby ascribe a continuity of consciousness to it."[11] However this does not mean that I have a reason to "arrive at the unity and inner connection of consciousness from its continuity." In other words, my attribution of substantiality to this other being does not warrant the affirmation that all of this individual's experiences are unified in virtue of a transcendental, logical I. Such a self can only be grasped from the first-person point of view. In sum, Schleiermacher is quite aware that (a) the transcendental function of uniting all representations in a single "I" does not imply a single substance that underlies this function, and

---

[11] The question here is what Schleiermacher means by the attribution of consciousness and its continuity to another being from such an "objective" point of view. This is especially troublesome given Schleiermacher's immediate admission afterwards that from the substantiality attributed to this other, I cannot conclude to the transcendental unity and identity of that person's consciousness. One might assume that such a logical unity is the *sine qua non* of the attribution of consciousness. However, on this point Schleiermacher also follows Kant. In the first paralogism Kant notes that the claim that thinking can only follow from the absolute unity of a thinking being is not an analytic one; as such we are not precluded from attributing thinking, and thereby a kind of consciousness, to a being without also attributing to it the analytic unity of thought. On this point see note 12 below.

(b) the substantiality that I attribute to another conscious being, from a third-person point of view, does not warrant the attribution of a single, identical I that makes the "unity and inner connection" of its experiences possible.[12] This is most certainly the "double doubt" that Schleiermacher affirms is not only possible, but even necessary concerning personal identity.

Given this discussion, Schleiermacher then gives an account of the three kinds of person. The designations originally provided had only to do with "their formulas," but now he provides an account "in accordance with their content." Given the possible combinations between the "personality" and the "principle of personality," the first possibility concerns a being that has both personality and the principle of personality. He defines it, under (a) as "a personality, where the unity of self-consciousness is necessarily connected with the identity of substance of the transcendental subject" (*KGA* I.1, 541). Unlike Schleiermacher's preceding account of the first kind of person, this definition highlights a *necessary* connection between the personality and the principle of personality. Only given such a necessary connection between the two can we be certain that a single being possesses both. Schleiermacher notes that this necessary combination of the two is applicable to the "highest being in a necessary and complete way" (*KGA* I.1, 541), that is, in God both are necessarily combined. This is because God's thought is (a) not discursive, like our own, and (b) the *content* of God's thought does not come from the *outside*, that is, God's thoughts do not stand in relation to (and therefore do

---

[12] The idea that thought, or consciousness, might be possible without attributing simplicity to the subject is discussed by Kant in the first paralogism. As Margaret Wilson has convincingly argued ("Leibniz and Materialism," *Canadian Journal of Philosophy* 3, [1974]: 495–513), Kant is here arguing against an essentially Leibnizian claim. Kant notes that the proposition "A thought can only be the effect of the absolute unity of a thinking being" cannot be treated as analytic. This is because a concept through which many representations are brought together has multiple parts, namely, the multiple representations themselves; hence the unity of such a thought is the unity of a collective. As such, it is conceivable that this unity be "related to the collective unity of the substances cooperating in it (as the movement of a body is the composite movement of all its parts)" (*KRV* A353). Kant seems to be arguing here that it is quite conceivable to think of something extended, and that is thereby composed of parts, as acting in the same way as a being that synthesizes its representations through the functional unity of the "I." However, it is important to note that such a view of a thinking being is possible only insofar as it is viewed from the third-person, objective point of view.

not depend in any way on) anything existing *independently* of God.[13] Rather, in God the unity of thought is equivalent to the complete dependence of these thoughts on God. This kind of personality "is completely problematic" (*KGA* I.1, 543), that is, we cannot know whether such a being exists.

This combination is also attributed to human beings "by dint of faith." However, given the discursive character of human thought, we can affirm no necessary connection between personality and the principle of personality in human beings. This then brings us to the second kind of personality, (b). This is "a personality where the unity of self-consciousness is fully formed, but the identity of the substance is not knowable from the same grounds, and therefore a doubt regarding the complete connection of the two is possible." Under (b) from the first-person point of view, we begin with the transcendental unity of the self, but cannot from there arrive at the substantial identity of the self. As such, the second part of this definition, regarding the identity of substance, "is also completely problematic" (*KGA* I.1, 543). Schleiermacher notes "this personality befits human beings, in that, namely, each directly ascribes to him/herself the unity of self-consciousness and, according to the analogy, the identity of substance; each ascribes to the other identity of substance, and according to the analogy, also the unity of self-consciousness" (*KGA* I.1, 541). We ascribe to others a transcendental unity of consciousness in virtue of the fact that we think of their consciousness as analogous with our own. And we ascribe substantiality to the unity of our own consciousness in virtue of an analogy between our own consciousness and that of others. However, while in our everyday life we proceed in accordance with such analogies, strictly speaking unity of self-consciousness and identity of substance are not necessarily combined. Schleiermacher describes (c) as "a personality in which the identity is formed by a substance equipped with consciousness. In the third category are animals: in them, the "unity of self-consciousness in accordance with the analogy is highly unlikely" (*KGA* I.1, 541).

---

[13] Interestingly, in §16 Kant also distinguishes our own understanding from that of God's. He notes, "An understanding, in which through self-consciousness all of the manifold would at the same time be given, would intuit; ours can only think and must seek the intuition in the senses" (*KRV* B135).

Schleiermacher claims that his own understanding of self-consciousness is "completely parallel to the Kantian." Significantly, he notes that given this way of conceiving consciousness, "the unity of self-consciousness (whether one take it as ground or consequent of consciousness) relates itself always only to the phenomenal" (*KGA* I.1, 542). What does Schleiermacher mean by ground and consequent here? The *ground* of the unity of consciousness is, no doubt, the analytical unity referred to by Kant in §16 of the first *Critique*. It is the I that must accompany all my representations if they are to be mine and is, as such, the *ratio essendi* of self-consciousness. Although it is transcendental, it relates itself only to the phenomenal. It is a necessary condition for the possibility of experience, that is, it functions to unify representations belonging to the phenomenal, empirical world. Such a ground cannot be thought without also thinking the *consequent* of the unity of self-consciousness, namely, the synthetic unity. This synthetic unity is constituted by the successive representational states of the subject bound together in accordance with necessary rules. As Kant had noted, the identity of the subject "does not yet come about by my accompanying each representation with consciousness, but rather by my adding one representation to the other and being conscious of their synthesis." In other words, "the analytical unity of apperception is only possible under the presumption of some synthetic one" (*KRV* B133). The analytical unity means nothing without a possible content for it to unite. Moreover, I can only become conscious of this analytical unity in and through the synthetic unity. Hence the synthetic unity is the *ratio cognoscendi* of consciousness. The importance of this latter fact for both Kant and Schleiermacher cannot be stressed too much. The identity of the subject is only cognizable in and through the synthesis of the manifold of intuition.[14] This means that the identity of the subject is

---

[14] The point is key to the argumentative strategy of Kant's transcendental deduction. The connection between the identity of the transcendental subject and the unity of the synthesis of the self's representations is explored in depth by Dieter Henrich in his article "Identity and Objectivity." As Henrich notes, for Kant "self-consciousness comes about only in conjunction with the consciousness of the synthetic functions of the subject" (192). Furthermore, "The thought of the identity of a subject in all its representations must also, from the outset, be formulated with reference to the unity of all its representations. It knows itself as the identical subject only when

wholly bound up with the identity of the world to which the subject relates. It is, therefore, completely bound up with the phenomenal sphere.

However, from that which we know of the self as phenomenon, "no conclusion is valid as to what it may be as noumenon" (*KGA* I.1, 542). Schleiermacher agrees with Kant that from the theoretical point of view, insofar as the identity of substance relates to noumena, "it is even for this reason an empty concept." As noted in the previous chapter, according to Kant, insofar as we posit appearances and therefore phenomena, we must also posit *that which appears*, and which can be thought in abstraction from its relational properties. We must, therefore, posit things as they are in themselves. Schleiermacher moves beyond Kant in speculating about the possible character of such noumena. If we attempt to think them,

two cases can be portrayed. First, it is possible that a multiplicity lies at the ground of experienced consciousness, to which we ascribe the 'I' as phenomenon. That is, the so-called consciousness has already been several transcendental subjects throughout the entire time series. This is what Schmidt understood by the Kantian expression that consciousness can be passed along. Another case is, however, yet also possible, namely, absolutely no noumenon lies at the basis of the I of consciousness for itself alone, but rather this I is merely a fluid property of another thing, having only to do with time. Such a case strikes me in the Spinozistic business.   (*KGA* I.1, 542)

The first case Schleiermacher mentions is the one discussed above in the analysis of Kant's third paralogism, that is, for all we know

representational states replace other representational states. However, it is the subject of representations, all of which it knows to be its own only if it is equally conscious of the mutual referability of the contents of its representational states. In this awareness it has original cognizance of the simplicity and identity of itself in equal measure" (196). In other words, the self recognizes itself as the selfsame subject insofar as it can connect all its representations according to a rule. It is in and through these rules (the categories) that the content of one representational state is referable to another. And it is through the referability of any given representational content to every other representational content that the unity of the experience of the *identical* subject is constituted. As such, the identity of the I is knowable only in the unity of experience.

the functional unity of the self and the content it unites is passed on baton-like from one substance to another. The second possibility is the Spinozistic one, where the I is merely a fluid property of another thing. In such a case, the I has no independent existence, since it is merely a mode of something else. Moreover, insofar as Schleiermacher envisions it as a merely "fluid" property, it has only a fleeting duration.[15] Significantly, Schleiermacher leaves out another possibility. This is the alternative favored by Jacobi, in which there exist many substances standing in interaction with one another. However, Schleiermacher argues against this possibility in the latter part of *Spinozism* for the reasons enumerated in the previous chapter: first, we can have no epistemic access to the *vinculum* of the monads, and hence to the individuating principles of things, and second, whenever we attempt to think the ground of phenomena, we are inexorably led to the conclusion that there can only be one such ground.

---

[15] Once the Spinozism controversy had erupted, several authors were prepared to recognize an affinity between Kant's philosophy and Spinozism, in particular in regard to the question of the self. If what we know of the self always relates—in one way or another—to the empirical, phenomenal self, then the possibility of Spinozism is left open, since we are not required to posit a plurality of noumenal selves. The possibility that Kant's transcendental self is a mere mode was already entertained by Hermann Andreas Pistorius in a 1786 review of Schultz's *Erläuterungen*. There Pistorius notes, "The author's [i.e. Kant's] theory would secure [Spinoza's] pantheism against the important objection that an infinite thinking substance cannot be put together out of an infinite number of finite thinking substances, for, if according to [that theory] our substantiality is merely logical and apparent, if our I is nothing but self-consciousness, and this only a subjective pre-requisite of the synthesis of representations, a modification of other modifications; what then prevents it from being the case that all these representations are modifications of the sole substance? Thus reason finds all its demands satisfied in Spinoza's system, if time determinations and all representations related to them are merely apparent and subjective, and reason would be unjust, after such a satisfaction, if it still wanted to seek a particular Godhead, at any rate the interest of truth demands no Godhead other than the intelligible world." (Cited and translated by Franks, *All or Nothing*, 95–6; originally in Landau, *Rezensionen zur kantischen Philosophie 1781–87*, 329–30). Pistorius makes the point—not lost on Schleiermacher—that even the transcendental self is intelligible only in relation to the synthesis of representations and calls it merely a "subjective pre-requisite," and as such can be understood as a mere "modification of other modifications."

PRACTICAL REASON, DETERMINISM, AND THE MECHANISM OF NATURE

The ultimate significance of all metaphysics concerning personal identity is found in the sphere of morality. It is no accident, then, that Schleiermacher proceeds to apply the results of his investigation to the practical sphere. He begins by characterizing Kant's definition of a person in the following way: "a person is a rational subject that sets itself ends independently of the mechanism of nature, and in this regard personality is the property of a subject to be its own end" (*KGA* I.1, 543). Importantly, however, he claims,

no equation allows itself to be made between identity of consciousness and rational self-determination or independence from the mechanism of nature. Even so little does the necessary and universal connection come to mind, for the original meaning of person and personality has only to do with a certain property of consciousness and has the least to do with the matter at hand.

(*KGA* I.1, 543)

What can be deduced from the identity of consciousness? If we follow Kant, as Schleiermacher here seems to be doing, then: if there is to be identity of consciousness there must also be a thoroughgoing connectedness of our representations in accordance with the categories. As such, only if there is unity among our representations (which constitute our world) is there an identity of self-consciousness. The proof of this proposition is central to Kant's transcendental deduction. However, Schleiermacher notes that identity of consciousness does not imply "rational self-determination or independence from the mechanism of nature," that is, it does not imply transcendental or intelligible freedom.

Schleiermacher's intimate acquaintance with Kant's paralogisms plays a key role here as well. In the paralogisms Kant had argued that neither the identity of consciousness nor the spontaneity of the intellect in determining objects allows us to equate self-consciousness with an intelligible substance. And neither does it allow us to infer the transcendental or intelligible freedom of such substances (rational self-determination). The concepts of an intelligible substance and transcendental freedom mutually imply one another. As Kant had noted in *Reflexion* 5653, "The concept of freedom is already by itself necessarily connected with the concept of a substance with respect to the intelligible, because the substance must be the ultimate subject of its actions and cannot itself be the mode of action of another substance."[16] But while the concepts of substance and intelligible freedom imply one another, both Kant and Schleiermacher claimed that neither is implied by the identity of consciousness and the spontaneity of the intellect. Schleiermacher's reasons for this, as we shall see, closely follow those of Kant. Both Kant and Schleiermacher affirm the irreducibility of thought to matter in motion. But this irreducibility of thought to the mechanism of nature does not preclude the possibility that both thought and the changing determinations of the spatial substrate are expressions of a single underlying ground. This thereby excludes the existence of both individual noumenal substances and intelligible freedom. In the chapter on the paralogism Kant had argued:

But now although extension, impenetrability, composition, and motion—in short, everything our outer senses can transmit to us—are not thoughts, feelings, inclinations or decisions, and cannot contain them, as these are never objects of outer intuition, yet that same Something that grounds outer appearances and affects our sense so that it receives the representations of space, matter, shape, etc.—this Something, considered as noumenon (or better transcendental object) could also at the same time be the subject of thoughts, even though we receive no intuition of representations, volitions, etc. in the way we are affected through outer sense, but rather receive merely intuitions of space and its determinations. But this Something is not extended, not impenetrable, not composite, because these predicates pertain only to sensibility and its intuition, insofar as we are affected by such objects (otherwise unknown to us) ...

If matter were a thing in itself, then as a composite it would be completely distinguished from the soul as a simple being. But it is merely an outer appearance, whose substratum is not cognized through any specifiable predicates; hence I can well assume about this substratum that in itself it is simple, even though in the way it affects our outer senses it produces in us the intuition of something extended and hence composite; and thus I can also assume that in the substance in itself, to which extension pertains in respect of our outer sense, thoughts may also be present, which may be represented

---

[16] *Kants gesammelte Schriften*, vol. 18, 311.

with consciousness through their own inner sense. In such a way the very same thing that is called a body in one relation would at the same time be a thinking being in another, whose thoughts, of course we could not intuit, but only their signs in appearance…

But if we compare the thinking I not with matter but with the intelligible that grounds the outer appearances we call matter, then because we know nothing at all about the latter, we cannot say that the soul is inwardly distinguished from it in any way at all.   (*KRV* A358–60)

Thoughts, feelings, and desires are irreducible to space and its determinations. But this does not imply an irreducible dualism between the thinking self and matter, since both may be the expressions of a single underlying ground. An irreducible dualism between thought and the material world only follows if we think of matter as if it were a thing in itself. Since, however, a necessary characteristic of matter, namely its extension, cannot be a feature of things in themselves but is, rather, only a feature of outer appearances (that is, of how things must appear to us given the forms of sensible intuition),[17] it is not impossible that what is given in inner sense and what appears in outer intuition have the same ground. As such, while the mechanism of nature would not *directly* determine the spontaneity of thought, yet since both are the expressions of a single underlying Something, mental occurrences could *appear* to supervene on physical occurrences. The correspondence between changes in thought and extension would not be the result of one being the cause of the other, but of both being the expression of a single underlying ground expressing itself in two distinct ways. Given that we have no positive concept of a noumenon, Kant notes that this idea of a single underlying ground to both thought and extension cannot be excluded.

Schleiermacher provides much the same argument at the beginning of *Spinozism*. There Schleiermacher answers Jacobi's charge that Spinoza is forced to conclude that "discussion is a pure thing of the body," that is, that thought is merely the product of the mechanism of nature. First, he notes that

as changeable in causal relationships, finite things bring one another forth. Spinoza certainly depended not only on the *ex nihil nihil fit*, but also on

---

[17] On this point see Allison, *Kant's Transcendental Idealism*, 237–54.

the *nihil ex nihilo fit*. Rather, each thing must have something from which it springs, that is, each thing must be understood as an effect, and therefore too, each change in that which thinks. As change, effects are not brought forth from the infinite directly (from the Infinite as *causa libera*), for each finite thing springs directly only out of the finite, thereby from the finite.

(*KGA* I.1, 528)

The Infinite in no way directly institutes a change in the finite. Rather, each change in the realm of the finite relates to a previous state of the finite. However, changes in thought do not stem directly from changes in the physical, extended stuff, "for thinking does not stem from extension." Thought, rather, stems "from that which thinks." Schleiermacher notes that according to Spinoza, "each change in that which thinks, viewed as an effect, is related to a prior thought." Spinoza, he argues, does not think of thought as the mere product of physical changes. It is true that such a change in thought "cannot exist for itself alone, but rather only makes up the change of thing taken together with a change in what is extended." In other words, while the genesis of each thought must be understood in terms of prior thoughts alone, this does not preclude that for each change in representational states there must be a corresponding change in the physical, material substrate. Hence it may be the case that there exists a necessary correspondence of changes in thought with changes in the physical, such that no change in thought takes place without a change in the extended, physical substrate. Changes in the material substrate, however, must be accounted for in terms of prior states of the material substrate, just as changes in thought must be accounted for in terms of prior representational states. The one to one correspondence between changes in thought and matter does not in any way mean, however, as Jacobi surmised, that thought can be understood as an effect of physical changes, or that thought is in any way reducible to physiological events. Moreover, consciousness of physical changes is not a "mere accompaniment" of such changes. Schleiermacher claims:

If I myself take the hardest case of a moral action, it can very well be thought in the spirit of the system that insofar as the decision contains judgment and desire, it is an effect of what has been previously thought. However, actual determination of the physical faculty, with which together it comprises only a change of the thing, is the consequence of a previous change of what is extended, only that we admittedly must resort to such changes which somewhat coincide with the material ideas or changes of the animal organs of the psyche. Thus the doctrine of harmony leads always to such subtleties, whether it be Leibniz or Spinoza who has put them forward. How can Jacobi thereby say that discussion is a pure thing of the body? How can he say the inventor of the watch has not invented the watch? The idea of it [the watch] developed itself as a consequence of other ideas; that its bodily accompaniments were a consequence of the movements of its body is irrelevant. So it is with what he says of the effects of the affections. The consideration which here drives him back from Spinozism is, however, only morality, and this really loses nothing through this, that the determinations of the physical faculty stem from changes in what is extended (especially when their necessary coincidence is assumed), since he actually comes to the decision insofar as it is judgment and desire. The last of Jacobi's words leave in doubt whether he means that what is extended determines actions, or whether the infinite thing has this function. I have clarified myself regarding the first, and the last seems to me to fully contradict the system and the sentences already put forward. Even so I cannot grasp how he can say that sensation and thought would be only concepts of extension, movement and speed. There certainly belongs a simple distinction to it, in order to here follow Spinoza correctly and exactly, but Jacobi is also equal to this task. I think the matter so: Each change of a thing is a new relation of it to other things; the relations of a thing can however be regarded from two points of view and at the same time consist of two parts exactly harmonized to one another. The expression of this new relation consists in the outer part in what is extended and the representation of it in the inner part, which consists of what thinks. Because both relate to the whole relation, so all that is in the expression is also in the representation, and all that is in the representation is also in the expression. Therefore I can correctly say: thought and sensation are nothing but concepts of extension, movement, and speed. I can also say: extension, movement, and speed are nothing but expressions of spirit, will and talent. In this way do I think Spinoza will have understood his system in this part.   (*KGA* I.1, 529–30)

For Kant, the notion that thought and extension are both the appearances of an unknown Something is a possibility left open by his critical idealism. Schleiermacher, however, here declares this to be his considered view. To think a change in a representational state, and to view a physiological change, is to understand the same thing from two points of view or two standpoints. Both extension and thought relate to the "whole relation," that is, each is in its own way an appearance fully expressive of the infinite. Because both have the same common ground, "all that is in the expression [physical reality] is also in the representation, and all that is in the representation is also in the expression." The two parts will thereby "be exactly harmonized to one another."

When Schleiermacher claims that "no equation allows itself to be made between identity of consciousness and rational self-determination or independence from the mechanism of nature," his discussion of the *harmony* of the progression of thought with physiological change, which mirrors Kant's discussion of the possible relation of inner and outer sense in the paralogisms, needs to be taken into account. Given this discussion, Schleiermacher cannot be claiming that thought (and hence the identity of consciousness in thinking) is reducible to the mechanism of nature, or that it is simply an effect of this mechanism. Thought is not independent of the mechanism of nature only in the sense that both thought and nature express a single underlying and common ground. It is because both are expressive of the same underlying ground in such a way that harmony results. What follows in Schleiermacher's text, however, poses some difficulty to this interpretation:

Even so little does the necessary and universal connection come to mind, for the original meaning of person and personality has only to do with a certain property of consciousness and has little to do with the matter at hand. For on the one hand, if one assumes a receptivity that is completely free and open, and is not limited to certain organs, it very well allows itself of a faculty of representation and a consciousness without a faculty of desire, and on the other hand, I do not see why an identical consciousness, a being that possesses unity of self-consciousness, nevertheless could not be completely passive in its actions and dependent upon the mechanism of nature, for just as Kant had himself deduced, indisputably self-consciousness does not touch upon self-determination.   (*KGA* I.1, 544)

The question at issue here is, once again, whether the identity of consciousness implies that the self is a substance. Kant had correctly argued that the category of substance and intelligible freedom mutually imply one another. Something is a substance if its mode of action can be explained in terms of its intrinsic or monadic properties, that is, the substance must in some way ground its accidents.[18] If all the changes that a thing undergoes are merely the effects of something acting upon it, then it is a mere mode of that other thing, since nothing about the thing functions to ground its properties in any way that is independent from other things. Schleiermacher claims there is no contradiction in thinking the identity of self-consciousness along with the notion that this consciousness is completely passive in its actions. He claims, in other words, that there is no contradiction in affirming the identity of self-consciousness, and in denying that the self is a substance and that its mode of action can in any way be grasped *independently* of the mechanism of nature. This would mean that whatever changes occur in self-consciousness can be explained completely through the mode of action of something else.

In this regard, several difficulties present themselves. First, it is unclear how Schleiermacher's idea of self-consciousness as completely passive or receptive does not contradict the *spontaneity* of thought required in the activity of synthesizing one representational state with another.[19] The only way that the two do not contradict

---

[18] Kant distinguishes between a substance and its powers and argues that the two cannot be identified. The relation of power belongs to the category of causality, and the relation of inherence in a substance is entirely different from it. In the Pölitz metaphysics Kant argues that "power is the concept of the relation between substance and accidents *insofar* as the substance contains the ground of the accidents." Moreover, this distinction is crucial to the avoidance of Spinozism: "For the concept of substance … is thereby (sc., by identifying substance and power) in reality completely lost … just as Spinoza would have it, since he affirmed the universal dependence of all things in the world on an original being as their common cause, and by making the universal, effective power itself into a substance, he converted this dependence into inherence" (cited in Henrich, "On the Unity of Subjectivity," 27).

[19] So Kant, "Yet the human being, who is otherwise acquainted with the whole of nature through sense, knows himself also through pure apperception, and indeed in actions and inner determinations which cannot be accounted at all among impressions of sense; he obviously is in one part phenomenon, but in another part, namely in regard to certain faculties, he is a merely intelligible object, *because the actions of this object cannot at all be ascribed to the receptivity of sensibility*" (A546–7/B574) [Italics mine]. And in *Reflexion* 4220, Kant notes that "The expression 'I think' indicates already that I am not passive in regard to the representation, that it must be ascribed to me, and that its counterpart depends on me." As Allison notes, "Largely against the empiricists, he [Kant] argues that the senses provide the mind with the data for thinking objects, but not with the thought or knowledge thereof. The latter, he maintains, requires the active taking up of the data by the mind, its unification in a

one another is through the argument Kant provides at A358, discussed above and echoed by Schleiermacher. Henrich summarizes the results of this argument in a way that illuminates Schleiermacher's point: "For even if consciousness is aware of itself in all its thoughts as the ground of their being thought, it is still possible to imagine that the conditions that bind consciousness to the laws for the production of its own thoughts are not at all different from the conditions that underlie the material appearances in their transcendental substrate."[20] Hence what seems to be the spontaneity of self-consciousness *could* be accounted for in terms of the transcendental substrate, which also grounds the material appearances. Only in this way can we think the *spontaneity* of thought as intrinsically related to the material conditions, but such a relation would only take place through their common ground, namely the transcendental substrate. On such a scenario, there are ultimately no noumenal substances that are intelligibly (transcendentally) free in their actions. Insofar as, for Kant, transcendental freedom is inherently bound up with the concept of a moral person, Schleiermacher is correct to claim that the idea of the identity of consciousness does not imply moral personhood.

Our analysis thus far has shown that what can be inferred from an analysis of the conditions of the possibility of experience (the identity of consciousness) does not allow us to conclude that there are noumenal, transcendentally free substances. We cannot, in other words, move from experience and its conditions to a positive concept of noumenal substances, which is what would be required in order to affirm the self's independence from the mechanism of nature. The move from noumena to phenomena is equally problematic:

If Kant wants to proceed, not from the phenomenal concept, but from the noumenal, then I see even less how he could make such a use of a clearly known concept and say something. If something corresponds to this concept, then it must express itself through rational determinations of the will.

---

concept or synthesis, and its reference to an object. All of this is the work of judgment, which is simply the spontaneity of the understanding in action" Allison, *Kant's Theory of Freedom*, 36.

[20] Henrich, "On the Unity of Subjectivity," 29.

Even this would be a true contradiction. For since we know so little of the connection between noumena and phenomena, then it would be laughable to claim that a certain noumenon must produce such a phenomenon.

(*KGA* I.1, 544)

In his chapter "Phenomena and Noumena" in the first *Critique*, Kant had argued that we have no positive conception of noumena.[21] In other words, we cannot think noumena through the categories, for we have no guide as to how noumena are to be subsumed under the concepts of the understanding. Hence Kant concludes, "that which we call noumenon must be understood to be such only in a negative sense" (*KRV* B309). Such a concept is merely a "boundary concept," allowing us to distinguish between things as they are given to us in experience and their unknowable ground. Schleiermacher emphasizes that since we can have no positive conception of a noumenon, if we begin from the idea of a noumenon, we can have no understanding of the connection between noumenon and phenomenon. He thereby argues that even if we agreed that the noumenal, intelligible self must "express itself through rational determinations of the will," we have absolutely no insight into how the noumenal, intelligible self might manifest itself in the phenomenal sphere.

But what of the connection that comes from "the other side," that is, that begins from the point of view of morality? In his *Critique of Practical Reason* Kant had argued that morality is a fact of reason and that morality and transcendental freedom mutually imply one another. Allison has termed this claim the "Reciprocity Thesis."[22] While we do not understand it, "freedom," Kant argued, is "the

[21] Kant notes that "the transcendental use of a concept in any sort of principle consists in its being related to things *in general* and *in themselves*" (*KRV* B298). This merely transcendental use of the categories is "in fact no use at all, and has no . . . determinable object" (*KRV* B304). Without the formal conditions of sensibility, the pure categories lack "the formal conditions of the subsumption of any sort of supposed object under these concepts" (*KRV* B305). Hence if "we wanted to apply the categories to objects that are not considered as appearances, then we would have to ground them on an intuition other than the sensible one, and then the object would be a noumenon in a *positive sense*. Now since such an intuition, namely intellectual intuition, lies absolutely outside our faculty of cognition, the use of the categories can by no means reach beyond the boundaries of the objects of experience."

[22] Allison, *Kant's Theory of Freedom*, 201ff.

condition of the moral law which we do know" (*KprV* 5:5). We *know* we are bound by the moral law, and this implies that we must be transcendentally free. In *Spinozism*, Schleiermacher stands in fundamental disagreement with Kant on this point. While each "moral subject that can act in accordance with laws" is a person, Schleiermacher affirms that this is true only in a "phenomenological" or subjective sense. Even if "action in accordance with the representation of rules presupposes the faculty of concepts and the ability to synthesize our acts of consciousness in one [consciousness]," this does not imply that moral subjects must be noumenal selves. In other words, Schleiermacher admits that action in accordance with rules presupposes both the analytic and the synthetic unity of consciousness. In order to act in accordance with such rules, the self must be conscious of the distinction between itself and the world. This further presupposes the ability to construct complex concepts in accordance with necessary laws and to make judgments about objects. And in order to act in accordance with rules, the self must be conscious of itself and its desires; coherence in action is possible only through the structuring of desire. It is clear that all of this involves the identity of self-consciousness. But this identity of self-consciousness, Schleiermacher argues once again, does not imply the substantiality of the noumenal self:

action in accordance with laws, and even so to be an end in itself, and set ends for oneself, is nothing other than a certain identity of the rules of desire. In any case, this relates itself to the transcendental self-consciousness, to the I, and at the same time thereby, along with this [transcendental self-consciousness, it] can just as well change from one transcendental substrate to the other, and so be a property that is passed on.   (*KGA* I.1, 545)

Schleiermacher's argument is that "action in accordance with laws" does not presuppose the identity of a noumenal, substantial self that remains identical throughout its changes. For the possibility exists that the practical imperatives structuring desire are passed along baton-like, along with the transcendental unity of consciousness itself. In such a case, one need not presuppose the identity of a *subject* that acts in accordance with laws; rather all that is needed is the preservation of the identity of the rules themselves, along with the functional identity of the transcendental I. Schleiermacher does

concede that "self-consciousness in the production of a representation, unity of self-consciousness in the production of a series of
representations, and ... identity of the rules of desire" are necessary
conditions of moral personhood. They are not, however, *sufficient*
to establish that the self is a transcendentally free noumenal subject.
While Schleiermacher notes that for Kant "we stand in the intelligible world for the sake of the moral law" (*KGA* I.1, 545) his own
view in *Spinozism* is that no element of our phenomenal experience,
including that of morality itself, requires us to posit that there are
substantial, noumenal selves.

Kant's considered view was that it is our moral experience that
leads us to conclude that we are transcendentally free and members
of an intelligible world. The moral law confronts us as a fact of
reason. While as late as 1785 Kant is still trying to ground moral
insight in the spontaneity of theoretical reason,[23] his mature view in
the *Critique of Practical Reason* recognizes such attempts as futile;[24]
he then posits moral insight as a fact of reason.[25] Moral insight

---

[23] In the *Groundwork* Kant argues "one cannot possibly think a reason that, in its
own consciousness, would receive steering from elsewhere in regard to its judgments;
for then the subject would ascribe the determination of its power of judgment not
to its reason but to an impulse." Immanuel Kant, *Groundwork for the Metaphysics of
Morals*, 65 (4: 449).

[24] For instance, in *Reflexion* 5442, Kant distinguishes between what he calls "logical
freedom" and "transcendental freedom." He notes, "Logical freedom can be found in
rational acts, but not transcendental freedom." Karl Ameriks argues that by the time
Kant produced the second edition of the first *Critique* in 1787, he had come to doubt
the argument that the cogito can establish transcendental freedom. He notes that in
the "general note" with which Kant concludes the revised section of the Paralogisms,
"he brings under critique the idea that dominates the arguments of all the moral texts
we have analyzed, namely, the spontaneity of thought. Kant does not deny that thinking exhibits a 'pure spontaneity,' but now he emphasizes that this represents merely a
'logical function' and that although it 'does not exhibit the subject of consciousness
as appearance,' it also does not 'represent myself to myself as I am in myself' (B428)."
Karl Ameriks, "Kant's Deduction of Freedom and Morality," 71.

[25] For an in-depth discussion of the differences in Kant's views as presented in
Groundwork III and the second *Critique*, see Ameriks, "Kant's Deduction of Freedom
and Morality," 45–65. Ameriks notes that in the *Groundwork*, "the assertion of our
freedom seemed to be based on the assertion of morality, which in turn rested on
an appeal to freedom. Now instead of the last step, which does involve a circular
grounding, no step at all and so no theoretical grounding is offered. In the place of
ambitious but understandable attempts at a strict deduction Kant has fallen back into
the invocation of an alleged a priori fact of practical reason" 66. See also Karl Ameriks,

consists not only in rationally determining what the moral law is, but also in the fact that the moral law confronts us as a *demand*. As Henrich has put it, the moral law is "not an arbitrary matter of fact." Rather, it must be "originally affirmed" by us, since to say that something is good is also to accept it "in its being."[26] This grounds Kant's understanding of positive freedom, that is, the moral law can function as an incentive to action. This means that our fundamental commitment to morality has consequences for our ontological commitments. Morality cannot be grounded in theoretical or speculative thought. Rather, our theoretical reflections must be informed by our moral commitments. For the mature Kant, it is the fact that morality confronts us in this way that leads us to posit our transcendental freedom and the idea that we are members of an intelligible world. Our affirmation of the absolute value of the moral law as the standard of action cannot simply be taken as one empirically conditioned desire among others. It is through *reason* that we recognize its unconditioned character and validity. But as I argued in Chapter 1, the recognition of such an unconditional demand and its capacity to influence us also implied, for Kant, transcendental freedom and the causality of reason. And since the category of substance and freedom mutually imply one another, this has the implication that we must think of ourselves as intelligible substances.

By the time that Schleiermacher writes the *Monologen* in 1800 we find that a major reversal has taken place in his thought. Instead of the monism he defends in Spinoza essays, he affirms a qualified monadic individualism. This reversal is ultimately informed by some of the same ethical concerns driving Kant's philosophy, although in Schleiermacher the problems and their solutions will be developed quite differently. But it is important to recognize that Schleiermacher does not so much repudiate Kant's thought as move beyond him. His own achievements in ethics, which are quite significant, would have been impossible without his predecessor.

Kant's Theory of Mind, in particular chapter VI, "Independence." Cf. Henrich, "The Concept of Moral Insight," 55–87, especially 82.

[26] Dieter Henrich, "The Concept of Moral Insight," 61.

4

The World is the Mirror of the Self

Schleiermacher's notes from 1797/8 show him preoccupied, once more, with Leibniz's philosophy.[1] He did not think Leibniz was a good philosopher, however. He wrote "Leibniz was a poor philosopher; from time to time he developed better insights" (*KGA* I.2, 79). Nevertheless, there is little doubt that Leibniz had a substantive influence on Schleiermacher's thought.[2] Schleiermacher continued to be preoccupied with the question of individuality and its relation to the absolute, and Leibniz's philosophy, for which this problem was a central concern, was a natural starting point for Schleiermacher to reflect on these issues. Two points in particular stand out in this regard. First, Schleiermacher's core notion of the feeling of absolute dependence clearly echoes Leibniz. For instance, in his *Discourse on Metaphysics*, Leibniz notes "in rigorous metaphysical truth, there is no external cause acting on us except God alone, and he alone communicates himself to us immediately in virtue of our

---

[1] Schleiermacher's sources for his commentary on Leibniz are: Louis Dutens' six volume edition of Leibniz's work (*Leibniz: Opera omni*, 6 vols.); the two-volume edition of the exchange between Leibniz and Bernouilli (*Leibnitii et Bernouilli Commercium philosophicum et mathematicum,*) and finally, de Jaucourt's biography of Leibniz, along with the two-volume edition of Leibniz's *Theodicée* (*Leibniz: Essais de Théodicée, Augmentée de l'Histoire de la Vie et des Ouvrages de l'Auteur*. On this point, see Günter Meckenstock's historical introduction to the materials in *KGA* I.2, xxv–xxvi. The contents of the Dutens edition are discussed in Emile Ravier, *Bibliographie des Oeuvres de Leibniz*, 175–8.

[2] As Grove notes, Schleiermacher's 1797/8 study of Leibniz marks a decisive shift. Henceforward we find an affirmative element in his reception of Leibniz's philosophy. It is during this period that he first studied Leibniz's philosophy directly, that is, through a careful examination of the original sources themselves. Grove, 168.

continual dependence."[3] Second, despite the continual influence of the insights reached in *Spinozism* and the *Short Presentation of the Spinozistic System,* Schleiermacher remained preoccupied with the problem of individuality. Even if, from an *ultimate* standpoint, only God is real, and whatever reality creation has derives from the reality of God,[4] Schleiermacher acknowledged that fundamental ethical concerns require us to investigate the nature of the individual and the relation of the individual to God and to other human beings. Hence, even when he understood fundamental notions in Leibniz to be inadequate, Schleiermacher significantly revised Leibnizian ideas in light of his earlier conclusions and then adopted them as his own. This is especially true of the theory Schleiermacher develops in his *Monologen,* a text that appeared in four editions in Schleiermacher's life, in 1800, 1810, 1822, and 1829. In the first part of this chapter I discuss Schleiermacher's grappling with key Leibnizian concerns regarding the relation of both the individual and the world to God. The second, lengthier section explores Schleiermacher's transformation of Leibniz's understanding of the self in light of his appropriation of Kant's analysis of self-consciousness. As we have seen in the previous chapter, Schleiermacher appropriates Kant's critique of rational psychology and affirms that we have no knowledge of the self as it is *in itself.* Self-knowledge is only of the empirical self, and this means that the self knows itself only in its *relation* to that which is different from it and stands outside it. It is, therefore, through the *world* that

---

[3] Ariew and Garber, 1989, 59; §28 of the *Discourse on Metaphysics.* As Robert Adams has pointed out to me in correspondence, Schleiermacher could not have had access to Leibniz's *Discourse,* as it was found in the Royal library in Hannover only in 1846. Nevertheless, the ideas that Leibniz presents in the *Discourse* are echoed in other writings such as the *Monadology, The Principles of Nature and Grace,* and *A New System of the Nature and Communication of Substances.* Schleiermacher's notes on Leibniz show him well acquainted with these texts. The "continual dependence" of creatures on God, as well as the idea that there is no cause acting upon us except God alone, is one of the main ideas put forth in the *Monadology,* where Leibniz notes that "all created or derivative monads are products, and are generated, so to speak, by continual fulgurations of the divinity from moment to moment" (Leibniz, *Philosophical Essays,* 219). In this chapter, I sometimes cite the *Discourse,* since in it Leibniz's ideas are presented especially clearly. When I do so, however, I will also refer to other works by Leibniz containing the same ideas, and which are contained in the six-volume Dutens edition of Leibniz's work.

[4] This is the final upshot of Schleiermacher's remark in *Spinozism* that while all things *have* substance, there do not exist separate, independent substances.

the self comes to know itself. However, this Kantian understanding of the self is qualified by Schleiermacher's adoption and transformation of key Leibnizian themes concerning the relations of God to the self, and the self to the world. This section is further subdivided into two other parts. The first develops Schleiermacher's exposition of the freedom of the self in relation to the world. In the second I discuss the significance of Schleiermacher's emphasis on the individual in the *Monologen*, its relation to his adoption and transformation of Leibnizian themes, and the way in which these ideas allowed him to move beyond Kant's ethics.

GOD AND WORLD

In his notes on Leibniz, Schleiermacher was concerned with the problem of the relation of the self to God, the finite to the infinite. In what way does God, who is infinite, relate to the finite? Does the relation not imply that God had to limit God-self in order to create? How can God remain infinite if the finite is different from God, and thereby limits God? In §28 of the *Discourse on Metaphysics*, Leibniz had noted

Thus we have ideas of everything in our soul only by virtue of God's continual action on us, that is to say, because every effect expresses its cause, and thus the essence of our soul is a certain expression, imitation or image of the divine essence, thought, and will, and of all the ideas comprised in it. It can then be said that God is our immediate external object and that we see all things by him. For example, when we see the sun and the stars, it is God who has given them to us and who conserves the ideas of them in us, and it is God who determines us really to think of them by his ordinary concourse while our senses are disposed in a certain manner, according to the laws he has established. God is the sun and the light of souls, the light that lights every man that comes into this world, and this is not an opinion new to our times.[5]

Similar ideas can be found in Leibniz's *New System*. There Leibniz notes,

It is quite true that, speaking with metaphysical rigor, there is no real influence of one created substance on another, and that all things, with all their

---

[5] Leibniz, *Philosophical Essays*, 60.

reality, are continually produced by the power [*vertu*] of God. . . . Therefore, since I was forced to agree that it is not possible for the soul, or any other true substance to receive something from without, except by divine omnipotence, I was led, little by little, to a view that surprised me . . . That is, we must say that God originally created the soul (and any other real unity) in such a way that everything must arise for it from its own depths [*fonds*], through a perfect *spontaneity* relative to itself, and yet with a perfect *conformity* relative to external things.[6]

From this it follows that all things must be perceived in God; the soul apprehends what is other than itself only in and through its relation to God. This is because (a) the soul does not stand in any real relation to other things, and (b) it only stands in a real relation to God, and it is through this relation that it is "continually produced." If it is to apprehend something other than itself and God, it can do so only through God. The soul's relation to God grounds the very depths [*fonds*] of the soul, and it is from within these depths that the soul relates to the rest of the creation. Hence, all perception stems from these depths.

Commenting on Leibniz's understanding of perception Schleiermacher remarks: "Leibniz denied that perceptions could be discontinuous, although he admitted this of apperception. Where do these then come from? Not from outside. Therefore they either arise naturally—through an act of human will, or supernaturally through an act of God's omnipotence. Thus, we are continually remade as human beings, or we thereby make ourselves" (*KGA* I.2, 83). For Leibniz, the soul is what it is insofar as it *expresses* its cause; this is what it means for it to be an effect of God. God continually imparts being to the soul, and we are, as Schleiermacher put it, "continually remade." Whatever being the soul has, it has in virtue of its being an effect, an expression of God. The mystical depths of these Leibnizian insights were not lost on Schleiermacher.[7] In his notes on Leibniz

---

[6] Leibniz, *Philosophical Essays*, 143.

[7] There is no doubt Leibniz was influenced by mystical literature. In the *New System* he refers to "the manner of speaking used by a certain person of great spiritual elevation whose piety is renowned." He is very likely referring to St. Teresa of Avila; cf. *Discourse on Metaphysics*, §32. In a letter from 1696 he wrote, "In [her] writings I once found this lovely thought, that the soul should conceive of things as if there were only God and itself in the world." On this point see Leibniz, *Philosophical Essays*, 64, n. 104. Also significant is that Leibniz cites Nicolas of Cusa in his *Principles of Nature*

he comments, "Without mysticism it is impossible to be consistent, because one cannot trace back one's thought to the unconditioned, and hence one cannot see the inconsistencies" (*KGA* I.2, 83). But if God is the fullness of reality, and the soul is what it is in virtue of its expressing God's reality, how then do we account for limitation, that is, the finite character of the soul? Schleiermacher's preoccupation with this question is evident in his remark: "Leibniz's philosophy is really highly Manichean and stands completely in need of the devil. God makes only the real, and he (the devil) must make the limitations." Later he reflects that since "eternal truths do not depend upon God's will, but on his understanding, and are its inner objects," this must mean that God, too, has limits (*KGA* I.2, 84). God cannot, through an act of will, simply establish what the eternal truths are. These are, rather, the inner objects of God's understanding, and God's establishment of the world is constrained by them.

Leibniz's idea of the divine fulgurations made a special impression on Schleiermacher, and even as he reflected on these he was preoccupied with the question of how God's infinite power could be communicated to the finite. He quotes from Leibniz's *Monadology* and notes, "Especially remarkable is proposition 48: 'Thus God alone is the primitive unity or the first [*originaire*] simple substance; all created or derivative monads are products, and are generated, so to speak, by continual fulgurations of the divinity from moment to moment, limited by the receptivity of the creature, to which it is essential to be limited.' Here is the Leibnizian fullness... the confusion of the ideal and the real (*creatae aut derivatae*) and its incompletion, for here there must be creatures before the monads are generated, and once again there are limitations of God in his fulgurations, which however, hopefully belong to the [divine workings]" (*KGA* I.2, 85). In defense of Leibniz, it might be argued that on his view it is the receptivity of the creature that limits the effect of the fulgurations, or determines how the fulgurations are received. However, as Schleiermacher later argued in his discussion of the divine causality, this causality, which is infinite, is different from finite causality in that it does not act

and Grace. There he notes: "It has been said quite nicely that he [God] is like a center that is everywhere, but that his circumference is nowhere, since all is present to him immediately, without any distance from this center" (Leibniz, *Philosophical Essays*, 211).

on something pre-existing and different from itself. It is not limited by what is *other* than it. Rather, it is infinite in that it continuously establishes its effect. As a result of this idea, in §38 of *The Christian Faith* Schleiermacher collapsed the doctrine of creation with that of preservation.[8] On such a view, however, we cannot account for the limitation of the effect of the fulgurations through the limited receptivity of the creature, for the creature, *as* limited and *as* having a determinate receptivity to the divine influence, is itself established by the fulgurations. As such Schleiermacher is right to claim that the fulgurations must themselves be limited, and that "there must be creatures before the monads are generated."

A principal concern of Schleiermacher's 1799 book *On Religion: Speeches to its Cultured Despisers* is the mystical dimension he discussed in his comments on Leibniz; similar concerns can also be found in his earlier essays on Spinoza. The self's relation to the unconditioned or absolute is at the heart of all genuine religion. As such all true religion springs from the depths of the self, since in its inmost part the self stands in immediate relation to the absolute. From it springs the "inner fire" that is the source of a living faith having the capacity to transform the self completely, since it has a vital and integral relationship with all the deeper forces of a person's psyche. No thought remains unillumined by it, no desire not redirected by it, and no goal not recast by it. It stands at the heart of all the world's confessions; Schleiermacher notes "If you investigate them at their source and their original components, you will find that all the dead slag was once the glowing outpouring of the inner fire that is contained in all religions..."[9] However, this inner fire has been

---

[8] As Schleiermacher notes in *The Christian Faith*, "For the divine causality is only equal in compass to the finite in so far as it is opposite to it in kind, since if it were like it in kind,... it too would belong to the sphere of interaction and thus be a part of the totality of the natural order" (*CF* §51.1, 201–2). In other words, in finite causality something different from the cause is acted upon. This something is passive, receiving the effect of the cause. To the extent that it is receptive to the activity of the cause, it is *independent* of the cause itself, for its *receptivity* is not due to the workings of the cause. On the other hand, absolute causality admits of no material extrinsic to itself on which it can have an effect. Key to the difference between finite and absolute causality is the all-comprehensive character of the latter. On this point see my discussion in "Schleiermacher's Christology Revisited: A Reply to his Critics."

[9] Friedrich Schleiermacher, *On Religion: Speeches to its Cultured Despisers*, 99. Future references to Schleiermacher's 1799 edition of the *Speeches* will be to Crouter's

in most places covered over by "the kind of people who best like to dwell only in the dilapidated ruins of the sanctuary and who cannot live even there without disfiguring and damaging it" (*OR* Crouter, 4). On the other hand, "if the holy fire burned everywhere, fiery prayers would not be needed to beseech it from heaven ... " (*OR* Crouter, 8).

What is our access to this inner fire? The *Speeches* already contain the heart of Schleiermacher's insight that our access to it is *immediate*. Religion, he tells us, is "sensibility and taste for the infinite" (*OR* Crouter, 23). Its essence is defined as "neither thinking nor acting, but intuition and feeling" (*OR* Crouter, 22).[10] Through religion we are put in touch with the unconditioned absolute, that is, with that which lies beyond the polarities of both self and world, and which is the ground of both. As Richard Crouter has noted, "how best to account for the ground of unity between the human self and the world" was the most pressing concern of post-Kantian idealism.[11] Schleiermacher recognized that this was not simply a theoretical problem of interest only to metaphysicians, however. The problem of religion, and hence the problem of the ground of both self and world, stands at the fundamental root from which all human thinking and action spring. Because this root also grounds the unity between both self and world, the ultimate object of religion cannot be known through a concept.[12] Our access to this ground is only immediate; it is not an object *for* consciousness and hence it cannot be *grasped* through the structures of consciousness, although it can *transform* them. In

1996 edition of his translation. They will be indicated by "*OR* Crouter" along with the page reference.

[10] Julia Lamm eloquently notes that intuition is "the 'touchstone' (*Prüfstein*) between ourselves and the world, between the finite world and the infinite universe. It is that point of unity which insures a correspondence and connection between our inner life and external nature, between our spiritual and bodily natures" Lamm, *The Living God*, 83.

[11] See Crouter's introduction to his 1988 edition of the *Speeches*, 60, as well as Dieter Henrich's "On the Unity of Subjectivity."

[12] As Crouter notes, "Reflection necessarily separates. Such an unavoidable separation immediately occurs not only in active reflection (speaking and writing) but also in our innermost reflection ... To recognize this level of being, which is presupposed in conscious self-awareness, is necessarily to move away from it." Richard Crouter, *Friedrich Schleiermacher: Between Enlightenment and Romanticism*, 199. See also Manfred Frank, "On the Unknowability of the Absolute," in *The Philosophical Foundations of Early German Romanticism*, 55–75, and my discussion in the last chapter of this book on religious pluralism.

the famous second speech Schleiermacher describes the immediacy of the moment in which the soul stands in contact with the absolute: "That first mysterious moment that occurs in every sensory perception, before intuition and feeling have separated, where sense and its objects have, as it were, flowed into one another and become one, before both turn back to their original position—I know how indescribable it is and how quickly it passes away" (*OR* Crouter, 31). This mysterious moment, Schleiermacher claims, is integral to religion. It is the fleeting instant in which the self intuits the fundamental unity between self and world. This fundamental moment of unity grounds the depths of consciousness and must be presupposed if the duality and interrelation of subject and object is to be possible. It is important to keep in mind, however, that Schleiermacher stands with Kant, and against Fichte and Hegel, in affirming the unknowability of the "common root"—the fundamental power of the soul grounding both sensibility and understanding. In the introduction of the first *Critique* Kant had claimed: "All that seems necessary for an introduction or preliminary is that there are two stems of human cognition, which may perhaps arise from a common but to us unknown root, namely sensibility and understanding, through the first of which objects are given to us, but through the second of which they are thought" (*KRV* A15/B29).

The question of the common root is also the locus of the basic problem of the unity of all reality, that is, of self and world. According to Kant's philosophy, the influences of the world upon us are received through sensibility; through the understanding, which Kant had linked with the spontaneity of the self, the self acts upon the material it has received from the senses. If there is such a common root, both self and world must be given together in a fundamental moment of consciousness. This is the possible Leibnizian moment in Kant's philosophy, to which Schleiermacher is also heir. However, Kant had recognized the mystery under which transcendental consciousness stands, and hence the impossibility of affirming with certainty the existence of such a root. This is the significance of the "perhaps" in his pregnant remark. The "I" is an "original consciousness" that must be presupposed if the analytic treatment of logical phenomena is to be possible; it does not, however, follow *from* the conditions of the possibility of logical phenomena. Henrich notes the "peculiar difficulty" that Kant finds himself in, "of not being able to determine in turn this supreme principle of all thought and knowledge."[13] He further provides an insightful analysis and defense of why Kant thought this determination was *not* possible:

it is even doubtful whether the problematic idea of a common origin of the faculties can at all be thought through the concepts of substance and power. That point becomes even clearer when one remembers that the common root can only be assumed as the object of some intellectual intuition. For such an intuition, however, the separation of self-consciousness and pre-given being, which first defines the concept of the category, does not apply. It is therefore at least questionable whether the categories of a finite self-consciousness have any meaning at all with reference to an intellectual intuition. To be sure, finite self-consciousness is required to employ the categories when attempting to grasp the very concept of the unity of the cognitive faculties. But at the same time it knows that it employs the categories only analogically, and that therefore the idea of the common root merely indicates an "empty space."[14]

Recall that for Kant, a concept is always a representation of a representation, that is, it a mark through which several representations (whether they be intuitions or concepts) can be thought together under one representation. This is what makes our thought discursive. Only through intuition is a representation *directly* related to an object. For finite beings such as ourselves, intuitions are always given through sensation.[15] An intellectual intuition, then, would be a representation relating *directly* to an individual, not given to us through

---

[13]　Henrich, "On the Unity of Subjectivity," 37.　　　[14]　Ibid. 35–6.

[15]　Kant's discussion is worth quoting at length: "Now we cannot partake of intuition independently of sensibility. The understanding is therefore not a faculty of intuition. But besides intuition there is no other kind of cognition than through concepts. Thus the cognition of every, at least human, understanding is a cognition through concepts, not intuitive but discursive. All intuitions, as sensible, rest on affections, concepts therefore on functions. By a function, however, I understand the unity of the action of ordering different representations under a common one. Concepts are therefore grounded on the spontaneity of thinking, as sensible intuitions are grounded on the receptivity of impressions. Now the understanding can make no other use of these concepts than that of judging by means of them. Since no representation pertains to the object immediately except intuition alone, a concept is thus never immediately related to an object, but is always related to some other representation of it (whether that be an intuition or itself already a concept). Judgment is therefore the mediate cognition of an object, hence the representation of a representation of it" (*KRV* A68/B93).

sensation but through the spontaneity of thought. But if our concepts are always representations of representations, some determinations of an individual thing must stand outside of our concept of it, and the individual cannot be grasped completely by the concept.[16] This is related to why we cannot think the common root, for to think it would mean for us to cognize, in one thought, the ground of all the determinations of self and world, that is, the ground of both what is thought and what lies outside of thought, namely, what is given in sensation.

Schleiermacher sided with Kant, against Fichte and Hegel, in affirming that mind cannot completely penetrate the world. Were it to be able to do so, the mind that cognizes reality must also be identical with the origin of reality. The problem of the knowability of the common root therefore becomes—at one and the same time— the problem of the thing in itself, which Kant affirmed must remain unknown and unknowable. In the *Speeches* Schleiermacher affirms

All intuition proceeds from the influence of the intuited on the one who intuits, from an original and independent action of the former, which is then grasped, apprehended, and conceived by the latter according to one's own nature. If the emanations of light—which happen completely without your efforts—did not affect your sense, if the smallest parts of the body, the tips of your fingers, were not mechanically or chemically affected, if the pressure of weight did not reveal to you an opposition and a limit to your power, you would intuit nothing and perceive nothing, and what you thus intuit and perceive is not the nature of things, but their action upon you.

(OR 24–5)

What is apprehended is not the thing in itself, but rather, the thing in its relation to us, that is, how it affects us. Things, according to Schleiermacher, stand in genuine community and interaction with one another. Insofar as we know things through their interaction with us, what is known is the outer of things, how they stand in relation with other things, and not the inner, that is, what the things are in themselves. What we perceive is not the "nature of things," but rather "their action" on us.

---

[16] On these and related points see my essay, "Schleiermacher Between Kant and Leibniz: Predication and Ontology," 59–77.

Along with Kant, Schleiermacher affirms the impossibility of absolute knowledge. This is why in the 1814/15 lectures on *Dialektik* he claimed that, with respect to knowledge, "beginning in the middle is unavoidable."[17] He further claimed that "just as the idea of the Godhead is the transcendental *terminus a quo,* and the principle of the possibility of knowledge as such, so the idea of the world is the transcendental *terminus ad quem* and the principle of the possibility of knowledge in its becoming." This understanding of the world as the *terminus ad quem* implies that "we can say of the idea of the world that the whole history of our knowledge is an approximation to it."[18] Complete knowledge stands as an ideal that can only be approached asymptotically. The absolute, as the locus of the unity of the ideal and the real, transcends the self: it is the transcendental *terminus a quo* that is a condition of the possibility of knowledge. For Schleiermacher this ground of unity between self and world, spontaneity and receptivity, however, stands *outside* the self and cannot be thought.[19] Schleiermacher is thereby in fundamental disagreement with Leibniz, for whom the self, along with all its experiences of the world, was completely determined through the complete concept of the individual. As such, for Leibniz the world, and everything the individual is to experience, is *contained* in each monad. These monads "have no windows through which something can enter or leave."[20] For Schleiermacher, on the other hand, it must be said that the world stands outside the self, and that the self genuinely *interacts* with other selves. The locus of this interaction is the ground of self and world, and it is what Schleiermacher would call the "Whence of our receptive and active existence" in §4.3 of *The Christian Faith.*[21]

---

[17] Friedrich Schleiermacher, *Dialektik* (1814/15), *Einleitung zur Dialektik* (1833), 105.

[18] Ibid. 70.

[19] Wolfgang Kasprzik puts it quite nicely: "Können wir diesen Grund denken? Nein, denn nichts, was wir denken können, kann der Grund der Stetigkeit unseres Bewußtseins in allen Übergangen sein. Der Grund muß den Zusammenhang als Ganzen bestimmen, so daß wir uns bei jedem Übergang in diesem Zusammenhang von dem Woher dieser Bestimmtheit des Zusammenhangs abhängig fühlen (DO 290 C, vgl. GL I 27f., §4.3)." Wolfgang Kasprzik, "Monaden mit Fenstern? Zur Konzeption der Individualität in Schleiermacher's *Dialektik*," 120.

[20] *Philosophical Essays,* 214.

[21] A related idea can be found in Kant's *Inaugural Dissertation,* 2: 410. There is an analogy between space, grounding the interaction of physical substances, and

The idea of the common root thereby indicates an "empty space" made possible by God, which in turn conditions the possibility of transitions in consciousness.[22]

SELF AND WORLD

Schleiermacher's *Monologen*, first appearing in 1800, can be fruitfully understood in terms of his encounter with, and critique of, Leibniz. Schleiermacher adopts key Leibnizian notions, but transforms them

God, who is the ground of the metaphysical community. Space is the "phenomenal omnipresence" of God; as Franks put it, it is "the derivative expression of the absolute ground." Franks, *All or Nothing*, 35. Here too, the absolute ground conditions the possibility of the relation between substances.

[22] This is one of the most profound and difficult problems in the metaphysics of the self and its relation to the world, and stands at the heart of one of Kant's most fundamental differences with Leibniz. In his chapter "Metaphysical Foundations: A Look at Schleiermacher's *Dialectic*," Manfred Frank notes the following: "Schleiermacher understands the feeling of Being as the 'ground of the soul.' This expression comes from Baumgarten, but Schleiermacher changes its function. In the second speech of *On Religion*, he speaks of a 'ground-feeling (*Grundgefühl*) of infinite and living nature.' As in his later writings, 'immediate self-consciousness' has two dimensions: an inner-temporal psychic phenomenon and a supra-temporal (the manifestation of the transcendent unity). In the early writings, feeling already has the character of a unity that exists before, or better founds the synthetic 'grasping-together' of individuals. It is furthermore not 'thinking in another.' This means it is not grounded in a conscious turning to a second object, in the manner of a reflection. Rather, it rests in itself. The remaining 'concepts' and 'modes,' such as willing and thinking (as Schleiermacher notes in terms that resemble those of Spinoza) 'inhere' in it. If the opposite were true, how the different concepts and modes transition from one to the next would be unintelligible. This transition presupposes a qualitative identity between the *terminus a quibus* and the *terminus ad quos*. Like Eberhard, Schleiermacher thought of the river of the soul's life and the arising transitions between types of representation as continuous. Consequently, thinking and sensing are fundamentally one and the same, although each accords with the changing predominance of one determination over the other." He notes further that Schleiermacher contradicts "Kant's dualism, which drives an unbridgeable wedge between not only sense and thought, but also thinking and willing." In Frank, "Metaphysical Foundations," 27. For such a dualism to be consistently denied, however, one must return to the Leibnizian conception of the monads as windowless. On such a view what is "outside" the self cannot affect it, and different selves cannot genuinely interact. Once the monads have windows, one cannot consistently hold to seamless transitions between the moments of spontaneity and receptivity occurring *within* consciousness itself. The transitions can only occur at the ground of the unity of the soul, which is completely unknowable, and which is also the locus of interaction between self and world.

in light of Kant's critique of rational psychology, explored in the previous chapter. The result is Schleiermacher's unique understanding of subjectivity and metaphysics of the self. Two important clues reveal Schleiermacher's play on key Leibnizian doctrines. The title of this work, the *Monologen*, serves to remind the reader of Leibniz's *Monadology*. More important still is his fundamental inversion of a key Leibnizian metaphor standing at the heart of the *Monologen*: for Leibniz, the soul is the mirror of the world.[23] For Schleiermacher, however, the *world* is the mirror of the soul. In what follows I discuss Leibniz's understanding of self and world and Schleiermacher's engagement and transformation of it.

Leibniz's *Discourse on Metaphysics* contains a succinct explanation of his understanding of substance and its relation to his notion of the complete concept. In §8 he notes: "the nature of an individual substance is to have a notion so complete that it is sufficient to contain and to allow us to deduce from it all the predicates of the subject to which this notion is attributed."[24] Elsewhere he tells us "a complete concept is the mark [*nota*] of a singular substance."[25] Later in §8 of the *Discourse*, he clarifies what he means through the following example: "Thus when we consider carefully the connection of things, we can say that from all time in Alexander's soul there are vestiges of everything that has happened to him and marks of everything that will happen to him and even traces of everything that happens in the universe, even though God alone could recognize them all."[26] At any

---

[23] In §83 of the *Monadology*, Leibniz notes: "Among other differences which exist between ordinary souls and minds, some of which I have already noted, there are also the following: that souls, in general, are living mirrors or images of the universe of creatures, but that minds are also images of the divinity itself, or of the author of nature, capable of knowing the system of the universe, and imitating something of it through their schematic representations [échantillons architectoniques] of it, each mind being like a little divinity in its own realm" Leibniz, *Philosophical Essays*, 223.

[24] Ibid. 41.

[25] The English translation of this passage is from Donald Rutherford's *Leibniz and the Rational Order of Nature*, 110; the passage is originally found in Eduard Bodemann, *Die Leibniz-Handschriften der Königlichen Öffentlichen Bibliothek zu Hanover*, LH IV 7C, Bl. 111–14.

[26] Leibniz, *Philosophical Essays*, 41. Similar ideas are expressed in Leibniz's *New System* and his *Principles of Nature and Grace*. I have already cited the *New System*, where Leibniz remarks that "God originally created the soul (and every other real unity) in such a way that everything must arise from it from its own depths [*fonds*] ... " (Leibniz, *Philosophical Essays*, 143). In the *Principles of Nature and Grace* Leibniz

given moment, the essence of the existing soul contains traces of its past and seeds of its future; all the soul's commerce and relations with the rest of creation, past, present, and future, are already given with this essence. Hence the soul can be likened to a compact disk containing the information of a whole life, and the light of consciousness a kind of laser illuminating the present.

Leibniz's theory of *independent* substance drives his notion of the complete concept. Contrary to Descartes, who defined substance as an *ens a se*, that is, in terms of the independence of its existence, Leibniz and the Wolffians who followed him conceived of substance as an *ens per se*.[27] The Cartesian definition of substance was a driving factor in Spinoza's conclusion that there is only one substance, that is, only one independently existing thing. For Leibniz, on the other hand, who wanted to avoid Spinozism and preserve the distinct reality of the soul,[28] a substance is what it is in virtue of its *intrinsic* properties. As such, there can be many different substances having distinct sets of intrinsic properties. Intrinsic properties are properties that a thing has independently of anything else, and they are to be contrasted with a substance's relational properties. A relational property, on the other hand, requires two substances in relation with one another for its instantiation. For example, that there is a certain distance between me and the chair across from me is a relational property that we normally think cannot be instantiated unless we assume both my own existence

---

claims: "For everything is ordered in things once and for all, with as much order and agreement as possible, since supreme wisdom and goodness can only act with perfect harmony: the present is pregnant with the future; the future can be read in the past; the distant is expressed in the proximate. One could know the beauty of the universe in each soul, if one could unfold all its folds, which only open perceptibly with time" (Leibniz, *Philosophical Essays*, 211). The concept through which God creates such complete individuals is the complete concept.

[27] On this point see Franks *All or Nothing*, 109.

[28] In his comments on Spinoza's philosophy, Leibniz notes the following: "it is a mockery to call souls immortal because ideas are eternal, as if the soul of a globe is to be called eternal because the idea of a spherical body is eternal. The soul is not an idea, but the source of innumerable ideas. For over and above a present idea, the soul has something active, that is, the production of new ideas. But, according to Spinoza, at any given moment, a soul will be different, since, when the body changes, the idea of the body is different. Hence, we shouldn't be surprised if he takes creatures for vanishing modifications. Therefore, the soul is something vital, that is, something that contains active force" (Leibniz, *Philosophical Essays*, 277).

and that of the chair. Leibniz's philosophy sought to explain all (what seem to be) relational properties in terms of intrinsic properties. On Leibniz's understanding of substance, even if nothing existed outside of me, I would still perceive the chair. It is likely that Leibniz's attempt to explain all so-called relational properties in terms of intrinsic properties (hence the windowless character of the monads) has to do with his attempt to avoid Spinozism. For if the windows are open, then things stand in mutual interaction with each other. This implies, however, that all the properties a thing exhibits or expresses are what they are in virtue of that thing's standing in relation to other things. This includes a thing's spatial, temporal, and causal properties. They are *all* relational properties. Kant had already noted this in his 1755 *Nova Delucidatio*: "All substances, in so far as they are connected with each other in the same space, reciprocally interact with each other, and thus they are dependent on each other in respect of their determinations."[29] The principle makes its way to Kant's first *Critique* as the third analogy of experience: "All substances, insofar as they can be perceived in space as simultaneous, are in thoroughgoing interaction" (A211/B256). One might still posit intrinsic properties, but as such, they would never appear. Kant arrives at this conclusion as well: a substance cannot determine another substance "by means of that which belongs to it internally."[30] This is because the way its power manifests itself always also presupposes the particular character of that which will receive the effect. It could then simply be a matter of Occam's razor to dispense with intrinsic properties.[31] Leibniz may have suspected that to open the windows would lead to Spinozism, and for this reason he insisted on the complete isolation of the

---

[29] Immanuel Kant, *Nova Delucidatio* 1:415.   [30] Ibid.

[31] Franks puts the matter succinctly: "It has been argued that no intrinsic properties of finite things can explain any of their spatial, temporal, or causal properties. But then which effects of finite things *can* be explained by their intrinsic properties? It would seem that intrinsic properties do not explain *any* other properties of finite things. Rather, the *assumption* that finite things have intrinsic properties is introduced solely to explain the fact that finite things have non-intrinsic properties. But why is this necessary? It is necessary only if finite things are substances. But what grounds that assumption? Thanks to B1 [God is all-sufficient], an absolute cause is already available to explain everything else. So what warrant is there for introducing intrinsic properties that do no explanatory work that is not already being done?" Franks *All or Nothing*, 122.

monads from each other.[32] Kant, too, had recognized the problem. Appearances are all mere relations. His solution, however, differed from that of Leibniz: space and time, through which the appearances are ordered and stand in relation to one another, are not features of things in themselves. Were they features of things in themselves, he argued, the result would be Spinozism.

Now for Leibniz, this independence of substance has the following implications. First, excepting its relation to God, the being of a substance does not depend on anything outside of itself. Second, if substance is truly independent, it must itself be the source of all its modifications. As such, it contains within itself its own entelechy. This principle, along with the first, is what leads Leibniz to conceive of his monads as "windowless," that is, they cannot be affected from without. Leibniz notes, "[From] the notion of an individual substance it also follows in metaphysical rigor that all the operations of substances, both actions and passions, are spontaneous, and that with the exception of the dependence of creatures on God, no real influx from one to the other is intelligible. For whatever happens to each one of them would flow from its nature and its notion even if the rest were supposed to be absent."[33] Third, a substance persists throughout its changes. Fourth, substance is a true or *per se* unity, that is, all of its attributes should be derivable from a fundamental principle that articulates its essence. The third and fourth conditions of substance are intrinsically interwoven, since insofar as substance is a *per se* unity, it can be said to persist through all its modifications. Lastly, substances are uniquely identifiable. Given this characterization of substance, Leibniz's understanding of the complete concept is uniquely suited to articulate the nature of the intrinsic connection of a substance's attributes to its essence. If substance is truly independent (the monads are windowless), all of its changes must flow from its

---

[32] In Leibniz's *New System*, he notes: "we should rather say that we are determined only in appearance, and that, in rigorous metaphysical language, we have a perfect independence relative to the influence of every other creature. This also throws a marvelous light on the immortality of our soul and the always uniform conservation of our individual being, which is perfectly well regulated by its own nature and protected from external accidents, appearances to the contrary not withstanding" (Leibniz, *Philosophical Essays*, 144).

[33] Leibniz, *A Specimen of Discoveries about Marvellous Secrets*, in *Philosophical Writings*, 79.

own spontaneous action. The complete concept expresses the unique essence of individual substance from which all of its modifications flow, since God creates through it. As Rutherford notes, "a complete concept is an appropriate way to conceive of God's knowledge of a being, which is, by its nature, a spontaneous source of change."[34] In Leibniz's system, the notion of a complete concept is inherently bound up with his notion of substance. It is Leibniz's commitment to independent substance that leads him to the notion of the complete concept.

The consequences for Leibniz's understanding of the creation of substances in terms of their complete concept is then worked out in §9:

Moreover, every substance is like a complete world and like a mirror of God or of the whole universe, which each one expresses in its own way, somewhat as the same city is variously represented depending upon the different positions from which it is viewed. Thus the universe is in some way multiplied as many times as there are substances, and the glory of God is likewise multiplied by as many entirely different representations of his work. It can even be said that every substance bears in some way the character of God's infinite wisdom and omnipotence and imitates him as much as it is capable. For it expresses, however confusedly, everything that happens in the universe, whether past, present, or future—this has some resemblance to an infinite perception or knowledge. And since all other substances in turn express this substance and accommodate themselves to it, one can say that it extends its power over all the others, in imitation of the creator's omnipotence.[35]

Each monad "expresses" all of the other monads and is "like a mirror of God or of the whole universe." It does so in virtue of the internal principle through which it was created, namely, its essence. This means, further, that each monad expresses all other monads in virtue of its intrinsic properties. Monads do not relate directly to one another, they "have no windows through which something can enter or leave."[36] They are, rather, "harmonized" with one another by God, and it is in virtue of this pre-established harmony that each monad must accommodate itself to other monads. In the *Monadology*

[34] Donald Rutherford, *Leibniz and the Rational Order of Nature*, 139.
[35] Leibniz, *Philosophical Essays*, 42. The same points are also made in §§51, 57, and 83 of the *Monadology*.
[36] Ibid. 214.

Leibniz notes that "this interconnection or accommodation of all created things to each other, and each to all the others, brings it about that each simple substance has relations that express all the others, and, consequently, that each simple substance is a perpetual, living mirror of the universe."[37] Two things stand out in this regard. First, as already noted, all of the soul's actions and experiences, according to Leibniz, are already "written," so to speak, into its essence; they are given to it at the moment of its creation. The monads are active forms or entelechies, each with its own drive to play out its life, but it is only *really* in active relation to God.

Now this doctrine can have pernicious ethical consequences. At its heart is a kind of metaphysical and ethical solipsism, since the self is never really in interaction with other selves and cannot be in any way transformed through this interaction. For Leibniz, the self never changes in *response* to another self. It is very likely this point that led Schleiermacher to aver that Leibniz was a bad philosopher. If we look at the *Monologen*, we find Schleiermacher taking over some of the central metaphors of Leibniz's philosophy and inverting them. According to Schleiermacher, at the heart of the self is consciousness, through which the self both stands in relation to the infinite and eternal and also *opens out* into the world. Yet no longer is the soul the mirror of the world, but, rather, the *world* is the mirror of the soul. The inversion of Leibniz's metaphor is reflective of the fact that Schleiermacher understands consciousness as essentially given to itself in its world. Schleiermacher begins the first section of the *Monologen* entitled "Reflection" in the following way: "Even the outer world with its most eternal laws and its most fleeting appearances reflects back to us, like a magic mirror, the highest and innermost dimension of our being [Wesen] in a thousand tender and sublime allegories" (*KGA* I.3, 6; 10).[38] And later he continues

---

[37] Leibniz, *Philosophical Essays*, 220; *Monadology* §56.

[38] This is Brent Sockness' translation of this passage. Large chunks of his translation of the *Monologen* can be found in his article "Schleiermacher and the Ethics of Authenticity: the *Monologen* of 1800." The translated passage can be found on page 490. A complete English translation of the *Monologen* can be found in Horace Leland Friess, *Schleiermacher's Soliloquies*. Subsequent references to the *Monologen* will be to the first edition of 1800 found in *Schleiermacher Kritischegesammtausgabe: Schriften aus der Berliner Zeit 1800–1802*. References are shown parenthetically in the text as *KGA* I.3, with page numbers following. Reference to the pagination of the Friess

What they call world, is for me the human, what they call human is for me the world. For them the world is always primary, and spirit is only a humble guest upon it, uncertain about its place and powers. For me spirit is the first and only thing; for what I recognize as world is spirit's most beautiful work, its self-created mirror.   (*KGA* I.3, 9; 16)[39]

In understanding these passages it is important to recall Schleiermacher's echo of Kant's critique of rational psychology in *Spinozism*, discussed in the previous chapter. There Schleiermacher had noted that "the consciousness, which is the sole *ratio cognoscendi* of self-consciousness, relates itself only to the outer of the thing, not to its inner...." (*KGA* I.1, 540). The self is conscious of itself in and through its relation to the manifold of its representations, through which it both apprehends and "constructs" the empirical world. All these representations are relational; they are the representations of *a self that stands in relation to the world* and apprehends the world *from a particular standpoint*. We can perceive only the outer of consciousness, that is, the "succession of representations and sensations" (*KGA* I.3, 6; 11). And it is in the *outer* that the self sees itself reflected, as if in a magic mirror.

This stands at the heart of the non-Fichtean character of the ideas Schleiermacher puts forward in the *Monologen*.[40] For

---

translation will follow after a semicolon. I have often significantly altered the Friess translation; when necessary passages have been completely retranslated.

[39] I made a few small changes to the translation found in Sockness (2004), 490–1.

[40] Although when the book first came out anonymously some mistook it for the work of a disciple of Fichte, Schleiermacher's intent in writing the *Monologen* was not to produce another bit of Fichtean philosophy. It is true that even today there are those who read the *Monologen* in light of Fichte; see, for instance, Ulrich Barth, "Der ethische Individualitätsgedanke beim frühen Schleiermacher." Peter Grove also makes a good case for significant Fichtean influences on Schleiermacher in *Deutungen des Subjekts*, 157–248. Nevertheless, while it is true that (a) there is no doubt that Schleiermacher was quite engaged with Fichte's thought, and (b) that Schleiermacher made use of certain Fichtean formulations (for instance in his *Notes on Ethics* he notes that "through every cognition a personal existence is posited" (43)), it is significant that Schleiermacher himself frequently expressed his distaste for the Fichtean philosophy. In a letter to the *Monologen's* publisher Johann Carl Philipp Spener, he affirms that the "*Monologen* contains something different than, say, what every Fichtean tends to put forward" (*KGA* V/3:321). And writing in 1803 from Stolpe, he criticized Fichte for separating philosophy and life, and expressed suspicion at Fichte's arrival at an entire system through a single starting point (*Aus Schleiermachers Leben. In Briefen* IV, 94ff). While there are certain influences, the divergences from Fichte's thought are more

Schleiermacher's self-consciousness really does open out into the world, a world that it shares with other selves and which results from the interaction of spiritual beings. Hence there genuinely exist "outer contact points, wherein the energies of the self meet with external things" (*KGA* I.3, 7; 11). *That* the world impinges upon us in certain ways, and that our representations must be brought to a unity in accordance with certain laws, is not a matter under our control. Even our emotions may not be fully under our control:

> To necessity belong also the rising and falling tides of emotion, the train of images that passes before us, and everything that changes in our soul with time. Such images and feelings are a token that the spirit and the world have met in harmony, ever renewing the kiss of friendship between them in a different manner. The Dance of Hours thus proceeds, melodious and harmonious, according to a necessary rhythm. But Freedom plays the melody, selects the key, and all subtle modulations are her work. For these proceed from an inner determination and from the individual's unique disposition.
>
> (*KGA* I.3, 10; 18)

Nevertheless, while the self knows itself in its world, the point of the first monologue is to avoid both a slavish empiricism, where the self *mistakes* itself for what is outer (instead of recognizing the outer as its mere reflection) as well as to eschew the Leibnizian notion of an inner essence of the soul through which the whole course of life has been determined at the outset. Against the latter, Schleiermacher's remark concerning those who "think some hidden hand pulls the thread of their lives along, drawing it sometimes more loosely, sometimes more tightly together" (*KGA* I.3, 6; 11)[41] may be an oblique reference. Against the empiricist who recognizes only the outer, and who is blind to the inner transcendental unity that holds together the outer impressions Schleiermacher affirms:

> Freedom seems to him nothing but an illusion, spread like a veil over a hidden and uncomprehended necessity. Moreover, such an empiricist, whose action and thought look outward, sees everything as finite and particular. He cannot imagine himself as other than a sum of fleeting appearances,

important still; I discuss these here and in Chapter 6. Some of the divergences are also discussed by Giovanni Moretto, "The Problem of the Religious in the Philosophical Perspectives of Fichte and Schleiermacher" 47–73.

[41] Sockness, "Schleiermacher and the Ethics of Authenticity," 489.

each of which supplants and cancels the other, so that it is impossible to conceive them as a whole. A complete picture of his being thus eludes him in a thousand contradictions... But within the spirit all is one, each action is but supplementary to another, in each the other also is preserved.... Each of my acts reveals the whole of my being, undivided, each of its manifestations goes with the rest...   (*KGA* I.3, 12; 21)

Such an empiricist, focused only on the outer, knows only the empirical self, and as such thinks of herself as determined by outside forces through inexorable causal necessity. "Whoever sees and recognizes only the outward spectacle of life instead of the spiritual activity that secretly stirs his inmost being...may never set foot within the sacred precincts of freedom, even though he thinks he has attained self-consciousness. For in the image he constructs of himself, this very self becomes something external, like all else, and everything in such an image is determined by external circumstances" (*KGA* I.3, 9; 15).

FREEDOM AND INNER REVELATION

Moreover, the empiricist cannot account for the *unity* of the self. All that s/he sees is the fleeting appearances that stand outside and alongside one another in the river of the soul's life. S/he cannot account for their principle of unity. What the empiricist fails to take into consideration is the transcendental unity of consciousness, which is not itself determined by any sensation, representation, or emotion. It is this transcendental unity, according to Schleiermacher, which is the source of the unity of a whole life. All the psychic forces of the self are grounded in it. This unity is *free* in relation to the world, for it is not a moment in the self's consciousness *of* the world and cannot be determined by the play of previous impressions. The transcendental unity does not contain within itself, or ground, what is other than the self (and this is the key point at which Schleiermacher stands at odds with Fichte), but it does determine *the way* in which the impressions of the world are received. Hence Schleiermacher notes that "All those feelings that seem to be forced upon me by the material world are in reality my own free doing; nothing is a mere effect of that world upon me" (*KGA* I.3, 10; 17).[42] This is Schleiermacher's doctrine of the preponderant synthesis: even the way that we *receive* impressions from the world is conditioned by our spontaneity. To give an example from ethical life: the loveless actions of another can be received either as an affront or as a sign of the impoverished life of the other, and therefore as a call for help that must be met in the spirit of forgiveness. One is receptive to the world and to others, but the light in which those actions are received is the province of human freedom. As such, the self is free in relation to the world; as Schleiermacher puts it, insofar as the self is free, it "plays the melody, selects the key, and all subtle modulations are her work. For these proceed from an inner determination and from the individual's unique disposition" (*KGA* I.3, 10; 18). The manner in which the impressions of the world are received (and even the way that the individual's imagination works to understand them) is not determined by what is outside the self. Rather an inner principle of the self is at work.

As noted in the previous chapter, in *Reflexion* 5653 Kant had observed, "the concept of freedom is already by itself necessarily connected with the concept of substance with respect to the intelligible, because the substance must be the ultimate subject of its actions and cannot itself be the mode of action of another substance."[43] Schleiermacher no doubt recognized this connection in the *Monologen*; here a significant change has taken place in Schleiermacher's thought. In the *Monologen* the self is not a mere modification, a moment in which a play of outside forces come together. This is likely the way that Schleiermacher thought of the self in *Spinozism*, and this determinism was also a significant factor in his earlier ethical work.

[42] Schleiermacher recognized that the passage as written could be misinterpreted in terms of a Fichtean idealism, and in later editions changed it to read as follows: "Thus for me the earth is the stage of my own free activity, and in every feeling, however much the outer world may seem to force it upon me, in those feelings too wherein I sense the kinship of material existence with universal being, there is free, inner action on my part." These changes serve to highlight the fact that Schleiermacher recognizes that the self receives genuine influences from the world. At issue, however, is *how* they are interpreted, and hence, received. What is given to the self is never simply the sheer, formless stuff of receptivity. Rather, what is given is received through the powers and dispositions of the self, and hence in some way is received as already interpreted. If the self is changed—and hence too its powers and dispositions—what it receives will be different as well.

[43] *Kants gesammelte Schriften*, vol. 18, 311.

Here, however, the self must be considered as a substance *insofar as* it is free in the way that it receives and responds to what stands outside of it.

Two things are important in this regard. First, the freedom that Schleiermacher speaks of in the *Monologen* is not the freedom of the self over against the Infinite and Eternal. Rather, God is the source of whatever freedom the self may possess in relation to the world. The self as substance is established and preserved in its being by God; as regards this point there are traces of Leibniz in Schleiermacher's thought. And because the soul is directly receptive to the divine influence, it is not a mere turnspit, reacting mechanically to *outside* influences. The transcendental light of consciousness that opens out into the world is a light preserved in its being in and through spirit's relation to the infinite and absolute. Schleiermacher describes the transcendental self as a "point" which "cuts a line" but which is "not part of that line."[44] This point is "truly and more immediately related to the Infinite than to the line, and anywhere along the line you can place such a point." It is itself "no moment of . . . temporal existence;" in it one becomes conscious of one's "relations to the Infinite and Eternal" (*KGA* I.3, 7; 12). The soul is genuinely—although not absolutely—free in its relation to the world. However, all genuine freedom, all creativity, all the productive workings of the imagination and inspiration result from the psychic powers of the self being enlivened by the light of God, who stands at the ground of the soul. Schleiermacher affirms that in freedom the spirit "discovers its creative nature, the light of God begins to shine . . . banishing far hence the mists in which enslaved humanity strays in error" (*KGA* I.3, 11; 19). The transcendental self is not compelled to receive or imagine what comes to it from the outside world in any *fully* determinate way (although this does not mean that what the self receives is completely indeterminate, either). The successive series of apprehensions,

---

[44] In understanding the transcendental self as distinct from the manifold of its representations, and hence as "outside" of the temporal continuum of the individual's self-understanding of itself as in relation to its world, Schleiermacher is working with important elements of the Kantian understanding of the transcendental self that he worked through in his discussion of the self in *Spinozism*. Recall that for Kant, from a transcendental perspective, "time is in me," and hence that the transcendental self stands outside of time.

the fleeting representations and sensations that are the stuff of self-conscious life do not of themselves completely determine *how* these disparate elements of consciousness will be knit together through the imagination. And while there are rules for coming to know that must be observed if inter-subjective knowledge is to be possible, there is yet great room for the play of the imagination. The transcendental freedom of the self in its relation to the world is made possible by the "light that lights every man that comes into the world," as Leibniz had put it. This, no doubt, was one of the insights of Leibniz's philosophy that Schleiermacher found congenial. It is no surprise that Schleiermacher, like Leibniz, was so taken with the gospel of John.

Second, Schleiermacher does not here propose that we are *absolutely* free. Our freedom is curtailed by the material stuff of the world as well as by the freedom of other human selves. "The infinitely great and ponderous mass of corporeal stuff," Schleiermacher writes, "is but the great common body of humanity. It belongs to us just as the single body belongs to the individual; it is possible only through humanity, and is given to humanity for it to rule and to announce itself through it" (*KGA* I.3, 9–10; 16–17). How are we to understand this material stuff? Given what Schleiermacher says explicitly, it must be something like the unconscious product of spiritual beings as they interrelate with one another. In the following remarkable passage Schleiermacher affirms that the only reality is that of the community of spiritual beings and what they jointly produce:

I deem worthy to be called world only the eternal community of spirits, their influence on one another, their mutual reflections, the high harmony of freedom. Only the infinite totality of spirits sets the finite and particular over against me. Only this reality do I allow to change and mold the surface of my being, to work on me. Here, and here alone, is the province of necessity. My activity itself is free, not so my workings in the world, for those obey eternal laws. Freedom finds its limit in another freedom, and whatever happens freely bears the marks of limitation and community. Yes, holy Freedom, you are first overall! You live in me, and in all. Necessity is posited outside us; it is the determinate tone of the beautiful clash of freedoms, which announces its being. I behold nothing but freedom within myself. What is necessary is not my doing; it is its reflection, the appearance of the world that I help fashion in holy community with others. To it belong the works I build on common ground with others; they are my contribution to the creation expressing our inner thoughts.   (*KGA* I.3, 10; 17–18)

Significantly, Schleiermacher affirms that selves are in genuine communion with one another. Free *interactions* with other spiritual beings "transform and shape the surface" of a person's being. This is a very different picture from that offered by Leibniz with his windowless monads that never freely interact with one another. Schleiermacher's understanding affords a much more fruitful basis for an understanding of both religion and human ethical development. For Schleiermacher the community of others is of genuine importance for moral and spiritual progress. From the actual existence of other selves stems "necessity," that is, the curtailment of human freedom by what is genuinely other than the self. An infinite number of spiritual beings restrict the freedom through which the self can express itself. The self is thereby *receptive* to a world of others that stands outside of it.[45] However, there is a crucial moment of freedom even in the self's receptivity to what is other than the self. To a degree, the self determines *how* impressions from the outside are received, how they are interpreted through the work of the imagination, and how the self will, as a consequence, react to the world and to other selves.

It is important to note, however, that already in the *Monologen*, Schleiermacher recognizes the socially constructed dimension of that which is received from outside the self. This social construction of the world is something to which the self contributes; however, it is a joint effort, and the result, too, is jointly determined. The world that appears is one that "I help fashion in holy community with others;" it is a "creation expressing our inner thoughts" (*KGA* I.3, 10; 17). Hence the world is the reflection of the collective exercise of the freedom of human selves. The self *knows* itself in this world, for along with others it *expresses* itself into this world. Without the world, which is the joint product of the expression of free spirits, the self cannot find itself reflected in what is other than itself, and hence, cannot come to

---

[45] In contrasting Schleiermacher's philosophy with that of Fichte, Günter Meckenstock correctly notes "Schleiermacher's moral individual is thoroughly related to community." Meckenstock, "Schleiermacher's Auseinandersetzung mit Fichte," 35.

know itself. It cannot become *self*-conscious, for self-consciousness presupposes a duality between subject and object, and it implies that the subject can make itself its own object. Objectification of the self also implies the self's understanding of itself as *related* to others in the world. This is the "outer" self, that is, the empirical self without which the self cannot come to know itself. To be sure, apart from it the self might have a certain experience of itself in immediate apperception. And this immediate apperception is that "inner" dimension of the self's experience of itself that Schleiermacher urges the reader to attend to, lest s/he make the mistake of identifying herself completely with the empirical, outer self. He notes that "the conclusion from the outer to the inner" is but a "wavering conjecture" and hence urges us to build what is "immediately certain" (*KGA* I.3, 15; 27). However, these immediately certain inner realities are expressed into the world held in common by spiritual beings, and without the world, which is the common expression of human freedom, and which is also its reflection, there can be no *self*-consciousness.

It is important to note that here, too, we already find the seeds of Schleiermacher's preoccupation with language, which plays a key role in his ethics. Language is that through which the world is socially constructed, and through it the world becomes the common expression of free beings in communication with one another. Through language rules are given for the unification of perceptions and the integration of experience, and through its efficacy experience is always already, to a large degree, interpreted. Furthermore, because of the social dimension of the world in which the self expresses itself and finds itself, the self comes to know itself in its relation to the socially constructed world. Hence the "outer" empirical self is also, to a great degree, socially constructed. This stands at the heart of Schleiermacher's identification of sin as social. While the root of sin lies in the obstruction of consciousness of the infinite and eternal, this obstruction is a blocking of the *expression* of this God-consciousness towards the community of spiritual subjects. Hence social constructions of the self and of others can serve to block it, especially when individuals are encouraged to make the mistake of completely identifying themselves with these outer relations, rather than recognizing the outer as an opportunity for the expression of the divine light at the ground of the soul. All outer experience, and even the "unity of the transient stream of consciousness" is of little value if it is not recognized as the sign of "something of higher ethical value" (*KGA* I.3, 18; 31). In the third discourse on the world, Schleiermacher laments the fact that most persons identify themselves with purely outer things. Persons have "a sense only for outer communion with the world of sense," and they measure everything in its terms. They are interested only in "increase in outward possessions or in knowledge, protection and aid against fate or misfortune, stronger alliances to keep rivals in check" (*KGA* I.3, 34; 59–60). The "great battle around the holy standard of humanity" (*KGA* I.3, 37; 65) revolves around language, for it is through language that persons come to know both self and other as they stand in relation to one another. However, at present language is in the service of the world; it "has exact symbols and fine abundance for everything thought and felt in the world's sense" and hence is "the clearest mirror of the times, a work of art in which its spirit is revealed." As such, language becomes one of the principle vehicles through which the self is entangled in what is purely outer: "Before it has yet found itself, the spirit belongs to the world through language, and must first slowly extricate itself from its entanglement." And even when the individual has had a glimpse of what is at the heart of reality, language, routinely used to express only the value of tangible things, becomes an impediment to the communication of higher truths. Words can introduce "errors and corruptions" and language can be treacherous, "isolating and imprisoning its victims" in the common idiom, so that the individual who has at last "penetrated through to truth ... cannot communicate" what s/he has discovered (*KGA* I.3, 37; 64).

INDIVIDUALITY

Most striking in Schleiermacher's *Monologen* is its stress on the individual. In light of his critique of Leibniz's monads and his defense of Spinoza in *Spinozism* and in the *Short Presentation of the Spinozistic System*, this emphasis is surprising. Echoing many of the arguments of *Spinozism*, in the *Short Presentation* he writes:

Were each individual in the world of sense to correspond to one in the intelligible world, then we must be in a position to increase the number of things in themselves. This would be from the side of the extended things. The next transition from the world of sense to the intelligible world is alone the human being. Is it then certain that a noumenon stands at the ground of each consciousness? Does not this claim also belong to the paralogisms of reason? To me at least it seems that it has the same relation to the thinking things as to what is extended: the individuating consciousness concerns receptivity and relates itself only to the appearances. Exactly that which certainly depends on it most closely, that which really exists in us, namely reason, individuates us least of all, and its consideration all the sooner leads us back from the illusion of individuality. If one has no reason to affirm a plurality of noumena—and we should not say anything about it other than that which necessarily relates itself to appearances—then it is already a presumption when we express ourselves in any other way than: the noumenon, the world as noumenon. Even so little, however, does it presume to go further and to claim, with Spinoza, a positive unity and infinity. Yet, of this, which was alien to the critical idealism, it could know nothing. Thereby the great question remains to be discussed: what is the origin of the idea of the individual, and with what does it have to do?   (*KGA* I.1, 574)

In the *Short Presentation* Schleiermacher enumerates only two aspects of the self. The first is the self in the aspect of its outer relations to the world. This is the empirical self, the self as it appears. This empirical self is individuated in virtue of its *position* in *relation* to other things. Insofar as the empirical self is fully determined by the nexus of the outer appearances in which it has a place, "the individuating consciousness concerns receptivity and relates itself only to the appearances." In his early work *On Freedom*, Schleiermacher had already recognized that if we think of the self only as such a point for the unification of different forces,[46] the "agency" of the agent "dissolves into infinitely many infinitesimally small external forces that leave us with nothing to think of as firmly active in the subject" (*KGA* I.1, 257; 42–3). Furthermore, according to Kant's ethics, to which Schleiermacher is surely making reference here, the desires that emerge directly from the self's existence as an individual, embodied self are those of the lower faculty of desire, and as such are desires conditioned by self's causal history. On the other hand,

---

[46] In the *Short Presentation*, Schleiermacher had also described the individual as "nothing other than the cohesion, the identical unity of powers of a certain mass at a point" (*KGA* I.1, 574).

Schleiermacher points out, "that which really exists in us, namely reason, individuates us least of all, and its consideration all the sooner leads us back from the illusion of individuality." Insofar as reason is the province of the universality of thought, it cannot be the source of individuality.

No doubt referring to this past system of belief, Schleiermacher notes "for a long time, I too, was content with the mere discovery of reason" (*KGA* I.3, 17; 30). By the time he writes the *Monologen* however, something has changed. He no longer thinks that ethical reasoning deals with only two aspects of the self, namely, sensuous desires and the laws of universal reason. Beyond the discovery of reason there is yet a higher understanding of what the self is. This "higher" self is the seat of individuality.

> If the person attains consciousness of universal humanity, scorning the unworthy particularity of the sensuous animal life, and bows down before duty, it is still not possible for her to penetrate the higher individuality of development and morality, or to see and understand nature, which chooses freedom for itself. Most hold themselves in an undetermined, wavering middle, and really represent humanity only in rough elements, simply because they have not grasped the thought of a higher existence.
>
> (*KGA* I.3, 18; 30–1)

The discovery of this higher level of individuality, however, does not eliminate the need to adhere to universal moral laws. Schleiermacher makes this clear when he notes that while earlier he had thought that "there is but a single right way of acting in every situation" (*KGA* I.3, 17; 30) he now recognizes that there are a "thousand ways of acting differently, in a different sense and spirit, without offending against the law of humanity" (*KGA* I.3, 19; 33). What, then, does the discovery of individuality amount to for Schleiermacher, and how does it contribute to a deepened understanding of morality?

In the second monologue Schleiermacher affirms that the vision of "humanity within oneself" is the "inner and necessary tie between doing and seeing" (*KGA* I.3, 16; 28). In transcendental self-consciousness the self stands in immediate relation to the Infinite and Eternal; this stands at the heart of Schleiermacher's vision of the inner, higher self. However, since this immediate relation grounds the core of *all* human beings, it is still unclear how this is going to *individuate* persons. Schleiermacher insists that each person is "uniquely fashioned," (*KGA* I.3, 17; 30) and that each person "is meant to represent humanity" in his or her own way, "combining its elements uniquely, so that it may reveal itself in every way..." (*KGA* I.3, 18; 31). He provides the key to his view of what constitutes individuality only in passing: it is given in a person's *limitations*.[47] Hence he links coming to understand the "unique in his activity" with becoming conscious of "each action and limitation as the consequences of that free action" (*KGA* I.3, 18; 32). Later he notes that in order to find the "most characteristic efforts of one's nature," one might find what is "unique by virtue of its limitations" (*KGA* I.3, 19; 32–3). It is as if each individual is a window through which the divine light is refracted and expressed, yet only partially. Different persons are capable of refracting and expressing it differently, and some are not yet even conscious that this is the source of their true being. Hence they identify themselves with externals only.

Two important points follow from this. First, each person offers a unique perspective on the world. S/he views the world from a particular point of view that is not exactly the same as anyone else's. Each person's specificity—the way that they refract the divine light—is reflected in the mirror of how they have imagined other selves, the world as the common arena of their interaction, and their place in

---

[47] This idea is certainly also due to the influence of Leibniz. We have already seen that in his notes on Leibniz he mentions the idea of limitation and muses that limitation must come from the devil. In his book *Leibniz: Determinist, Theist, Idealist*, Robert Adams explores this issue in the context of his discussion of the relation of Leibniz to Spinoza. Adams argues that the mature Leibniz conceived of creatures as distinct from God in virtue of their limitations: "It is not hard to see how Leibniz might have thought the powers of creatures distinct from God's power. For the powers of creatures have limitations." On the other hand, "no limited perfection can be ascribed" to the *ens perfectissimum*. It is *because* there is a distinction of powers that there must be a distinction of subjects; the distinction of subjects "flows from the distinction of powers" (132). While the mature Leibniz affirmed that the reality of creatures is a limitation of the reality of God, he nevertheless claimed that the creatures are not "in" God but are distinct from God. In his paper entitled "On the Abstract and the Concrete," from about 1688 he notes "the reality of creatures is not that very reality that in God is absolute, but a limited reality for that is of the essence of the creature" (VE 1603=LH IV, 7C, 99–100, cited in Adams). Adams is right to conclude "Here the thought seems very clear that the limited and the absolute or unlimited reality are different, indeed incompatible, attributes and hence are not present in the same subject, so that the creatures are not 'in' God after all" (133).

it. To be sure, there are contact points between any given individual's outlook on the world and that of others. But each outlook is unique. In this regard, Schleiermacher's grasp of individuality echoes Leibniz's notion that "every substance is like a complete world and like a mirror of God or the whole universe."[48] However, for Schleiermacher, the self receives the divine influence and actively *expresses* it out into the world. Only in and through its expression does the self achieve consciousness of its relation to the infinite and eternal. Important, too, in this regard, is what Schleiermacher had learned from Kant's critique of rational psychology. While the self immediately apperceives itself, it can only *know* its own "outer," that is, how it stands in relation to what is other than itself. To be sure, the self also stands in *immediate* relation to the absolute and has an immediate experience of itself in apperception. But insofar as this relation is immediate, it cannot be conceptualized and made an object *of* knowledge. Instead, reception of the divine influence is refracted in its expression out into the world and can be grasped *there*; the world, as such, becomes the mirror of the self. This expression is limited in differing degrees to the extent that the self confuses itself with the world. Insofar as it does so, it understands itself as a mere product of the world and as determined by it. This constitutes the lower, purely sensuous dimension of human being.[49] Moreover, the socially constructed world can also be an impediment to the expression of the divine influence. This happens insofar as the individual first comes to self-knowledge in and through social relations with worldly persons, as well as through language, in which expression of these social relations has been imbedded.

The powers and dispositions of the self have a determinative influence on how the world is received and interpreted. Insofar as the self stands in communion with the whole world, it reflects the whole world from its own point of view. This idea, too, can be traced back to Leibniz, although at the hands of Schleiermacher it has been significantly transformed. According to Leibniz, each monad expresses the whole universe in its own way "somewhat as the same city is variously represented depending upon the different positions from which it is

---

[48] Leibniz, *Philosophical Essays*, 42.

[49] In the second monologue, Schleiermacher speaks of the "unworthy particularity of a sensuous animal life" (*KGA* I:3, 18; 30); the sensuous is a "culpably limited kind of external personality" (*KGA* I:3, 19; 32).

viewed."[50] However, it does so in virtue of how it was created from
the outset, and not because it stands in any real relation to other
spiritual substances in its own right. For Schleiermacher, on the other
hand, each self reflects the whole world in so far as it stands in genuine community with all beings. Hence Schleiermacher affirms that
"...everyone feels the influence of others as part of his own life; by
the ingenious mechanism of this community the slightest movement
of each individual is conducted like an electric spark, through a long
chain of a thousand links, greatly amplifying its final effect; all are, as
it were, members of a great organism ... (*KGA* I.3, 29; 52)." In regard
to himself, Schleiermacher notes "...whatever I embrace will bear
my mark. Whatever part of humanity's infinite realm I have apprehended will be in equal measure uniquely transformed and taken
up into my being" (*KGA* I.3, 24; 42). Friess eloquently summarizes
Schleiermacher's position in his introduction to the *Soliloquies:* "By
receiving the universe into his soul, he becomes, as it were, the soul
of a second universe where ... his individuality enters into the life of
all. The universe itself acquires a kind of infinity through being thus
received in individual souls, as if it were reflected and reflected again
in an infinite series of different mirrors" (xlix).

This insight into the individual character of each person is the
starting point for the ethical theory of the *Monologen.* The particular
position of each person, his or her perspective on the world, must
be taken into account if human beings are to negotiate "the determinate tone of the beautiful clash of freedoms" (*KGA* I.3, 10; 17);
each must strive to understand the particular place from which the
other views the world. It would be a mistake to assume that everyone
is exactly the same, and that universal rules are sufficient to guide
the specificity of the actions called for in each situation. To be sure,
because each individual has the capacity to reflect the divine, each is
of infinite value. But because each stands in a different situation, to
disregard both a person's outer circumstances as well as their general
approach to the world is to do her a grave disservice. To love a
person is love her "in the measure that I find and understand this
individuality" (*KGA* I.3, 26; 46). Hence right action calls for sensitivity to the other's situation: "The highest condition of individual

---

[50] Leibniz, *Philosophical Essays* 42.

perfection in a determined field is a general sensitiveness" (*KGA* I.3, 22; 38). This "sensitiveness" cannot occur apart from love, which recognizes the infinite worth of the other and strives to understand his or her point of view. Schleiermacher insightfully notes that "without love the very first attempt at self-formation would prove shattering because of the terrifying disproportion between giving and receiving; the mind would be forced to some extreme one-sidedness, and he who made the attempt in this fashion would either be wholly broken or else sink to the vulgar level" (*KGA* I.3, 22; 38–9). The giving and receiving of goods such as knowledge, culture and property, which go to constitute how a person comes to an understanding of herself and her place in the world, is fraught with danger. Those who have power in virtue of their possession of such goods can lord it over those who do not. The giving or withholding of those things through which the other comes to recognize him or herself as a valuable member of the human community can become an opportunity for the advancement of egoism in all its forms, where one person or group asserts superiority over others and refuses to recognize their intrinsic worth. Even giving can be an opportunity for the advancement of egoism, in particular when the person who is in power, and who demonstrates this power through the gift, comes to identify *herself* with this role. When human interchange occurs without love, all are impoverished. Only when both giving and receiving is a free interchange in which both parties recognize the infinite worth of the other is "brokenness" and "vulgarity" avoided. Hence there is "no development without love." Moreover, "without individual development there is no perfection in love; each supplements the other, both increase indivisibly" (*KGA* I.3, 22; 39). Perfection in love can begin to develop only when each recognizes the perspectival character of all knowledge and of all individual apprehensions of the world. Schleiermacher affirms, "I happily allow each other view to take its place beside my own; my mind peacefully completes the task of interpreting each and penetrating its standpoint" (*KGA* I.3; 23; 41). Only when the *limited* character of one's own knowledge and standpoint is acknowledged, along with an acknowledgement of the standpoints of others, is true moral development possible. In all action, attention must be paid to the particular situation of the other and, hence, to how one's own action will be received by the other. This is the key to moral growth, which occurs only through the gradual and mutual interpenetration of standpoints.

Key to a development of sensitivity to the other's standpoint is the moral imagination. Without it, loving action is almost impossible. "Imagination," notes Schleiermacher, "alone can free the spirit and place it far beyond any power and limitation" (*KGA* I.3, 48; 81). It is in virtue of imagination that "I can put myself in the position of any other person I notice" (*KGA* I.3, 48–9; 82). To be sure, one of the principle flaws in Schleiermacher's book is its excessive overestimation of the powers of the imagination. Schleiermacher even affirms that to live with another in imagination is as good as living with another in reality. No doubt, the imagination is integral to moral judgment, and without it one could not even begin to understand the other sufficiently for appropriate action. But the book also ignores the perils of the imagination, which can easily misconstrue the other and his or her motivations, imagining the most nefarious schemes and terrifying outcomes.

The standpoint of each individual is multivalent. Schleiermacher notes that the person that seeks to develop him or herself "belongs to more than one world...Like a comet, the cultured individual traverses many systems and encircles many a sun" (*KGA* I.3, 26–7; 47). Persons are capable of expressing many facets of humanity. Each of these facets, however, will resonate with some individuals, but not with others. In such a way, one expresses different facets of the self to different persons. Schleiermacher notes the wisdom of those who advise, "so much will that one understand you, there is another who will understand something else; you may embrace that one with a certain kind of love, but hold back from the other one" (*KGA* I.3, 26; 47). Furthermore, at one point a person will grow closer to this one; later that friendship might fade, and the individual grows closer to another. Throughout the phases of life the self changes, and throughout those changes different aspects of the self are revealed to different individuals. Yet Schleiermacher insists that this limitation must be transcended. This can happen in perfect friendship, where through steadfast loyalty to one another over time, the particular standpoints of two finite individuals are perfectly interpenetrated: "Where is the beautiful ideal of the perfect union, the friendship that is at once complete on both sides? Only when, in equal measure, both love and sensitiveness have grown almost beyond all measure. But then they are perfected at once through love, and the hour strikes— oh, for us it strikes much sooner!—to give up finite existence, and to return out of the world to the bosom of the infinite" (*KGA* I.3, 27; 48). The limitations of individuality are overcome in perfect love, in which there is no *mine* or *yours*, but only the infinite character of reflected love. The same theme is repeated in his meditation upon death in the fourth monologue. The perfection of the self means the death of the individual: "such a one must also perish for whom this balance is destroyed in a different way, who, having arrived at the goal of perfecting his individuality, surrounded by the riches of the world, no longer has anything to do. A completely perfect being is a god. It could not endure the burden of life, and no longer has a place in the human world" (*KGA* I.3, 51–2; 87). In this remarkable meditation upon the meaning of death, Schleiermacher affirms the significance of the other for self-knowledge and development:

I can well say that death will never part my friends from me, for I take up their lives in mine, and their influence upon me never ceases. But it is I myself who slowly perish in their death. The life of friendship is a beautiful sequence of harmonizing chords, to a keynote that dies out when the friend passes away. Of course, within oneself re-echoing tones are heard without cease for a long while and the music is carried on; but the accompanying harmony of him, of which I was the keynote, has died away, and it was this that gave me my key, just as I gave him his. What I produced in him is no more, and a part of life is thereby lost. Every creature that loves another kills something in that other through its death, and he who loses many of his friends is finally slain himself at their hands, since cut off from influencing those who were his world, his spirit is driven inward and forced to consume itself.   (*KGA* I.3, 51; 86–7)

Without the other, there is no knowledge of the self. The person expresses him or herself to the other, and the self as thus expressed is reflected back to the self in the self-consciousness of the other. Loss of the other is therefore a loss of oneself. This once again picks up the theme developed in the last chapter, that the self has no *knowledge* of the inner self. Only as expressed and reflected in the self-consciousness of the other does the self arrive at this knowledge; hence, what can be known is the outer, the self in its relations to others and its influence upon them. This theme is also one that Schleiermacher shares with Hegel, especially as developed in Hegel's *Phenomenology of Spirit*. In Schleiermacher's hands, however, the idea grounds Schleiermacher's emphasis on the importance of the historical arena for moral development, where human persons act and react upon one another. This idea, furthermore, lies at the heart of Schleiermacher's claim that only in relation to a historical individual with a perfect God-consciousness can human beings achieve moral perfection. For only such a one who expresses the divine love perfectly knows the essence of all rational beings as their capacity to express the divine love. Such a one reflects this essence back to them so that they can thereby know themselves as beings that express the divine love; they thereby achieve the consciousness of God in doing so. On the basis of conclusions to which he comes through reflection upon Kant's critique of rational psychology, namely, his affirmation of our lack of knowledge of the inner self, Schleiermacher arrives at the insight that it is only in relation to the other that we can arrive at self-understanding and realization of the God-consciousness.

None of this is so much a refutation of Kant's ethics as a moving beyond him. Along with Kant, Schleiermacher reaffirms the importance of universal ethical laws that cannot be abrogated. His ethics of individuality does not give the individual license to do as he pleases; he stands in agreement with Kant that all moral beings are of infinite worth and cannot be treated as mere means. However, Schleiermacher goes beyond Kant in three important ways. First, in emphasizing the connection of each human being to the infinite and eternal in the immediate self-consciousness, Schleiermacher connects the source of each person's ultimate value with that element in self-consciousness that interpenetrates all aspects of a person's psyche, both rational and emotive. Kant, on the other hand, derived the moral law from the universality of reason, but was then unable to explain how reason could become a motive power for the will. Schleiermacher solves the problem through his understanding of the immediate self-consciousness influencing both reason and desire. Although still somewhat undeveloped, the idea is certainly already present in *On Religion* and the *Monologen*. Unlike Kant, Schleiermacher was not stymied by the philosopher's stone.

Second, Schleiermacher's adoption and inversion of key Leibnizian doctrines helped him to understand the significance of individuality for moral action. It is not enough to affirm the universal moral law; right judgment and right action requires one to take into account the individual circumstances, limitations, and capacities of the other in relating to him or her. Each individual has a unique perspective from which s/he understands both herself and the world. The mutual interpenetration of subjectivities requires the use of the imagination in order to understand the other's perspective; only love makes possible sensitivity to the other's standpoint. Self-development occurs by breaking through limitations of the self through sympathetically entering further into the situation of the other.

Third, and most importantly, Schleiermacher's understanding of the conditions of the possibility of self-knowledge allowed him to move significantly beyond Kant's ethical theory. For Kant, personification of the moral ideal (Christ) is not necessary for moral development. In his *Religion within the Bounds of Reason Alone*, Kant had argued that having the moral ideal of perfection in one's reason is enough to make moral action possible. However, Schleiermacher came to understand that self-knowledge, and therefore moral development, is only possible in relation to the other, through which the self comes to know itself. This idea grounds Schleiermacher's later claim in *The Christian Faith* that it is only in relation to Jesus Christ, who expresses the God-consciousness perfectly, that both ethical and religious perfection is possible for human beings.

5

The Highest Good

In the last chapter I have shown how, by the time that Schleiermacher writes the *Monologen*, many of the fundamental metaphysical concepts driving his ethical system have been put in place. At the ground of the self is a point of contact with the divine, and it is in virtue of its dependence on this absolute that the self is *free* in relation to the world, that is, that the self is not completely determined through its outer relations alone. The idea that the self stands in absolute dependence upon God echoes Leibniz, yet unlike Leibnizian monads, for Schleiermacher selves really interact with other selves. Most importantly, the self comes to know itself only in and through its relation with other selves, that is, it knows itself in virtue of its expressive activity, which is received and reflected back to it through others. As such, the ethical activity through which the self relates to others is fundamental to a person's ability to know him or herself as absolutely dependent upon God. The individual can come to know him or herself as a locus receptive and expressive of the divine love only insofar as s/he expresses this love to others and sees herself reflected *as loving* in the consciousness of the other. As I will argue in this and in subsequent chapters, Schleiermacher's understanding of the highest good is ultimately guided by this quasi-Leibnizian vision. Each self expresses all other selves, but from a particular point of view. The idea is well captured by Leibniz's metaphor of the same city reflected by different individuals from differing points of view. Contra Leibniz, however, (a) individuals stand in genuine interaction with one another; (b) here we have a much more complex understanding of the particular way in which each self expresses all other selves than that of Leibniz; and (c) each individual develops organically, in relation to the whole community of individuals. Organic development occurs in nature. However, the possibility of development stands in the closest possible unity with the capacity to come to know the community of other selves and to express this knowledge. The complete development of all individuals in relation to each other is the *terminus ad quem* of all existence and can be thought of as the highest good.

Important to an understanding of Schleiermacher's philosophical ethics is the fact that it stands in the closest possible unity to his theology. It is, in the end, a description of how divine causality expresses itself in the natural world through individuals. Its starting point is the eschatological conviction that the highest good will be realized. This is the *terminus ad quem*, the goal of all human knowing and willing. Theologically, this idea can be expressed as the idea that "God will be all in all," and in reading Schleiermacher it is important to keep in mind that this idea is what ultimately drives his philosophical ethics, which describes how this eschatological goal works itself through in the human and natural world. Because Schleiermacher's ethics begins with this eschatological conviction, his ethics is a purely descriptive one. In his *Notes on Ethics* from 1805/06 (*Brouillon zur Ethik*), which we will examine in this chapter in some detail, he declares that "the appropriate form for ethics is simple narration."[1]

In this regard Schleiermacher's ethics is quite different from that of Kant, whose fundamental ethical principle confronted human beings always as an ought, as something that *should* happen through the efficacy of reason, but which does not always happen, and which certainly does not always happen simply as a matter of course. Moreover, for Kant the activity of reason stands over against that of the naturally given desires: the moral law, as a fact of reason, commands respect and sets limits to the fulfillment of the empirical desires. The virtuous self must be always on its guard, lest the unruly inclinations take the upper hand.

Schleiermacher found Kant's bifurcation between what ought to occur, as given through *reason*, and the realm of the contingently existing desires, as found in *nature*, as a significant problem in Kant's philosophy. What kind of assurances does Kant offer us that the

---

[1] Friedrich Schleiermacher, *Brouillon zur Ethik/Notes on Ethics* (1805–1806); translated by John Wallhausser. All subsequent references to this translation will be indicated by *Ethics* with the page number following; in this case: *Ethics* 34.

Good grounds all of nature as a whole, and that as such the natural world in which we live, move, and have our being, is in fact moving towards moral perfection? Can Kant's philosophy offer any hope that nature itself will be perfected, that is, that it will one day become a perfect expression of the moral order? If nature is to be perfected in such a way, then it must be possible for reason to transform desire. Contra Kant, Schleiermacher's fundamental ethical insight springs from the confidence that the highest good, which he understood as "the ensouling of human nature by reason" (*Ethics* 40) *will* occur, for it is, after all, the working out of God's efficacy in the world. This was not an assurance that Kant's ethics was capable of making intelligible, and in Schleiermacher's mature view, this was the fundamental problem with Kantian ethics.

In this chapter, I explore Schleiermacher's understanding of the highest good, as well as what he means by the "ensouling of human nature by reason." My analysis is divided into two parts. In the first I discuss Schleiermacher's early views on Kant's understanding of the highest good. These early views will help us to determine how Schleiermacher himself understands the concept. In the second half of the chapter I discuss his overall critique of Kantian ethics. Since this critique propelled him to develop his own ethical system, a grasp of it is key to understanding Schleiermacher's views.

THE EARLY SCHLEIERMACHER'S UNDERSTANDING OF THE HIGHEST GOOD

As early as 1789, in his youthful essay "On the Highest Good," Schleiermacher noted the following:

Kant expels the reality of this joining of virtue and Happiness from our world and is correct in doing so. The grounds on which he does this are very convincing, but there are still a thousand others that are no less persuasive. Yet, should it be more readily conceivable in the next world? I do not think so. *First*, if one assumes that in every other state possible for us we will continue to be sensuous beings, then the *laws of nature* attached to our faculty of desire will also forever differ from the *commands* of practical reason, and Happiness as a result of observing the laws of nature will not merely be an effect of observing the commands of practical reason. *Second*, if one assumes the opposite, it cannot be demonstrated that anything like Happiness will then still be of concern to us. Thus we will also not regard it as part of the highest good.[2]

The young Schleiermacher is very well aware that Kant's concept of the highest good, especially as developed in the Dialectic of the second *Critique*, is a synthetic concept, comprised of two heterogeneous elements, namely virtue and happiness.[3] In the Analytic of the second *Critique* Kant defined happiness as a "rational being's consciousness of the agreeableness of life which without interruption accompanies his whole existence" (*KprV* 5:22). The maxim to seek one's own happiness, no matter how much the understanding is used, "contains no other determinants for the will than those which belong to the lower faculty of desire" (*KprV* 5:24). This lower faculty of desire is itself affected through the feeling of pleasure, which can be determined differently in different persons through causes lying outside the self. Kant notes that the "desires and inclinations...because they rest on physical causes, do not of themselves agree with the moral law, which has an entirely different source" (*KprV* 5:83–4). The lower faculty of desire is thereby conditioned by the *receptivity* of the inner and outer senses, that is, our susceptibility to pleasure and pain. Hence, for Kant happiness is always *empirical* happiness, i.e. satisfaction with our condition insofar as we are finite agents conditioned by sensibility

---

[2] Schleiermacher, *On the Highest Good*, translated by H. Victor Froese. Future references to this work will first indicate the *KGA* pagination, with references to the pagination of the Froese translation, indicated by *HG* following. In this case the reference would be: *KGA* 1.1, 102; *HG* 26.

[3] For a discussion of the highest good in Kant's philosophy, see my "Making Sense of Kant's Highest Good," 329–55. There I discuss two conflicting understandings of the highest good in Kant's philosophy, namely, the highest good as immanent within the world of sense, and the highest good as transcendent, that is, as an unconditioned condition. Since practical reason concerns itself with objects that are to be made real through its exercise, the absolute totality of conditions for a given conditioned thing must in this case be understood teleologically: it is the ultimate goal of all moral human striving, i.e. the highest good. As such an unconditioned goal, it is that for the sake of which all other practical actions are undertaken. The Dialectic of pure practical reason arises when this goal, which as an unconditioned condition cannot pertain to the world of appearances, is thought of as the final goal of appearances realizable *in* the empirical world.

with respect to what we desire.[4] The nature of this receptivity, upon which the susceptibility to pleasure and pain is based, entails that the will allowing it to become its fundamental determining ground is heteronomous, i.e. allows itself to be determined by a causal principle (i.e. nature) lying outside of the will itself.[5] As such, the feeling of pleasure cannot determine what is of universal value. Virtue, on the other hand, concerns the *spontaneity*, as opposed to the receptivity, of the will. The person with a virtuous disposition strives to adhere to the moral law, which commands *unconditionally*, that is, irrespective of whatever empirically given desires a person may happen to have. Recognition of the absolute value of the unconditional moral law is possible through our reason, which allows us to transcend the *particularity* of the sensuously given desires and to achieve a standpoint that comprehends the value of all rational beings. It is in virtue of this capacity that we are members of an intelligible order.

Insofar as virtue and the inclinations stem from two distinct faculties of human nature (spontaneity and receptivity), the maxims made in the pursuance of each will not necessarily coincide. Willing to be virtuous and striving after happiness cannot be joined analytically in one and the same maxim; they are two different principles, and as such the goal of becoming virtuous does not guarantee happiness. That virtue and happiness stem from two distinct faculties is the fundamental source of the heterogeneous character of the two elements comprising the highest good as understood by Kant. Because happiness refers to contentment with our state insofar as we are beings

---

[4] This is stressed by Michael Albrecht: "Daraus scheint zu folgen, daß jede inhaltlich bestimmte Materie des Wollens, auch wenn sie nicht in dessen Maxime aufgenommen wird, letztlich Glückseligkeit zum Ziel hat. Im Hinblick auf die 'Dialektik' ist diese Feststellung genauso wichtig wie die folgende: Die Glückseligkeit ist in der *Kritik der praktischen Vernunft* offensichtlich *empirische* Glückseligkeit; für die menschliche Vorstellung hat sie ihren Ort ausschließlich in der Sinnenwelt. Gerade weil 'alle Bestimmungsgründe des Willens, außer dem einigen reinen praktischen Vernunftgesetze (dem moralischen), insgesamt empirisch sind,' gehören sie 'also zum Glückseligkeitsprinzip' (A167). 'Es kommt [. . .] was unsere Natur als sinnlicher Wesen betrifft, *alles* auf unsere *Glückseligkeit* an' (A107). Denkt man an mögliche frühere oder an spätere Positionen Kants, so kann man sagen, daß es für den Kant der *Kritik der praktischen Vernunft* die Möglichkeit einer 'intellektuellen' oder 'moralischen' (nichtsinnlichen) Glückseligkeit nicht gibt." *Kants Antinomie der praktischen Vernunft*, 51 ff.

[5] This analysis of heteronomy has been convincingly developed by Andrews Reath in his article "Hedonism, Heteronomy, and Kant's Principle of Happiness," 42–72.

affected through our senses, its source, i.e. the world of nature and appearances, is completely different from that of virtue, which is possible insofar as we are members of an intelligible order. This means, moreover, that at the heart of the difference between the sources for happiness and virtue is a fundamental bifurcation of reason and nature in Kant's philosophy.

Now Kant argued that if the highest good is to be possible, then it must also be possible that virtue and happiness are *necessarily* combined. The differences in origin between virtue and happiness, however, imply that the two can be necessarily contained in the same concept only if we think of them as combined *synthetically*. Their connection is not logical, such that one of the concepts analytically contains the ground of the other, but *real*. When this connection is real, the two concepts comprising the highest good are necessarily combined in virtue of some third thing, i.e. the causal law. There are two ways in which this synthesis of the elements in the highest good can be thought: "either the desire for happiness must be the motive to maxims of virtue, or the maxim of virtue must be the efficient cause of happiness" (*KprV* 5:113). Kant had already argued that maxims aiming at happiness have no moral worth, so that leaves only the second alternative, namely the highest good might be possible if virtue were the efficient cause of happiness. This too, however, is impossible, "since every practical connection of causes and effects in the world, as a result of the determination of the will, is dependent not on the moral intentions of the will but on knowledge of natural laws and the physical capacity of using them to its purposes; consequently, no necessary connection, sufficient to the highest good, between happiness and virtue in the world can be expected from the most meticulous observance of the moral law" (*KprV* 5:113).

Schleiermacher recognizes that Kant "expels the reality of this joining of virtue and Happiness from our world and is correct in doing so." The synthesis of happiness and virtue, especially when this synthesis is further specified in terms of the proportionality between virtue and happiness, is impossible in this world. This is for two important reasons. First, the mechanism of nature seems to be indifferent to the morality of human intentions. Yet human happiness, grounded as it is on our finite condition as sensuously affected beings of needs, depends on the workings of the natural order. Second, Kant had argued that a rational creature cannot ever reach the stage of thoroughly liking to do all morality requires:

> To such a level of moral disposition no creature can ever attain. For since he is a creature, and consequently is always dependent with respect to what he needs for complete satisfaction with his condition, he can never be wholly free from desires and inclinations which, because they rest on physical causes, do not of themselves agree with the moral law, which has an entirely different source.   (*KprV* 5: 83–4)

Kant argued that insofar as we are sensuously conditioned beings, we will *always* have desires and inclinations that do not necessarily agree with the moral law.

Both reasons for the impossibility of the joining of virtue and happiness in this life stem from the bifurcation of reason, through which we are members of an intelligible order, and nature, through which we are sensuously affected beings. Schleiermacher acutely notes that the highest good, insofar as it is conceived as a synthesis of two distinct elements, is impossible to achieve. It cannot be achieved in this life, for the reasons enumerated above. And it cannot be achieved in the next life, either. Two possibilities arise. Either in that state we will still be sensuously conditioned beings standing in need of happiness—and then "the *laws of nature* attached to our faculty of desire will also forever differ from the *commands* of practical reason." In such a case we would never arrive at a state wherein we will thoroughly like to do what reason commands, for our happiness would still be dependent upon desires and inclinations determined by something other than the moral law. The second possibility is that we would no longer be sensuously affected beings. But on such a scenario, the need for happiness—as Kant defines it—is no longer operative. Happiness will no longer be "of concern to us," and we need not "regard it as part of the highest good."

It is for these reasons that the young Schleiermacher eliminated happiness from his understanding of the highest good. In 1789 he affirms that the holy will, which wills *only* what reason demands, should be thought of as the schema of the highest good: "If we imagine a will that can be determined by nothing but pure reason and that would thus be barely distinguished from pure reason in name, its reality would only prove reason's agreement with itself and the result of its perfection would be holiness, not virtue; but we could also regard this will simply as the schema of the highest good" (*KGA* I.1, 93; *HG* 15). Furthermore, the highest good should not be thought of "as containing something other than that which follows directly and necessarily from the idea of a will conforming without exception to the commands of practical reason and which is not simultaneously given with this conformity" (*KGA* I.1, 94; *HG* 16).

Schleiermacher continued to be preoccupied with questions surrounding the notion of the highest good in his 1792–3 essay *On What Gives Value to Life*. There he first reaffirms Kant's idea of the heterogeneity of virtue and happiness, as well as the Kantian notion that striving for happiness must be subordinated to striving after virtue: "Virtue reigns in my soul without limitation, but not generally; happiness would be able to fill any part of my existence through gratification and striving, but it must acknowledge subordination to virtue."[6] Nevertheless, he moves beyond his earlier essay on the highest good in affirming "Life ... must give me material with which to be happy" (*KGA* I.1, 413; *VL* 27). He seeks to show that happiness can, indeed, be found here, and that, moreover, there is justice in the way that happiness is apportioned in this life. Hence while there are sorrows that come into one's life unbidden, there is also a great deal of control that one can exercise in life concerning one's happiness. So Schleiermacher, "if I increase the unavoidable by letting it have consequences that bring sorrow to me, which is already an arbitrary application and determination of the impression, that is my work" (*KGA* I.1, 428; *VL* 43). He notes "I am certain of the justice of fate" (*KGA* I.1, 458; *VL* 76), and argues, in favor of that conclusion, "Greatness is permitted to be twisted into the scourge of the weak but never to be transformed into the cornucopia of the powerful." He argues that there are laws of interpersonal relations that prohibit the derivation of happiness through the oppression and control of others, and he affirms, "to the degree that one makes and has slaves, one becomes a slave oneself" (*KGA* I.1, 432; *VL* 48). The having of power over

---

[6] Schleiermacher, *On What Gives Value to Life*, translated by Edwina Lawler and Terrence N. Tice. Future references to this work will first indicate the *KGA* pagination, with references to the pagination of the Lawler–Tice translation, indicated by *VL* following. In this case the reference would be: *KGA* I.1, 413: *VL* 27.

others can never become the source of happiness, but to the contrary, leads to much unhappiness. Regarding those that oppress others he observes:

First, the feeling of the right of the oppressed to insubordination, hatred, and deception—a feeling that is never completely extinguishable—brings a dismal bitterness over their souls that sours all the joys of their thirst for power. Or, if they gradually accustom themselves to considering a person a useful machine, they must scorn that person to the same degree. How can their power give them a feeling of how privileged they are if they scorn those over whom they have elevated themselves by means of their privilege? ... At all levels there is nothing more difficult to rule and to bear than people who are dependent. Their love is just as dangerous as their spite, and their fear is just as burdensome as their complaisance.   (*KGA* I.1, 432–3; *VL* 49)

Insofar as one enslaves others, one enslaves oneself. This is for two reasons. First, the oppressor will always have to be on guard against the hatreds of those he oppresses. The second reason Schleiermacher gives for this result already foreshadows some of the ideas he would later develop, especially in the *Monologen*: self-knowledge depends on the recognition of the other. Insofar as one oppresses others, one cannot help but disdain them as well. But if I can only recognize myself as privileged (and hence as having a superior value) through the recognition of the other, the value I ascribe to the other will be of supreme importance in recognizing my own value as refracted through him. Hence insofar as I oppress and disdain the other, I really disdain myself. Only when I value the other can I value myself as reflected in the eyes of the other. Ultimately, Schleiermacher argues, those who have power over others will not derive any extra share of happiness through its exercise.

These musings reveal that the early Schleiermacher is preoccupied with the question of the laws connecting virtue and happiness. Already we find him moving beyond Kant in attempting to understand happiness in terms of the value that one can ascribe to oneself, which is, however, always refracted through the other. This way of thinking of happiness already brings it closer to the realm of the ethical. Happiness does not merely have to do with satisfaction of my sensuously conditioned desires. It is in large part determined through my interpersonal relations, and there are laws governing how happiness is apportioned in regard to these. I can only value myself insofar as I value the other, through which I come to know myself.

THE HIGHEST GOOD IN SCHLEIERMACHER'S LATER THOUGHT

Schleiermacher's own understanding of the highest good and its relation to his ethical theory can best be understood in light of his critique of previous ethical systems. These views are delineated in his lengthy and dense *Outline of a Critique of Previous Ethical Theories* (1803). The two principal kinds of theories that he critiques in this study are eudaimonistic ethics and the ethics of duty. Reflection on the shortcomings of these theories led him to come up with the original insight foundational to his own ethical theory.[7]

Schleiermacher stands in fundamental agreement with Kant that the principle of happiness cannot ground moral action. In his *Critique of Previous Ethical Theories*, he notes "through it [happiness] nothing specific can be determined." While happiness can, in general, be understood in terms of the fulfillment of desires,[8] "what that desire would be for each, in general or in particular cases, cannot be judged through the fundamental principle, but rather in each case can only be empirically determined" (*KGA* I.4, 116). The *Brouillon* echoes this idea: "Eudaemonism focuses on a rather base personal existence which, because everything in it is accidental, stands beneath the dignity of philosophy. If someone claims to be organized differently, nothing can be said against that person" (*Ethics* 33). The principle of happiness, which amounts to the injunction to act in such a way so as to derive the most lasting satisfaction with one's existence and fulfill one's most important desires, cannot be the ground of the validity

---

[7] On this point see John Wallhausser's introduction to the *Notes on Ethics*, 5–9, as well as the *Notes on Ethics*, third hour, 36.

[8] As Kant notes in his *Groundwork for the Metaphysics of Morals*, "precisely in this idea [happiness] all inclinations are united in a sum" (4:399; Wood 15).

of a moral law that is universally binding on all rational beings. For suppose one were to come up with the following moral principle: "Do not murder, for murder will bring great unhappiness and misfortune." An individual might still be able to object: "I am constituted differently and have different kinds of desires. Murder is what brings me happiness." Because the person is constituted differently, s/he will have different kinds of desires, the fulfilment of which will make her happy. Schleiermacher thereby stands in full agreement with Kant that the desire for happiness cannot ground morality. Moreover, the principle of happiness cannot even yield determinate principles for concrete action, that is, it cannot offer concrete guidelines as to what *specifically* must be done in order to achieve happiness. As Kant had already noted:

It is a misfortune that the concept of happiness is such an indeterminate concept that although every human being wishes to attain it, he can never say, determinately and in a way that is harmonious with himself, what he really wishes and wills. The cause of this is that all the elements that belong to the concept of happiness are altogether empirical, i.e., have to be gotten from experience, while for the idea of happiness an absolute whole, a maximum of welfare, is required, in my present and in my future condition. Now it is impossible for the most insightful, and at the same time most resourceful, yet finite being to make a determinate concept of what he really wills here ... In short, he is not capable of determining with complete certainty, in accordance with any principle, what will make him truly happy, because omniscience would be required for that.[9]

The harmonizing of the satisfaction of all the desires that might make up a person's happiness is very difficult, not only because the satisfaction of one desire often requires the thwarting of others, but also because one cannot foresee what the ultimate effects of the satisfaction of a given desire will be on one's entire life as a whole. Given these observations, as well as the fact that what one thinks makes up one's happiness will depend upon how one happens to be constituted, Schleiermacher affirms, "the counsels of eudaemonism turn toward arbitrariness" (*Ethics* 34). Moreover, while the "content" of happiness "lies in personal existence," "the form expressed by the concept cannot itself be generated from personal existence." This form is the

---

[9] Immanuel Kant, *Groundwork for the Metaphysics of Morals* 4:418; Wood 35.

harmony of desires, the fulfillment of which produces the "highest and most fully satisfying feeling of life." However because "the diverse factors of life appear in relative contrasts,"—that is, because the raw desires will conflict with one another, the best that can be hoped for is a situation in which one manages to constrain some desires in order to fulfill others. But on such a scenario the individual is still at war with him or herself. The form, namely, the harmony of desires, "can be provided only if reason has entered life as soul" (*Ethics* 37). In other words, a complete harmony between one's desires can be achieved only when reason not only orders, but also transforms, desire.

While Kant's philosophy had made a deep impression on Schleiermacher, by the time he wrote his *Critique of Previous Ethical Systems*, he is quite critical of Kantian ethics. Kant's ethics is found wanting on two principal grounds, both inherently connected. The first has to do with the familiar critique of formalism in Kant's ethics; Schleiermacher argues that the categorical imperative on its own can provide no ethical content:

> Let us consider…the operation of the derivation and determination of the individual [practical principles]. First is to be noted how just these three, which are always found together, namely Kant, Fichte, and the Stoics, concur in this as well, that they cannot determine or build anything from their fundamental principle alone—since it expresses a mere relation—without at the same time bringing in another concept which first gives this relation its content. For one may consider all three Kantian formulas, of the fitness of lawgiving, or of the treatment of humanity as an end, or also of the kingdom of ends, from all angles. It will thereby reveal itself to be impossible to derive a genuine law from here, or a virtue, or a duty. Rather, for itself, in this form, the fundamental principle can only serve to examine a given principle…
>
> (*KGA* I.4, 126–7)

Schleiermacher argues that, "the fundamental principle reveals itself as insufficient." This is because Kant's categorical imperative is merely formal, that is, it expresses a required *relation* among the principles of action of all moral agents (the principles of action of all moral agents must harmonize with one another), but it does not express any content on its own. In order to derive actual content, the agent's subjective principles of action (i.e. maxims) must be presupposed as the "matter" which is then tested through the categorical imperative:

only those maxims that are universalizable can be acted upon.[10] As such, the categorical imperative functions as a *second order* principle selecting among an agent's actual maxims, which s/he forms on the basis of the desires s/he contingently has. The problem with Kant's fundamental principle, Schleiermacher claims, is that *by itself* it cannot determine any *ends* for the will. It must always presuppose a material given to it from the outside in order for it to come up with any concrete content whatsoever. As such, it merely *organizes* those ends that finite rational agents already have in virtue of the constitution they happen to have. Later on Schleiermacher claims that Kant has a "natural tendency to the British school, however little he may also himself be conscious of it," and he concludes that his ethics ends "in the attempt to give a scientific form to that political eudaemonism" (*KGA* I.4, 130).

How fair are these criticisms of Kant? First, it should be noted that in Kant's philosophy the virtuous agent makes conformity of the will with universal lawgiving his or her ultimate end, so it would be unfair to Kantian ethics to say that it does not specify *any* ends for the will. Nevertheless, Schleiermacher seems to have put his finger on a fundamental problem in Kantian ethics, and that is that it cannot explain how the *material* of willing, that is, the given desires and their attendant maxims supplying the content to Kant's ethical formalism, could *themselves* be transformed.[11] Rather, what we are given through the CI is a principle of selection for pre-existing maxims, and there is no mechanism for transforming this given pool. How the faculty of desire generating subjective practical principles could *itself* be transformed, so that the desires one begins with (prior to testing)

---

[10] See H. J. Paton's discussion of this problem in Kant's ethical theory in his book *The Categorical Imperative* 73.

[11] Kant strove to deal with this problem in some of his later writings, in particular in *Religion within the Boundaries of Mere Reason* as well as in the *Anthropology*; his views on the matter are quite sophisticated and capable of withstanding many of the criticisms often put forward against his ethics. Nevertheless, Schleiermacher's fundamental criticism regarding the bifurcation of nature and reason in Kant's philosophy is still a valid one. For a discussion of Kant's views on the transformation of the self, see my "Transformation and Personal Identity in Kant." Recently, several treatments of Kant's theory of virtue have appeared, for instance, G. Felicitas Munzel, *Kant's Conception of Moral Character.*

might become ethical desires, is a question that is left completely unanswered.

This brings us to Schleiermacher's second fundamental criticism of Kant, for Kant's inability to give an account of how desire might itself be transformed is inextricably tied to it. This is the fundamental bifurcation between reason and nature pervading Kant's philosophy. For Kant, nature is given to us through the senses and conceptualized through the understanding. Every item found in nature is conditioned by nature as a whole. For instance, every event encountered in the natural world has a cause. This means, further, that all the empirically conditioned desires that we happen to have are determined by factors lying outside the will (as practical reason). On the other hand, insofar as we recognize the value of the universal moral law, we are free members of an intelligible world that in some way grounds the world of sense.[12] But the fundamental interrelation between reason and nature—in this case between our sensuously conditioned desires and our capacity for morality—is left unexamined. In the first *Critique*, Kant mentions the possibility of an unknown root grounding both our faculty of concepts and that of sensation, but nothing else is said. The relation between the two faculties remains fundamentally mysterious, and, as such, it is impossible to come up with a theory grounding the *rationalizing* of nature—or, as Schleiermacher would call it, "the ensoulment of nature through reason." Only if such an "ensoulment" is possible can the sensuously conditioned desires be raised above mere contingency and particularity. Only in this way

---

[12] In the *Groundwork* Kant notes, "The human being who in such a wise considers himself as an intelligence, sets himself thereby in another order of things, and in a relation to determinate grounds of an entirely different kind, when he thinks of himself as an intelligence with a will, consequently as endowed with causality, than when he perceives himself as a phenomenon in the world of sense (which he actually is too), and subjects his causality, regarding external determination, to natural laws. Now he soon becomes aware that both can take place at the same time, indeed even that they must. For that a *thing in its appearance* (belonging to the world of sense) is subject to certain laws, of which the very same thing *as thing* or being *in itself* is independent, contains not the least contradiction; but that he must represent and think of himself in this twofold way rests, regarding the first, on the consciousness of himself as an object affected through sense, and as far as the second goes, on the consciousness of himself as intelligence, i.e., as independent in his use of reason of sensible impressions (hence as belonging to the world of understanding)." Kant, *Groundwork for the Metaphysics of Morals*, 4:457; Wood 73.

can the individual, insofar as s/he is *part of the natural world*, come to stand in a harmonious relation—one that is not merely accidental—with the rest of nature as a whole.

Here then, is the fundamental difference between the ethical theories of Kant and Schleiermacher. Given his definition of happiness and his understanding of the sensuously conditioned desires as being determined by factors lying *outside* the will (as practical reason), Kant could not account for the existence of the highest good *in this world*, namely the proportioning of virtue to happiness. Kant was well aware that in *this* world, happiness is in fact not proportioned to virtue. Here the wicked prosper, and the commitment to morality often has significant costs; it can even require one to forego earthly happiness altogether. The only way that Kant could finally give a coherent account of the highest good, as the final goal of all human willing, was by having it transcend nature altogether. On such a scenario, however, consistency demands we must give up *empirical* happiness as an element of the highest good. The highest good would then be thought of as the ideal of the harmonious co-existence of all the members of an intelligible world. The empirical happiness of this world is replaced by bliss, in which the moral law is all that is willed. As such it is something that completely *transcends* the world of sense, although we must think that the natural world is ordered to this goal.[13] For Schleiermacher, on the other hand, *the natural world itself* is to become the arena in which each being harmonizes his or her being with all other beings. The whole of nature itself is in the process of transformation, that is, of becoming the arena of the ethical. Schleiermacher's ethics is, as such, the description of this process.

To sum up our results thus far, Schleiermacher takes over from Kant the critique of eudaemonism: nature as it is *currently* constituted, and the sensuously conditioned desires that arise from it, cannot be the ground of morality. In the *Brouillon* he notes that "universal conformity to law cannot be found within the interest of personal existence, for predetermination of action there appears as simply arbitrary, as something absolutely lacking in conformity to

---

[13] I argue for this point at length in my article "Making Sense of Kant's Highest Good."

law" (*Ethics* 37). This current state of affairs does not imply, however, that nature will not *develop* to be all that it should be, that is, that it will not be "ensouled" through reason. But if it has to be possible for nature to be thus transformed, then we must come up with a theory allowing us to overcome the bifurcation between reason and nature posited by Kant. It must be possible for nature to be taken up into reason. In terms of metaethical theory, this means that it must be possible for the sensuously conditioned desires to be infused with ethical content. This is the significance of Schleiermacher's comments in the *Brouillon* that "the ought formula is totally unacceptable for ethics. Even its advocates expound it as a bifurcation contrary to law...In bifurcation there is no blessedness, not even in the loftiest categorical morality" (*Ethics* 34). At the bottom of Kant's moral theory is the notion of the *ought*. As Kant notes in the *Groundwork:*

if the will is not *in itself* fully in accord with reason (as it actually is with human beings), the actions which are objectively recognized as necessary are subjectively contingent, and the determination of such a will, in accord with objective laws, is *necessitation* . . . The representation of an objective principle, insofar as it is necessitating for a will, is called a 'command' (of reason), and the formula of the command is called an **imperative**. [14]

For Kant the moral law must always confront us as a command. This is because the subjective inclinations do not necessarily stand in accord with the moral law, and must thereby be constrained. As noted above, the inclinations have an entirely different source from the moral law. The former arise from the fact that the individual, insofar as s/he knows herself as appearance, is an object affected by sense; the latter from the fact that s/he is an intelligence, and as such a member of an intelligible world. We are members of two different orders. Insofar as the human being is a finite, sensuously conditioned being of needs, s/he could never come to the point of thoroughly liking to do what morality requires. The "bifurcation contrary to law," of which Schleiermacher speaks, refers to the fact that for Kant the sensuously conditioned desires and inclinations have a completely different source from the moral law. As such, there is no mechanism for transforming the desires and inclinations. It is for this reason, too,

---

[14] *Groundwork* 4: 413; Wood 30.

that Schleiermacher claims there is no "blessedness, not even in the loftiest categorical morality," for in Kant there is always some material left over that cannot be infused with reason and with ethical content.

In the *Brouillon* Schleiermacher discusses three possible fundamental ethical principles. We have already analyzed two, namely, universal conformity to law and the principle of happiness. Both have severe shortcomings. Schleiermacher presents a third principle, which he calls "the principle of God-likeness." He notes:

It appears that the principle of God-likeness cannot be presented where absolute knowledge is treated only as the soul of the particular. Yet, ancient philosophy posited the universe in just this way, first as living and ensouled, and then again as *nous*. It considered the idea of God-likeness as principle, as the soul of this soul, precisely as is given in our fundamental moral intuition, which is thus fully contained within this ancient view.   (*Ethics* 37)

It is this third that comes closest to Schleiermacher's considered view. On it, reason permeates nature and elevates it: "the accidental should be grasped and overcome, transformed into the essential" (*Ethics* 38). Such a view allows for the possibility that all of a person's desires will be transformed, such that they can (a) harmonize with one another and (b) harmonize with the desires of all other beings within nature. As Schleiermacher notes, however, in order for such a principle of God-likeness to work, reason must be understood as ensouling both the particular individual as well as the whole of the natural order. Only if reason ensouls both can an ultimate harmony be achieved between the desires of the different individuals comprising the whole of nature. So Schleiermacher:

Reason should be soul. The ensouling principle forms and sustains body and life; we must thus discover reason as appropriating human nature and maintaining itself as soul in reciprocity with the whole. This principle, conceived in its entirety, is the theory of the highest good.   (*Ethics* 38–9)

The principle of God-likeness is inherently connected with the highest good, which stands at the pinnacle of Schleiermacher's ethics. Nevertheless, Schleiermacher includes both virtue theory and deontology as moments within his ethical system. Hence he affirms, "a better perspective is provided by making a comparison with nature. The highest good is the cosmography, the entire organization of the theory of virtue is the dynamics, and the theory of duty is the speculative perspective of those single oscillations through which the whole is generated" (*Ethics* 38). The demands of reason first confront the individual as duties, since they originally stand in conflict with the arbitrariness of natural inclinations. But these natural inclinations are to be overcome and transformed; the process of this transformation is the theory of virtue. Schleiermacher describes the theory of virtue as the theory of the "productivity" of nature insofar as nature has received "a new dignity through the ensouling of reason" (*Ethics* 39). The unifying factor, which takes into account the dynamics of both reason and nature as whole, is the overarching theory of the highest good.

The rest of the *Brouillon/Notes on Ethics* describes the character of nature's productivity and its ensouling through reason. Schleiermacher understands the individual as firmly ensconced in the natural world, as operating from a point of view that is organically, historically, and culturally conditioned. The "ensouling" of nature is the process through which historically situated individuals become self-consciously related to the whole of nature, that is, to the whole community of individuals capable of such ensouling. The highest good is reached when each individual comes to know herself in and through the community of individuals, and when the community knows itself in each individual. Individuals develop naturally and organically; in and through this development they come to relate to other individuals. This relation to others, in turn, is taken up as a key factor in self-development. Schleiermacher's account of the organic development of the self in and through the community is the subject of the next chapter.

6

Individual and Community

One of the most important elements in Schleiermacher's ethics is his attempt to underline the value and ethical significance of the individual *qua* individual. Schleiermacher recognized that this was not something Kant's ethics was capable of doing. Certainly Kant acknowledged—especially prominently in the second formulation of the categorical imperative—that each person must be respected as an end in him or herself. However, given the purely formal character of Kant's ethics, the categorical imperative ultimately expresses what Franks has aptly called "the unconditional value of a will that is capable of unconditional valuation."[1] As such, what grounds the unconditioned value of the will is its capacity to reason practically and thereby to recognize that which has universal value, that is, that which must be of value to all rational wills. This means, however, that what grounds the absolute value of the will in Kant's system is that it is "the will of a rational agent as such."[2] Yet as Schleiermacher

---

[1] Franks continues, "In this special case, willing suffices for reason-giving. Thus, to will for the sake of the moral law is to will one's own will, or to act for the sake of one's own act. But this is true only because the will and act in question are not *individual*, but rather express *the will of a rational agent as such*" (Franks, *All or Nothing*, 283).

[2] Cited in previous note. I make the same point in "The Religious Significance of Kant's Ethics." There I note, "Rationality is thus the capacity to take an interest in that which has unconditioned worth. But just what has such unconditioned worth is in fact this very *capacity* of moving beyond self-interest and entering into community with the other-as-one that must be considered an end in him or herself. The other has such worth because s/he too can transcend her merely subjective desires and enter into community. Hence the ability to enter into communion with other rational selves is just what constitutes rationality and is the ground of the claim that the person has upon another's regard." The ability to act in accordance with reason's demands and not to be completely determined by the empirically conditioned desires is transcendental freedom; what reason demands, however, is respect for the capacity

had already noted in the *Short Presentation*, "reason individuates us least of all" (*KGA* I.1, 574). What, then, of what is irreducibly particular in the individual—what grounds the value of his or her individuality *qua* individuality? How can the value of the individual be affirmed? Does not Kant's system lead to the absurd conclusion that persons are interchangeable, since what grounds their absolute value is the same in all? Is it not true that Kant's ethics *cannot* value the individual *qua* individual, since the only thing that individuates persons are the empirically conditioned desires, which themselves cannot have any absolute value? Schleiermacher had already critiqued Kant's ethics on these grounds in his *Critique of all Previous Ethical Systems*. There he charged that for Kant "pleasure [the lower faculty of desire] is that which especially represents the personality" (*KGA* I.4, 94). Fichte followed Kant in this: for him individuality did not move beyond the "relationship to one's own body, and to the plurality of human exemplars in general" (*KGA* I.4, 93). Fichte did not ground the particularity of persons in the "inner individuality of persons," but rather on "the point where each first encountered his freedom." Both Kant and Fichte could only account for the specificity of individuals in spatial and temporal terms, that is, through their position in the spatial and temporal continuum (*KGA* I.4, 92–3). As such, they regarded individuality as "something alien and accidental" to morality, "something absolutely physical" (*Ethics*, 73).

Schleiermacher's ethics, however, proceeds from the insight that a complete ethical system must be able to account for the ethical value of the individual *qua* individual. The task outlined in the *Notes on Ethics* is to "arrive critically at the recognition that the principle of individuation lies in morality itself, and that it must be the greatest principle, because if one neglects it everything pre-eminent is omitted from the presentation of moral action" (*Ethics* 74). Whereas Kant had made freedom the limiting factor in ethics, for Schleiermacher it is "personal existence that appears as the limiting factor" (*Ethics* 36). In

---

to act in accordance with reason's demands, which amounts to a respect for this freedom. Schleiermacher finds this way of thinking circular: "Thus, in this latter view only the interest of nature is the positive feature, and the result is: freedom is provided only in order to make possible the co-existence of individuated natures. But then one spins around in a circle, for if one asks why they should co-exist, the answer is because freedom is present within them" (*Ethics* 36).

Kant's system the validity of the moral law is intrinsically bound up with freedom. Positive freedom is the capacity to value the moral law *for its own sake*. However, what Kant's moral law ultimately expresses is the formula for the harmony of individual wills with one another in the kingdom of ends. Yet as Schleiermacher acutely notes, in such a system "freedom is provided only in order to make possible the co-existence of individuated natures. But then one spins around in a circle, for if one asks why they should co-exist, the answer is because freedom is present within them" (*Ethics*, 36). Kant's system did not penetrate to the heart of ethical matters. His ethics was an attempt to provide a formula for the harmony of wills with one another, but he never gave a convincing answer to the more ultimate question of why one individual *should* co-exist with another. In order to answer this deeper question, one had to answer the question of why what is *irreducibly particular* and individual in the person is of *ethical* value. The closest Kant came to recognizing the value of the individual was his second formulation of the categorical imperative. Even this formula, however, never penetrated the value of the individual as such; the formula could only affirm the value of the person *qua* rational being—it is because the person can affirm what is of absolute value through practical reason that s/he is herself an end in herself, one that should never be used as a mere means.

In this regard Schleiermacher's critique of Kant in his *Critique of all Previous Ethical Systems* is significant. As we have seen earlier, he there repeatedly accuses Kant of a political eudaimonism. This accusation refers to the fact that Kant's ethics does not specify any ends for the will: it is merely formal. The categorical imperative is a second order principle that selects among the maxims that an agent already has. As such, its principle function is the harmonization of the principles of action of different selves. As we have seen in the last chapter, the categorical imperative does not, however, function positively to determine which maxims an agent will form to begin with. Rather, the given pool of maxims that the moral agent tests through the categorical imperative are formed in virtue of the desire for happiness. The individual wills that are harmonized have naturally determined ends; it is *these* naturally determined ends—given through the lower faculty of desire—that provide the individuating characteristics for each will. Schleiermacher charges that Kant's ethics winds up being a system of political eudaimonism since it only harmonizes the wills of different individuals, each of which is individualized insofar as he or she seeks his or her own happiness. The categorical imperative does not specify the *matter* of action in the sense of *ends* that must be adopted. To be sure, Kant's second formulation of the categorical imperative does make mention of an end, but only in a negative sense, that is, Kant notes that "the end here has to be thought of not as an end to be effected *but as a self-sufficient* end, hence only negatively, i.e., never to be acted against, which therefore has to be estimated in every volition never merely as a means but always at the same time as an end."[3]

Schleiermacher's critique of Kant's system as expressive of a political eudaimonism is inherently bound up with his first criticism of Kantian ethics mentioned above, namely, that Kant cannot account for the *ethical* value of the individual *qua* individual. The problem ultimately has to do with the fact that Kant can only determine the specificity of the person through her empirically conditioned desires, and these can have only a conditioned value. This is because the capacity to reason practically and to be moved by the moral law is a characteristic of all rational agents, and as such cannot be a means to distinguish among agents. All that is left, then, to individuate agents is their empirically determined character and the desires arising from it. As a consequence, "…one regards individuality either as something to be negated by means of morality, or as something utterly alien and accidental to it, something absolutely physical" (*Ethics* 74).

Connected with this problem is Schleiermacher's charge that Kant has no way of conceiving the possibility of the "ensouling" of the individual in his or her *particularity* through reason, and of thereby granting an absolute value to the individuality of the individual as such. While in many ways the criticism is unfair to Kant, ignoring his theory of virtue,[4] it still points to an important lacuna in the

---

[3] Immanuel Kant, *Groundwork for the Metaphysics of Morals*, 4: 437; Wood 55.

[4] In important regards, this criticism does not take into account what Kant has to say in the *Metaphysics of Morals* as well as in *Religion within the Boundaries of Mere Reason*, where Kant's understanding of virtue, and of what it means to progress in virtue, becomes clearer. This progress in virtue involves not only the strengthening of the moral disposition in us, but also a deliberate self-affection through which one puts oneself in a position where affections, such as empathy—conducive to morality— are strengthened. For a helpful account of Kant's understanding of virtue see G.

groundwork of Kant's ethical system. Schleiermacher's project in the *Notes on Ethics* is to offer a corrective. In what way is the specificity of the individual—his or her particularity—foundational to morality? Schleiermacher's answer will involve re-conceiving the insights of Kantian ethics in light of two fundamental questions: (a) that of the relation of the individual to the community, and (b) the understanding of the relation between individuals in terms of a model of communicative praxis. On Schleiermacher's account, the other is not an end in the merely *negative* sense of that which is never to be acted against. It is that, to be sure—the humanity of the other must always be respected.[5] But Schleiermacher wants to stress that the other must become my end in a more positive sense as well. Not, of course, as an end to be effected. The other must become my end in that I must come to value him or her in his or her historically conditioned particularity, that is, insofar as he or she is an *individual.* I must therefore come to *know* and *value* the individuality of the other. As such, Schleiermacher supplements Kant's understanding of persons as ends in themselves who should not be acted against *in virtue of their rationality* with the understanding of persons as absolutely valuable also *in virtue their individuality.* At the heart of Schleiermacher's ethics is the non-transposable character of individuals and historical communities, each of which has a special character determined by a particular historical development. Individuality cannot be something to be merely overcome or superseded through rationality. It has, rather, a foundational role, for it is the foundation of community.

Key to this insight is Schleiermacher's rethinking of the implications of Leibniz's city, where each reflects the whole, albeit from a particular point of view. In the *Principles of Nature and Grace* Leibniz had affirmed "...each living mirror...represents the universe

---

Felicitas Munzel, *Kant's Conception of Moral Character: The Critical Link of Morality, Anthropology, and Reflective Judgment,* as well as the essay by Lara Denis, "Kant's conception of virtue," in *The Cambridge Companion to Kant and Modern Philosophy.*

[5] Schleiermacher affirms this point in the *Notes on Ethics* when he notes that "from the standpoint of personal existence this acknowledging of others appears as a personal restraint, because it would seem most opportune to treat human beings as things" (*Ethics,* 62–3).

according to its own point of view."[6] The same idea is very clearly expressed in §57 of the *Monadology:* "Just as the same city viewed from different directions appears entirely different and, as it were, multiplied perspectively, in just the same way it happens that, because of the infinite multitude of simple substances, there are, as it were, just as many different universes, which are, nevertheless, only perspectives on a single one, corresponding to the different points of view of each monad."[7] According to Leibniz rational souls are "not only a mirror of the universe of created things, but also an image of the divinity."[8] Furthermore, "all minds, whether of men or genies, entering into a kind of society with God by virtue of reason or eternal truths, are members of the City of God."[9] No doubt Leibniz's vision of this city also had an influence on Kant's ethics: the notion of the harmonization of the causality of the will of all rational beings in the kingdom of ends echoes the Augustinian and Leibnizian idea of the City of God.[10] In the *Groundwork* Kant defines this kingdom in the following way: "For rational beings all stand under the *law* that every one of them ought to treat itself and others *never merely as means*, but always *at the same time as end in itself.* From this, however, arises a systematic combination of rational beings through communal objective laws, i.e., a realm that, because these laws have as their aim the reference of these beings to one another as ends and means, can be called a 'realm of ends' (obviously only an ideal)."[11] Reflecting upon the metaphor of the city or realm, one immediately sees that the

---

[6] *Philosophical Essays,* 211; *Principles of Nature and Grace,* §12.

[7] *Philosophical Essays,* 220.

[8] *Philosophical Essays,* 211; *Principles of Nature and Grace,* §14.

[9] *Philosophical Essays,* 212; *Principles of Nature and Grace,* §15.

[10] On Kant's indebtedness to Augustine and Leibniz, see Frederick C. Beiser, "Moral faith and the highest good," in *The Cambridge Companion to Kant and Modern Philosophy,* 588–629, esp. 594ff. So Beiser, "in the first *Critique* Kant betrays the immediate source of his ideal: it is the Leibnizian 'city of God,' a republic ruled by God himself, who governs all souls according to love and the strictest principle of justice (B840). The ultimate provenance for this view was, of course, Augustine. Kant knew this perfectly well; in the 1785 Mrongovius lectures he explicitly identifies his highest good with what 'Augustine and Leibniz called ... the kingdom of grace' (29:629)," 597. In the first *Critique* Kant characterizes Leibniz's realm of grace: "Leibniz called the world, insofar as in it one attends only to rational beings and their interconnection with moral laws under the rule of the highest good, the realm of grace ..." (*KRV* B840).

[11] *Groundwork* 4: 433; Wood 52.

ultimate goal of all moral action is *community*. Notice that for *both* Kant and Leibniz, reason is the basis of the possibility of the harmonious interrelation between individuals; it is reason that makes community possible. Schleiermacher would not deny this. However, his fundamental insight is that the *moral community* envisioned by both Leibniz and Kant could never get off the ground without individuals to populate it. Individuals are the fundamental building blocks of community, and it is essential for a proper understanding of morality that the role that individuality plays in the founding of community be given its proper due. Hence Schleiermacher notes, "Insofar as it is possible to speak of higher and lower in ethics, individuality is the higher and community the lower. The impulse to community also presupposes the consciousness of individuality in such a way that the impulse of individualization does not presuppose the consciousness of community" (*Ethics* 72).

THE NATURE OF THE INDIVIDUAL

In what follows I will discuss four characteristics of the individual marked out by Schleiermacher in the *Notes on Ethics*. All four are intrinsically interconnected. These characteristics play an essential role in his ethical theory. They are: (a) the individual apprehends the world through feeling; (b) this implies the uniqueness or *nontransposability* of the individual; (c) all of the individual's knowledge is finite and perspectival; and (d) the individual is embodied.

The first characteristic of the individual is that the individual immediately apprehends its world through *feeling*. Schleiermacher notes: "Cognition, however, also emerges, on the other hand, in the character of uniqueness—that is, nontransposability. We call this, in its proper sense, feeling. To the extent that feeling is found in every concrete operation of life, non-transposability is also present within it. This non-transposability applies, however, not only among several people but also among several moments of the same life" (*Ethics*, 51). In order to unpack the significance of this, it is helpful to recall Kant's description of the human faculties of cognition, for the most part adopted by Schleiermacher. Fundamental to Kant's philosophy is the distinction between sense and intellect, intuition and concept. As Hegel had noted, this distinction is fundamental to all of Kant's dualisms.[12] In the Introduction to the first *Critique*, Kant notes "there are two stems of human cognition, which may perhaps arise from a common but to us unknown root, namely sensibility and understanding, through the first of which objects are given to us, but through the second of which they are thought" (*KRV* A15/B29). Furthermore, Kant emphasizes that "these two faculties or capacities cannot exchange their functions. The understanding is not capable of intuiting anything, and the senses are not capable of thinking anything" (*KRV* A51/B75). In the *Dialectic* of 1814/15 Schleiermacher echoes Kant's famous dictum that "thoughts without content are empty; intuitions without concepts are blind" (*KRV* A51/B75). There Schleiermacher notes "without unity and multiplicity the manifold is undetermined; without the manifold the determinate unity and multiplicity is empty."[13] The two activities are essential to human cognition. Schleiermacher, however, stresses that neither is ever found in its purity in human knowing. Reason is always present in the organic function, and all human reasoning occurs through language, itself always conditioned by the immediacy of perception.

When Schleiermacher mentions feeling, he is referring to the subjective pole of sensibility, that is, to the determination of the *subject* that results from an affection of the sensitive faculty. An intuition, however, refers to *what* is given in sensation.[14] Kant contrasts intuitions—which for us must be given through sensation—with a concept. In the *Jäsche Logic*, for instance, Kant defines an intuition as "a *singular* representation (*representatio singularis*)" and a concept as "a universal (*representatio per notas communes*) or *reflected*

---

[12] For an excellent discussion of the considerations that led Kant to this distinction, see Paul Guyer, "The Rejection of Kantian Dualism," in *The Cambridge Companion to German Idealism*, 37–56.

[13] *Dialektik* (1814/15). *Einleitung zur Dialektik*, 23.

[14] Schleiermacher makes this distinction in the *Notes on Ethics*: "What we posit as intuition we posit as a uniform relation to communal subjectivity, to human nature. What we posit as feeling we posit, in contrast, as personal, individual, local, temporal subjectivity. We consider intuition to be everywhere and unconditionally the same in everyone; about feeling we are convinced that in no one else is it completely the same as it is in us" (102). Insofar as intuition refers to the *object* of sensation, it stands in relation to all human subjects; characteristics of the object are inter-subjectively verifiable. On the other hand, feeling refers to the affections of the subject.

representation," namely, "a representation of what is common to several objects, hence a representation *insofar as it can be contained in various ones.*"[15] Moreover, not only is an intuition a *singular* representation, that is, the representation of an *individual*, it is also a representation that relates *directly* to individuals. In the *Critique of Pure Reason* Kant notes, "In whatever way and through whatever means a cognition may relate to objects, that through which it relates immediately to them, and at which all thought as a means is directed as an end, is *intuition*" (*KRV* A19/B33). Both characteristics of intuitions, their singularity and their immediate relation to objects, are mentioned later on in the *Critique* when Kant distinguishes between intuitions and concepts; an intuition is "immediately related to the object and is singular," and a concept "is mediate, by means of a mark, and is common to several things" (*KRV* A320/B377). Schleiermacher adopts Kant's understanding of sensibility: the individual's cognition of other individuals via sensibility (and hence feeling) is absolutely unique, since it refers to, among other things, the absolutely unique position of the individual to all other objects of possible cognition, but grasped *from* the reference point of the individual's own position. As Kant had recognized in his *Attempt to Introduce the Concept of Negative Magnitudes into Philosophy* of 1763, all our cognitions of real relations—such as those of cause and effect—"reduce to simple, unanalysable concepts of real grounds, the relation of which to their consequences cannot be rendered distinct at all."[16] Real relations, for instance, change—in which a substance undergoes differing determinations—or causation, are distinct from logical relations. They are given in *immediate* representations that cannot themselves undergo logical analysis.[17] They are, moreover, representations of

---

[15] *Immanuel Kant's Logic: A Manual for Lectures*, ed. Benjamin Gottlob Jäsche, §1 and note 1: in *Immanuel Kant: Lectures on Logic*, 589; cited in Guyer, "The Rejection of Kantian Dualism, 40–1.

[16] Immanuel Kant, *Attempt to Introduce the Concept of Negative Magnitudes into Philosophy* (2:204) translated in *Theoretical Philosophy, 1755–1770*, 241; cited in Guyer, "The Rejection of Kantian Dualism," 42–3.

[17] Guyer explains Kant's remark quite nicely: " ...the basis for such relationships, relationships of real opposition leading to equilibrium or of causation leading to actual change, cannot be revealed by the logical analysis of the composition of complex concepts, but must be immediately given and reflected in concepts that cannot themselves be analyzed by logical means;" Guyer, "The Rejection of Kantian Dualism," 43.

singular objects. As Kant would later recognize, these representations must be given immediately through a medium other than concepts, that is, through sensation.[18] The *immediacy* of these representations arises from the fact that they directly reflect the position of the object of cognition relative to the subject, a position that is calculated *from the standpoint of the subject* and not from the perspective of absolute space or time:[19] as such, this immediacy is inherently connected with the *uniqueness* of the representations given in sensation. Schleiermacher certainly followed Kant on this. In the *Notes on Ethics* he comments on the immediacy of feeling: "in feeling the way in which unfamiliar life grasps our own is given immediately" (*Ethics*, 75). And earlier he notes that what is cognized through the organs of sensation are singular objects: "nature that is personal is simply the point from which activity proceeds and apprehends all that can enter into association with it. For this function the entire external world consists only of singulars..." (*Ethics* 56–7).

The unique character of the cognitions given to the individual in sensation follows from what Schleiermacher calls the *non-transposability* of the individual. Schleiermacher notes that "Individuation is indeed the most complete formation, and yet it remains *unknowable* owing to its non-transposability, for it is precisely that which no other organ can be, and it can never become the organ of another without being destroyed" (*Ethics* 74). Cognitions given through sensation reflect the unique position of the individual in virtue of which the individual stands in a direct relation to all other individuals, and as such these cognitions cannot be made an object of abstract knowledge. They are only fully understandable from the first person standpoint of the perceiver herself, and this standpoint is something that cannot be transposed, for such cognitions depend on the unique position of his or her organs of sensation relative to

---

[18] Kant finally arrives at this position in the inaugural dissertation *On the Form and Principles of the Sensible and Intelligible Worlds* in *Theoretical Philosophy, 1755–1770*.

[19] While I cannot discuss this in more depth here, the immediacy and uniqueness of what is given in sensation is, for Kant, inherently connected with the character of space as a form of intuition: there are *characteristics* of the spatial structure and orientation of space that cannot be captured by concepts (general representations), but which must be given *immediately*, and which thereby reflect the position of objects in relation to *me*.

other individuals.[20] To be sure, the characteristics of particulars given in sensation can be abstracted and then serve as concepts that can then be communicated to others. But as *concepts* they are mediate and general representations under which many individuals can be ranged. Individual objects in their completeness, as they are perceived by *me* through my organs of sensation, can never be fully picked out by a concept. As such, the cognitions I have in virtue of my being a sensitive being can never be fully communicated to another. And insofar as my perspective on the world, the way I reflect it and engage it, cannot be transposed, my knowledge is absolutely unique. It is precisely the uniqueness of this perspective that is reflective of individuality, and in its uniqueness lies the unknowability of the individual. Schleiermacher notes, " . . . individuality is not something attainable by thought" (*Ethics* 74). As such, "the uniqueness of the other becomes only the object of acknowledgement, an object which one can never entirely or purely dissolve [through conceptual analysis]" (*Ethics* 48). This implies that knowledge of the individual and his or her perspective on the world can only be achieved through successive approximations: "By means of the correlated intuition of its particular externalizations described above, one achieves an approximation that, however, can never be completed" (*Ethics* 74). Given that a community is based on the individuals that constitute it, and given his extensive analysis of the uniqueness of the individual (which can, ultimately, only be the object of *acknowledgement*) Schleiermacher concludes that "a community of individuality must be founded, which, however, cannot be directed at anything except reciprocal intuiting and cognizing. This impulse to intuit inaccessible, nontransposable individuality is what one calls love in the narrower (but not yet narrowest) sense" (*Ethics* 74). That which grounds community, binding its members together while at the same time acknowledging their uniqueness, is love.

From the non-transposable and unique character of the individual follows the finite and perspectival character of all human knowledge.

---

[20] Schleiermacher notes further, "As uniqueness, however, the organizing activity of reason has the character of non-transposability, because in each person a fundamental relationship of the person is expressed that is not applicable to any other . . . " (*Ethics* 68). This fundamental relationship is the relationship of the individual to others, which originates from a unique position and which as such cannot be transposed.

The principal objects of our knowledge having ethical import are other individuals, their standpoints, and the cognitions and desires arising from those standpoints. The non-transposable character of such individuals and *their* knowledge implies the perspectival and finite character of knowledge for two reasons. First, there is no *absolute* standpoint from which to grasp the position of others. Others are always grasped from our own embodied perspective. As such, each perspective on the world is absolutely unique: "From every point from which it originates, a representation of the world must be a different one" (*Ethics* 112).[21] Second, the perspective of the other who is the object of my knowledge and desire is something that I can never fully know. I arrive at knowledge of the other and his/her standpoint through successive approximations, but the unique standpoint of the other must always remain a mystery to me: it is something that I can only acknowledge. Given the fact that the cognitions of the other, insofar as they are absolutely unique, must ultimately remain opaque to me, my knowledge is *finite*. Moreover, insofar as *my* organs of sensation are situated and my horizon of knowledge originates from a particular point, my knowledge is *perspectival*. Important to note, in this regard, is that it is Schleiermacher's emphasis on the foundational role of the individual that lead him to disagree so vehemently with his Berlin colleague, Hegel. For Schleiermacher there is no absolute knowing, no absolute philosophy.[22] Non-transposable individuals are what ground community. This fact is of ultimate significance, both for Schleiermacher's ethics and epistemology. There are limits to what persons can know about others; our knowledge of them must in principle remain finite. This finitude arises from the situatedness, not only of our organs of cognition, but also of the organs of others we

---

[21] In this he clearly echoes Leibniz.

[22] Crouter makes note of Schleiermacher's 1810 acceptance speech before the Berlin Academy of Sciences, where he "spoke against systematic philosophy and in favor of the historical-critical approach to philosophy...," and cites Harnack, who noted that "Schleiermacher feared the despotism of the Hegelian philosophy and at least the Academy was to be kept free of it" (Crouter, *Friedrich Schleiermacher: Between Enlightenment and Romanticism*, 87–8). Schleiermacher's suspicions of Hegel's speculative and absolute philosophy are in keeping with his own philosophical position that there can be no such thing as absolute knowing. Instead, we can only attempt to approach given historically conditioned positions regarding knowledge; this is reflected in Schleiermacher's preference for the historical-critical method.

strive to know as well. Standpoints can never be fully transcended. Schleiermacher recognized that not to acknowledge our situatedness can only lead to delusions of absolute knowledge having the most pernicious of consequences.

Lastly, individuals are embodied. Insofar as the knowledge of an individual is to be related to that of others, it must be understood as arising from a particular perspective or point of view. It is impossible, however, to understand cognition as arising from a point in relation to other points of view without also thinking of the individual as occupying a particular point in space, and hence as embodied. Schleiermacher notes "Nature that is personal is simply the point from which activity proceeds and apprehends all that can enter into association with it. For this function the entire external world consists only of singulars. As chaos, it stands in contrast to the ensouling principle" (*Ethics* 57). It is significant that throughout the *Notes on Ethics* Schleiermacher speaks of feeling and intuition, and of the *organs* through which the world is apprehended, namely, the body. Through the bodily organs of sensation, the individual stands in immediate relation to the world and to others: "In feeling the way in which unfamiliar life grasps our own is given immediately" (*Ethics* 75). As such the contents of the external world are apprehended through feeling as singulars by the organs of cognition.

Schleiermacher's emphasis on intuition and feeling follows from his emphasis on the role that *organs* of cognition play in knowledge. This emphasis on our embodiment follows from important ethical commitments. In order to recognize what these are, however, we will need to take a look at Schleiermacher's relation to Fichte, who thought of himself as someone who stood in genuine agreement with the spirit of Kant's philosophy. Schleiermacher took over important elements of Fichte's interpretation of Kant's philosophy, but also disagreed with him in important ways as well, and it is these disagreements with Fichte that lead him to stress the prominence of intuition and feeling in his own philosophy. In the *Wissenschaftslehre* Fichte points out that all consciousness of objects presupposes an immediate self-consciousness:

Hitherto, people reasoned as follows: We cannot be conscious of things posited in opposition to us, that is, of external objects, unless we are conscious of ourselves, i.e., unless we are an object for ourself. This occurs by means of an act of our own consciousness, of which we are able to become conscious only insofar as we, in turn, think of ourself as an object and thereby obtain a consciousness of our own consciousness. But we become conscious of this consciousness of our consciousness only by, once again, turning it into an object and thereby obtaining a consciousness of the consciousness of our consciousness, and so on *ad infinitum*. Our consciousness, however, would never be explained in this manner. Or else one would have to conclude that there is no consciousness at all—so long, that is, as one continues to treat consciousness as a state of mind or else as an object; for in proceeding in this manner one always presupposes a subject, which, however, one can never discover.[23]

Schleiermacher stands in agreement with Fichte on the need to posit the immediate self-consciousnesss. Its immediacy stands in the closest possible relation to the transcendental character of Kant's unity of apperception: the *act* of synthesizing representations can be reflected upon, to be sure, but insofar as the action is taking place, it can never be its own object, and as such, it always *transcends* the objective world that is given through the synthesis of the act. Schleiermacher touches on a related point in the *Notes on Ethics* when he notes " ... in the subject no unity can be posited that would actually be found once again within knowing, except this: that it contains the law by which to represent the world" (*Ethics*, 105). That is, the *unity* of the act of synthesis cannot itself be captured as an object of thought; at best it can be represented as the "law" through which representations are synthesized, and what is given externally is apprehended *as world*. In *The Christian Faith*, Schleiermacher speaks of the *immediate* self-consciousness, and what he refers to by the expression is no doubt indebted to Fichte's insightful interpretation of Kant.[24]

---

[23] J. G. Fichte, *Wissenschaftslehre nova methodo* (student lecture transcripts, 1796–99). *Foundations of Transcendental Philosophy (Wissenschaftslehre) nova methodo*, 30; Cited by Franks, *All or Nothing*, 226.

[24] Christian Berner also notes the similar function of Kant's transcendental I and Schleiermacher's immediate self-consciousness. He notes: "Que nous pensions ou que nous voulions, le sentiment comme conscience immédiate de soi, comme sentiment de l'unité, nous accompagne à chaque instant et il devient ainsi le fondement senti de toute réflexion. C'est à ce titre, nous le notions aussi, que cette 'conscience immediate de soi' semble jouer un rôle similaire à l'aperception transcendentale, au "Je pense" chez Kant. Mais si le "Je pense" est une forme vide, la conscience immédiate de soi est présence immédiate au fondement et de l'unité de l'être que la pensée par ailleurs

Now according to Fichte, it is through the *act* of the synthesis of its representations that the I posits itself. The "I" that accompanies all my representations has its character as an I in virtue of its synthetic activity; it just *is* constituted by this activity. There is no I that exists independently of, and prior to, this activity. Hence, Fichte would say, "The I posits itself as an I." Moreover, we have *immediate* access to this activity of self-positing through intellectual intuition, that is, through an immediate apprehension of the I as active and self-constituting. But Fichte would go even further. He eliminates Kant's thing in itself and all of Kant's dualisms. There cannot be anything distinct and "outside" of the self with which the self interacts, and which is, as such, in itself (apart from its *relation* to the subject) unknowable to the subject. This means that the self is not affected by that which is different from the self; the "matter" of sensation cannot be given to the self by something distinct from it. Fichte argued that in order for complete knowledge to be possible, there must be a subject–object identity, and hence, in any act of knowledge, the self really knows *only* itself. What appears to the subject as the object of knowledge is in fact also posited by the subject: "The absolute subject, the I, is not given by empirical intuition; it is instead, posited by intellectual intuition. And the absolute object, the not-I, is that which is posited in opposition to the I."[25] But if the I only knows itself, how is community between distinct subjects to be possible? Given that ethical concerns are at the forefront of Fichte's philosophy, the problem was especially pressing. In *The Vocation of Man*, Fichte asks: "How have free spirits knowledge of free spirits? We know that free spirits are the only reality, and that an independent world of sense, through which they might act on each other, is no longer to be taken into account."[26] He answers his own question in the following way:

In short, this mutual recognition and reciprocal action of free beings in this world is perfectly inexplicable by the laws of nature or of thought, and can be explained only through the One in whom they are united while separate

jamais ne peut atteindre par la voie de la réflexion." Christian Berner, *La Philosophie de Schleiermacher*, 129–30.

[25] *[Rezension:] Aenesidemus* (1794). "*Aenesidemus* Review." In *Fichte: Early Philosophical Writings*, 55–77; cited by Franks, *All or Nothing*, 225.

[26] Johann Gottlieb Fichte, *The Vocation of Man*, ed. by Roderick Chisholm (Indianapolis: Bobbs-Merrill, 1956), 136.

from each other; through the Infinite Will who sustains and embraces them all in His own sphere. The knowledge we have of each other does not flow immediately from you to me, or from me to you; we are separated by an insurmountable barrier. Only through the common fountain of our spiritual being do we know of each other; only in Him do we recognize each other and influence each other.[27]

God guarantees that alterations in what I posit as other than myself (and hence as my world) will harmonize with the changes that are posited by the other in his or her world. Hence there is no *direct* community between self and other in Fichte's philosophy. Schleiermacher, however, wants to posit a direct interaction between self and others. In order to do so, he comes to understand the immediacy of consciousness quite differently than Fichte. It is an immediate consciousness of the self in its *positional* relation to others. Insofar as the self stands in a relation such that others can in some way *affect* the self, this immediate self-consciousness must be one of feeling, that is, of receptivity to the givenness of the self in its juxtaposition to others. Hence in a note to §3 of the first edition of *The Christian Faith* of 1821–2, Schleiermacher defines feeling as the "immediate presence of all indivisible existence" (*KGA* I.7). However, if self and world are to stand in relation, there must be a ground unifying both the self and that which is other than the self. It is for this reason that Schleiermacher comes to the conclusion that the analogue of the immediate self-consciousness, through which self and other are given in their immediacy, is the absolute, the "Whence" of both our active and receptive existence. This "Whence" is the ultimate object of the feeling of absolute dependence. However, it is important to note that for Schleiermacher the absolute lies *outside* of consciousness itself. It is only signaled by the lacuna that consciousness must traverse as it shifts from a moment of activity to receptivity. Whereas, according to Fichte, what is given in immediate self-consciousness is consciousness of our own activity—a *Tathandlung* through which we are aware of our self-constitutive activity in intellectual intuition, Schleiermacher posits an immediate awareness of absolute *dependence*, the very opposite of such constitutive activity. We are immediately aware of both our activity and receptivity, the correlates of which are self

---

[27] Ibid. 136–7.

and world. Interaction between the two is possible because both are grounded in the absolute; in fact, it is through such interaction that we become immediately aware of the feeling of absolute dependence on the "Whence" of our receptive and active existence. In an important sense, for both Schleiermacher and Fichte, it is God that makes possible the interaction between self and others. There are, however, important differences between them. Schleiermacher strives to preserve both the transcendence of the absolute to consciousness, as well as the real character of the relation between self and others. The possibility of this relation is grounded in the absolute, an absolute which, however, *transcends* consciousness itself.[28] Moreover, just as the absolute transcends consciousness, the facticity of both self and other does so as well. The self is present to itself in the *immediate* self-consciousness; the other is given to me *immediately* as an object of acknowledgement. Neither, however, can be *fully* known as *objects* of knowledge, since what is immediately given can never be fully objectified. The *immediacy* of self-consciousness implies that the self can never fully know itself as its own object, and *as such* as standing in relation to all other objects that constitute the self's world. Therefore, there is a dimension of the self that always transcends objectification, and the transcendental self can never be *reduced* to the embodied self, certainly not from a first person perspective.[29] All of these claims, the

---

[28] On this point Schleiermacher differs significantly from Fichte. As Günter Zöller notes Fichte "insists on the presence of the absolute *in* the I. It is the absolute itself that manifests itself under the form of the thinking and willing I"; in "German Realism: the self-limitation of idealist thinking in Fichte, Schelling, and Schopenhauer," 206. See also Günter Zöller, "'On revient toujours.' Die transzendentale Theorie des Wissens beim letzten Fichte," *Fichte Studien*, Volume 20, Teil III.

[29] On this point I stand in disagreement with Thandeka, *The Embodied Self: Friedrich Schleiermacher's Solution to Kant's Problem of the Empirical Self*. Insofar as Scheiermacher recognizes, along with Fichte, the immediate self-consciousness, he must also recognize that Kant's transcendental self can in no way be *reduced* to the embodied self. The fact that this reduction is impossible does not, however, imply the loss of the embodied self. As such, it is not at all clear that Kant ever "lost" the embodied self, or that Schleiermacher must fundamentally disagree with him on the question of the relation to the transcendental self (having significant affinities with the immediate self-consciousness) to the empirical self. The relation of the transcendental self to the empirical self in Kant's philosophy is an enormously complicated and difficult subject, but for Kant the two are in no way cut off from one another. My chapter, "On Some Presumed Gaps in Kant's Refutation of Idealism," touches on some of these issues. Moreover, it is Fichte, not Kant, who clearly lost the empirical self, since for him, on a fundamental metaphysical level, the self does not stand in any

transcendence of the absolute, as well as the reality of the relations between self and world, are inherently interconnected.

It is the positing of real relations between the self and others that lead Schleiermacher to discuss the organs of cognition through which the self can both be acting and acted upon by others. In order for the self to genuinely interact with others, the self must be an embodied self, that is, it must be a self that is genuinely *receptive* to the influence of others, and for this is must have *organs* through which it can be affected, and through which it can act, in turn, on that which is other than itself. In *The Christian Faith*, Schleiermacher affirms "Thus the whole of this aspect of the original perfection of the world can be summarily expressed by saying that in it there is given for the spirit such an organism as the human body in living connexion with all else—an organism which brings the spirit into contact with the rest of existence" (*CF* §59.1). Because of this commitment to both genuine spontaneity and receptivity, Schleiermacher preserved Kant's dualisms. Most importantly for Schleiermacher's ethics, however, is the role that embodiment plays in all our coming to know. Later in the *Dialectic* he would note, "there is no choice but to ground the relativity of knowledge in an original difference of organic impressions. The deviation [Abweichung] in the process of schematization of different peoples, giving birth to the diversity of languages, is grounded in this way" (*Dial O*, 376).

Our coming to know is conditioned by our embodiment, which is inherently linked with the fact that we are individuals in community with others. But this means further that our coming to know must always begin from a particular perspective achieved in and through the organs of our embodiment. The organic impressions providing language with its materiality differ from one another for a variety of reasons. First, each individual has a distinct position vis à vis others. Hence Schleiermacher notes, "Each person has his place in the totality of being, and his thought represents being, but not independently of his place" (*Dial O*, 377). Second, in the *Notes on Ethics* Schleiermacher develops the notion of *organ formation*. There he notes, "the functions of life consist of the formation of nature into an organ

real relation to anything outside of it, but all of the self's objects are merely ideal, a projection of the self.

and the use of the organ for action by reason. There are no other functions than these, for in these the essence of the ensouling principle is exhausted ... Organs cannot be formed except through use; there is only self-formation, and with increased knowledge in their use new tasks of organ formation also arise" (*Ethics*, 43). Organs are that through which the self is both receptive to the world, and that through which the self *expresses* itself; as he notes here, organs are formed *through use*. Their use just is this process of interacting with the rest of nature, and this means being in community with it. Earlier in the *Notes on Ethics* he notes:

Self-contained existence is the binding of all natural powers in a center. Community is a taking-into-oneself and a bringing-forth from oneself. On the lowest levels the taking-into-oneself is simply organic bonding, the bringing forth from oneself is simply an inorganic deposit; on the higher levels the taking-into-oneself ascends to become perception, the bringing-forth-from-oneself issues in production. (*Ethics* 41)

The organs through which sensations are received develop to different degrees depending on their use; hence their receptive powers are also subject to degrees of development. Development of the receptive powers of organs is part and parcel of the "ensoulment of nature through reason"; life evolves through ever more complex interactions between the center of a self-contained existence and its world; through reason these are organized in such a way that the individual progressively becomes integrated into larger and larger circles of community. Through these complex interactions the individual develops his/her organs of cognition, and in doing so also changes the way s/he is capable of perceiving the world, much like the trained ear is capable of discriminating tones that the untrained ear would simply not apprehend.

COMMUNITY

How is it possible to apprehend the standpoint of another? Schleiermacher notes, "Through use an organ is formed and from forming arises an object for knowledge" (*Ethics*, 45). The organ that is formed for both receptivity and expression in turn becomes an object of knowledge for other embodied beings. Community is formed as the *way* that a being apprehends its world and reacts to it and in turn becomes an object of knowledge for other selves, and vice versa. Beings become objects of knowledge for others through their effects on the world and their visible traces: the more fully organized beings do not simply leave traces, but also produce and thereby *express* themselves. Schleiermacher's ethics is grounded on the presupposition that community develops through the interaction of different embodied beings, each with a different perspective on the world. First local communities are formed; these local communities also form part of larger ones. The individual stands in relation to both, and both condition his/her individuality: " ... the individuality of the particular person does not stand directly over against universality; rather it is rooted in larger individualities. These individualities must also be found in knowing and speaking" (*Ethics* 111). The ultimate moral goal is for the individual to stand in community with all of existence: "The good then consists in relating the subjective aspect of community to the identity of reason and organization—that is, to positing this identity as the relation of self-contained existence to everything else as a whole, as world in the proper sense, for only so does organization's being affected have a relation to reason. By this means feeling is raised to the potency of morality, and this process is nothing other than what we call religion" (*Ethics*, 121). Both reason and religion are fundamentally related: in both the relation of the individual to the totality of existence is a central concern. The following essential passage is worth quoting at length, since it encapsulates Schleiermacher's understanding of the relations of reason, morality and religion:

It is said, (1) that religion is the immediate relation of the finite to the infinite. Now, if the finite here is nothing other than reason enclosed in particular organization, then the infinite cannot be other than precisely the identity of reason with the totality of what is real; and so the content of this formula is entirely the same. (2) In the same sense, it is also said that religion is a striving toward reunification with the All. If this striving is then to proceed from the identity of reason with organization, its tendency cannot be to destroy organization. Thus, it can be absolute community of organization only as a particular, self-contained of itself with the whole. (3) It is said that religion is community not with the world but with God. Yet, however one might

place each in opposition to the other, God is always that in which the unity
and totality of the world is posited. Hence, the designated relation is at once
community with God. (*Ethics* 121)

Reason permeates both individual existences and the whole of nature:
it is both that through which the individual achieves its individual
existence (its form, or principle of organization), as well as that
through which individuals are related to all individual existences.
It is *in and through the organization present within individual existences that the organization between the individual and the totality is
to be forged.* This is the fundamental insight standing at the heart
of Schleiermacher's ethics. The organization of the individual—its
particularity—is therefore essential to its reunification with the All,
that is, to religion. Furthermore, relation to God cannot not be
understood apart from the goal of community with all that is real:
as such, there is no genuine religion without ethics. However, the
ultimate ethical goal, the highest good, is itself the proper object of
religion.

The philosophical questions that preoccupy Schleiermacher in the
years following the publication of the *Notes on Ethics* are concerned
with two questions that are the outgrowth of his foundational ethical
insights: First, given the perspectival character of the standpoint of
all finite individuals, how is knowledge possible? This is the material
that he would attempt to work out in the *Dialectic*. Second, given
the perspectival character of all human standpoints, how is mutual
understanding among different selves possible? The latter is material
that he would work out, through in his *Hermeneutics*. Both projects
are closely interrelated and are outgrowths of his ethical concerns;
they can only be properly understood in this context. Discussion
of the details of Schleiermacher's *Dialectic* and *Hermeneutics* is
beyond the scope of the present study, which seeks only to uncover
the metaphysical foundations of Schleiermacher's ethical system.
These foundations concern the nature of the highest good, as
well as the conditions of the possibility of its achievement. This
chapter and the previous one concerned Schleiermacher's understanding of the nature of the highest good. As a Christian philosopher, Schleiermacher understood Christ as the indispensable condition of the possibility of the highest good: he believed that it is

only in and through Christ that all individual rational beings can be united in perfect love. This is the subject of our next chapter. No doubt Schleirmacher's understanding of the nature and function of Christ stems from his Christian commitments. Nevertheless, his treatment of the significance of Christ is full of insights that are of ethical value, for among other things he shows how the actions of an individual can ethically transform the lives of others.

7

Transformation of the Self through Christ

In the previous chapters we have examined the progression of
Schleiermacher's metaethical commitments. He moves away from a
metaphysical monism in the early essays on Spinoza and towards a
qualified monadic individualism in the *Monologen* of 1800. Throughout this philosophical development, the influence of Kant remains
paramount. However, Schleiermacher moves significantly beyond
him as well, even while retaining important traces of Kant's thought.
Key to Schleiermacher's own position was Kant's critique of rational psychology: we have no access to the "inner" self, but only to
the "outer" self, the self in its relation to the world. How the self
brings together its representations and thereby "constructs" its world
is the window to the self: we know the self through its world. In
the *Notes on Ethics* Schleiermacher notes that "in the subject no
unity can be posited that would actually be found once again within
knowing, except this: that it contains the law by which to represent
the world (*Ethics*, 105). This is the closest that the self can come to
objectifying itself *as a unity*, through apprehending the law through
which the self unites its representations of the world. Already in the
Monologen, however, Schleiermacher emphasized that the self does
not construct its world by itself. The human, social world is the
joint expression of the way that many selves in community imagine
their common world. As such the self comes to construct the world
through which it will know itself through the building blocks of
language and the social institutions that are already given to it as
forms for organizing cognition of the world. Schleiermacher thereby
stressed the importance of the community and its activity for the
self's knowledge of itself, and, hence, for its ethical development.

Just as important is Schleiermacher's insight in the *Monologen* that the self comes to know itself through its influence on the other who reflects the self back to itself. The loss of the other is thereby the loss of oneself.

In the *Monologen* these two insights are developed in the context of Schleiermacher's growing recognition of the importance of the individual. Not only does Schleiermacher repudiate his earlier metaphysical monism in favor of a qualified monadic individualism, he also continues to reflect on the ways in which it is crucial to take into account the individuality of the person for a viable ethical theory. In affirming this monadic individualism, Schleiermacher moves past Spinozism and comes closer to Kant's own position. However, it is Schleiermacher's reflections on the importance of the individual that lead him to move past Kant in both the *Critique of all Previous Ethical Theories* and in the *Notes on Ethics*. The organization of the whole, that is, harmonization of rational beings with one another, occurs in and through the specific organization of individuals who are organized differently from one another. Individuality, and therefore difference, is at the heart of community.

All of these ethical insights will be crucial to the development of Schleiermacher's theology. In fact, his theology cannot be properly understood apart from his ethical theory. At the heart of Schleiermacher's philosophic and theological system is his conviction that the self-consciousness of one individual can transform the self-consciousness of all. Schleiermacher arrives at this conclusion through his previous work on the nature of the individual. The individual comes to know itself through the way that it represents its world as well as through its influence on others. The self thereby achieves its self-consciousness and individuality in and through community. As such, contact with another person and incorporation into a community founded by such an individual can be the occasion for ethical transformation. In this chapter, I will explore how Schleiermacher envisioned ethical transformation through contact with one individual and the community founded by him, namely Christ and the Christian community. The focus of this chapter is therefore the person and work of Christ.

Schleiermacher's Christology encapsulates the whole of his theology, as well as significant elements of his philosophy. Because he stresses the full and complete humanity of Jesus, and because, too, for Schleiermacher Jesus embodies *perfect* human nature, Schleiermacher's Christological doctrine contains significant elements of his anthropology. Insofar as Schleiermacher affirms a veritable presence of God in Christ, his Christology also contains a theory of how God relates to human self-consciousness and the world in which it develops itself. And finally, because Schleiermacher stresses that it is the *person-forming* activity of Jesus that is salvific, his theory of the work of Christ presupposes an understanding not only of human nature, but of the significance of history, that is, of how it is that what occurs in *history* can change the fundamental, inner disposition of a person. A fully adequate conception of Schleiermacher's Christology thereby has to touch on all of these questions. It is to these issues that I now turn. My discussion will be organized around Schleiermacher's presentation in §100 of *The Christian Faith* on the work of Christ. There he affirms that the proper, mystical view of the work of Christ is the "true mean between two others," namely, "the magical way, and the other the empirical."[1] It is in understanding what is wrong with both magical and empirical views that Schleiermacher's own mystical view of the work of Christ comes into focus.

EMPIRICAL VIEWS OF THE WORK OF CHRIST

In §100 of the *Christian Faith*, Schleiermacher tells us that an empirical view of the work of Christ "admits a redemptive activity on the part of Christ, but one which is held to consist only in bringing about an increasing perfection in us; and this cannot properly occur otherwise than in the forms of teaching and example." Such a view is found in Immanuel Kant's *Religion within the Boundaries of Mere Reason*, and it is likely that Schleiermacher had Kant specifically in

---

[1] I often provide my own translations of *The Christian Faith*; otherwise I cite the translation by Mackintosh and Stewart. Unless otherwise indicated, citations are to the 1830–1 edition of *The Christian Faith*, and will be indicated first by paragraph and section number, *KGA* pagination, and then to the Mackintosh and Stewart translation pagination, here *CF* §100.3, *KGA* I.13,2 110; 429.

mind in discussing the empiricist view. In a moving passage in the
Religion Kant notes that

However, the good principle did not descend among humans from heaven
at one particular time but from the very beginning of the human race, in
some invisible way (as anyone must grant who attentively considers the
holiness of the principle, and the incomprehensibility as well of the union
of this holiness with human sensible nature in the moral disposition) and
has precedence of domicile in humankind by right. And, since the principle
appeared in an actual human being as example for all others, this human
being "came unto his own, and his own received him not, but as many as
received him, to them gave he powers to be called the sons of God, even
to them that believe on his name"; that is, by exemplifying this principle
(in the moral idea) that human being opened the doors of freedom to
all who, like him, choose to die to everything that holds them fettered
to earthly life to the detriment of morality; and among these he gathers
unto himself "a people for his possession, zealous of good works," under
his dominion, while he abandons to their fate all those who prefer moral
servitude.[2]

What is significant in such a view is the following: First, the "good
principle" is not something that makes its first appearance in Jesus
Christ, and which then, through him, spreads through the entire
race. It is something, rather, the adoption of which is present as a
real possibility from the first beginnings of the human race. Second,
given the key position of human autonomy in Kant's ethical theory,
contact with an historical individual can be neither a necessary nor a
sufficient condition of human transformation. The decision to adopt
a good fundamental disposition must have its basis in the transcendentally free human will alone. As such, the influence of Jesus can at
most be an example or vivid representation of the moral ideal already
present in all human consciousness; it is through his example that
Jesus "opens the doors of freedom to all." At best such an example
can strengthen a resolve to goodness that is already present, but an
encounter with an historical individual (however good he or she may
be) cannot be, on Kant's view, what actually *occasions* the turning
away from evil and the beginning of a new life. Given Kant's stress on

---

[2] Immanuel Kant, *Religion within the Boundaries of Mere Reason* 6:83; in *Religion
and Rational Theology*, 121.

the importance of autonomy and transcendental freedom for genuine morality, a mere exemplar, providing a stimulus from the outside, cannot play a constitutive role in the adoption of a good disposition. Jesus cannot be the occasion for the recognition of the moral principle, since recognition and valuation of the moral principle must be presupposed in order for him to be recognized as good to begin with.[3] And neither, it seems, can he provide the incentive for the adoption of such a good disposition as one's own, since the very recognition of the moral principle *as* a moral principle already implies its valuation as an incentive to action.

Schleiermacher clearly wants to distinguish his own position from this one. He notes that on such an empirical view, the teaching and example in terms of which the redemptive activity of Christ is conceived are "general" forms having "nothing distinctive in them" (*CF* §100.3, *KGA* I.13,2: 111; 430). In other words, on such a view there is nothing unique about Christ's person and work. All human beings are able to discern the fundamental principle of morality in virtue of their status as rational agents, and, moreover, the moral law itself functions as an incentive to action for all of them. On such a view the work of Jesus is minimal and interchangeable: he functions merely as a vivid representation of an ideal independently accessible to consciousness. The work of such an exemplar is limited to strengthening the moral disposition that is already present. But for such a limited task, any other exemplar, provided he or she were good enough, would do just as well.

It could not have been lost on Schleiermacher that a key feature of such an empiricist view is that it is unable to ascribe genuine importance to the historical arena, the arena wherein we come into

---

[3] In the second section of the *Groundwork*, Kant notes, "Even the holy one of the Gospel must first be compared with our ideal of moral perfection before one can recognize him as holy; he says this about himself too: Why do call me (whom you see) good? No one is good (the archetype of the good) except the one God (whom you do not see). But where do we get the concept of God as the highest good? Solely from the *idea* that reason projects *a priori* of moral perfection and connects inseparably with the concept of a free will. In morality there is no imitation, and examples serve only for our encouragement, i.e., they place beyond doubt the feasibility of what the law commands, they make intuitive what the practical rule expresses universally; but they can never justify setting aside their true original, which lies in reason, and in directing ourselves in accordance with examples" *Groundwork for the Metaphysics of Morals* 4: 408–9, Wood 25.

contact with other human selves. For such a view cannot provide a compelling account of how it is possible that an encounter with another person in history can really be the occasion for human transformation. All of the resources for human transformation are, on Kant's account, already *within* the self, and, as such, the significance of the historical arena, and even the question of how moral education is possible, poses a special difficulty for his theoretical framework. For Schleiermacher, however, the historical arena, in which persons exercise their powers and can influence one another and their moral development, is of paramount importance. How it is that Schleiermacher is able to incorporate the significance of the historical arena within his theoretical framework is key to his understanding of his own "mystical" view of the work of Christ and his avoidance of an empirical view.

SCHLEIERMACHER'S AVOIDANCE OF EMPIRICAL VIEWS OF THE WORK OF CHRIST

How does Schleiermacher avoid such an empirical view of the work of Christ? Schleiermacher was himself accused of holding a view close to the empiricist one that he criticizes. Many of his critics concluded that *The Christian Faith* presents an anthropological transcendental philosophy of religion with an amazingly high Christology stuck in the middle. F. C. Baur complained to his brother that if the principle characteristics of Jesus "were derived from religious self-consciousness...I could think of the Redeemer only as a certain form and potency of self-consciousness...and the outward appearance of Jesus is not the original fact [from which Christian consciousness is derived]."[4] Such, too, was the verdict of Karl Barth, who accused Schleiermacher of an anthropological starting point logically committing him to understanding Jesus as a mere exemplar of human nature. He charged that for Schleiermacher "statements about sin and grace relate to those of the God-consciousness

---

[4] Cited in Strauss, *The Christ of Faith and the Jesus of History*, lii.

as *predicates* to a *subject*,"[5] that is, sin and grace are viewed as mere modifications of a human nature understood in its own right, from the perspectives of philosophy, psychology and anthropology. As such the revelation given in Jesus Christ cannot function as a supernatural event, that is, as the Word of God against which the natural man must be judged and through which he is redeemed. Rather, Jesus is viewed as functioning inside the parameters of a God-consciousness that is an element of an already given human nature; as such, Barth notes, the advent of Jesus is just about as novel as "the formation of a new nebula."[6] If such is the case, it is hard to understand Jesus as the archetype of the relation between God and persons such that all human relationship to God is rooted in him.[7]

Part of the reasons for which he was accused of holding such an empiricist view no doubt stem from the fact that even while he criticized him, Schleiermacher had learned much from Kant. Schleiermacher recognized that the ground of the unity of the self cannot be given in a representation, and cannot as such make its appearance *in* the world wherein objects appear alongside of one another and over against the subject. The act of thinking always transcends the representational contents of thought. Even if I were to make my thinking the object of my thought, this then becomes merely yet another representation among others, and my *act* of uniting this representation with others remains only *immediately* available to consciousness and transcends all objects of consciousness dependent upon the subject–object split. As such, the transcendental function of the self in uniting representations remains beyond that access that we have to both self and the world through the system of representations given to consciousness. It is in this important sense that the transcendental self is free in relation to the empirical world, that is, it transcends the causal nature system given in and through the series of representations.[8]

---

[5] Barth, *The Theology of Schleiermacher*, 205.   [6] Ibid.

[7] Emil Brunner also made similar charges in his book *Die Mystik und das Wort*. Brunner's point is discussed by Brian Gerrish in *Tradition and the Modern World*, 24.

[8] The point is also nicely made by Andrew Bowie, who notes, "Once the role of the 'spontaneity' of the subject in the constitution of an objective world is established the world cannot be said to be reducible to the objective physical laws that govern

As I argued in Chapter 4, Schleiermacher adopted Kant's transcendental turn while at the same time incorporating significant Leibnizian and Eberhardian influences into his own metaphysics of the self. As such, an important element in Schleiermacher's psychology is his focus on the grounding principle of the self that points to the whence of its active and receptive existence. This is the immediate self-consciousness; transitions between moments of the self's activity and its receptivity take place here. Earlier I cited Kant's remark that "there are two stems of human cognition, which may perhaps arise from a common but to us unknown root, namely sensibility and understanding..." (*KRV* A15/B29). While Kant suggests the possibility of single ground of both, he says nothing more on the matter; he considers that it is something that cannot be fathomed by our understanding. Schleiermacher, however, recognized the importance of such a ground linking spontaneity and receptivity, thinking and willing. In the *Dialectic* Schleiermacher speaks of the "living unity of the succession of the acts of thought." This is "the transcendent basis of thought, in which the principles of linkage are contained" and it is "nothing but our own transcendent basis as thinking being... The transcendent basis must now indeed be the same basis of the being which affects us as the being which is our own activity" (*Dial O*, 274–5). It is given in the "immediate self-consciousness," and is "that which links all the moments of both functions, of thinking and willing, [it is] the identity in the linking, it is real being" (*Dial O*, 291). As is well known, it is through the immediate self-consciousness, the transcendental ground of self-consciousness, that the self has access to the "Whence of our active and receptive existence"; this is the God-consciousness itself. In focusing upon such a transcendent basis of thought and action, Schleiermacher weds Kantian insights with

---

it. Establishing *objective* laws which could explain why the world becomes *subjectively* intelligible at all...involves the problem of how to objectify that which is inherently subjective, thus of how to come to knowledge of what is already supposed to be the *prior* condition of knowledge" Bowie, "Introduction," in *Schleiermacher: Hermeneutics and Criticism*, x. Strictly speaking, however, as I argue in the third chapter of the present study, while the transcendental character of consciousness implies its irreducibility to objective physical laws, this does not by itself imply transcendental freedom. The irreducibility of thought to the mechanism of nature does not exclude the possibility that both thought and the physical world are expressions of a single underlying ground.

Eberhard's notion of a fundamental power of the soul (*Grundkraft der Seele*) guaranteeing the unity of the life of the soul;[9] following both Eberhard and Reinhold, he understands this fundamental power as a kind of drive that grounds both the faculties of desire and of representation.[10] The conditions of the possibility of the self's relation to God are thereby to be found in the transcendental structure of selfhood itself, and thereby in what might be called a religious *a priori* which, while beginning with experience, does not arise *from* it. As such this fundamental power of the soul is the ground of both religion and morality. This fact alone poses several difficulties for Schleiermacher, not the least of which is how he will be able to account for the effectiveness of an *historical* event for human redemption given this religious *a priori*, operative—even if only to a limited degree—in all human beings.

Because Schleiermacher stresses the full and complete humanity of Jesus, he understands Jesus' God-consciousness as arising in accordance with these general conditions of human nature. But if so, it would seem that his consciousness is, once again, a mere exemplar. His possibilities would seem to be the same as those of all other human beings. In this regard, another significant problem arises as well. Because all human beings share this general structure of human consciousness with him, it is hard to see why any given human person could not have developed the God-consciousness as fully as Jesus independently from him. Jesus shares the same general structure of consciousness as all of us; insofar as he does, there is nothing distinctive marking him as the individual destined to redeem the whole race. Jesus would then seem to stand in the same line as Hillel or Buddha.

---

[9] Eilert Herms traces the genesis of Schleiermacher's thought to both Eberhard and Kant; he argues that from Eberhard Schleiermacher adopts the notion of the "fundamental power of the soul." According to Herms, Schleiermacher's reception of Kant is more piecemeal, so that by the early 1790s he has only adopted Kant's thesis of the phenomenal character of all knowledge. On this point see Herms, *Herkunft, Entfaltung, und erste Gestalt des Systems der Wissenschaften bei Schleiermacher*, 96–7. As the present study shows, Schleiermacher's reception of Kant is more significant than Herms allows.

[10] This idea is present in *On Freedom*, where Schleiermacher notes, "In general, I understand by drive (*Treib*) the capacity grounded in the nature of the representing subject to bring about representations." The link with both Eberhard and Reinhold is noted by Herms, 95.

Contra Schleiermacher's theological critics, it is important to note that this is a problem having a peculiarly theological provenance, one stemming from the need to affirm Jesus' full and complete humanity. Insofar as Schleiermacher explicates the structure of human consciousness, the question involves major philosophical issues. But what motivates the affirmation of Jesus' humanity are purely theological concerns. If Jesus is to be fully human, as affirmed by Chalcedon, then the fundamental structure of his consciousness must be fully like our own. Schleiermacher fully recognized that only if the full and complete humanity of Jesus is affirmed can we think of Jesus as having a genuine influence over us; in the *Life of Jesus* he notes that "if we think of him as an absolute model we must think of his action as wholly human, for otherwise I cannot follow him."[11] We can only understand and follow Jesus insofar as what is realized in his person is a genuine possibility for us. But if our humanity is to be redeemed through our fellowship with him, and if this redemption is to be understood as our participation in the divine love, then we can only enter into this divine love *in and through* his humanity. Consequently Jesus' divinity must be present in and with his humanity. Schleiermacher understands the fundamental structure of human consciousness present in Jesus in terms of the immediate self-consciousness and its relation to self-consciousness as mediated through the representations of self and world. As argued above, the immediate self-consciousness functions as a fundamental power of the soul (*Grundkraft der Seele*) conditioning the transition between representations, between knowing and doing, as well as between spontaneity and receptivity. As such, in his *Life of Jesus* Schleiermacher argues that the divine in Jesus is not a discrete consciousness, but is rather "something that lies at the basis of the total consciousness" (*LJ* 97). Hence, the divinity of Jesus is fully integrated with his humanity; humanity and divinity are coextensive.[12]

[11] References to the *Life of Jesus* are to the Gilmour translation and will be indicated in the text by *LJ* with page number following, in this case *LJ* 84.

[12] Schleiermacher argues that as soon as one conceives of the divine element in Jesus as a real, discrete consciousness coexisting *alongside* the human "we clearly put an end to the unity of the personality" (*LJ* 96). And if the unity of the personality is done away with, one is clearly headed in the direction of the Nestorian heresy. On the other hand, if the divine in him is thought of as a vital principle lying at the ground of his consciousness, then we can conceive of it as something

Schleiermacher is able to counter the accusation of his critics that his is a merely "empiricist" Christology through several crucial moves. The first is a purely theological one. According to Schleiermacher, it was ordained in the original divine decree that redemption should occur through Jesus Christ. It is in virtue of this decree that Jesus has distinctive status. Schleiermacher argues that the impartation of the God-consciousness to both the first Adam, in which the God-consciousness remained sunk in sensuousness, and to the second Adam, in which its impartation reaches its perfection, "go back to one undivided eternal divine decree" (*CF* §94.3; *KGA* I.13,2 58; 389) ordaining that the first Adam should reach completion in the second. There is, therefore, no creation of human nature independent of Jesus Christ, but both go back to a *single establishing action* on God's part. As a consequence of this decree, human nature only achieves its perfection in Jesus Christ, whose perfect God-consciousness was destined from the very beginning to quicken that of the entire race. Hence, for Schleiermacher "Christ is...the completion of the creation of man" (*CF* §89.1; *KGA* I.13,2 29; 367). From the first moment of its creation the human race was ordered to its completion in Jesus Christ: "For although in the first creation of the human race only the imperfect condition of human nature made its appearance, yet the appearance of the Redeemer was already eternally implanted within it" (*CF* §89.3; *KGA* I.13,2 31; 368). Jesus not only achieves distinctive status in and through this decree, but his distinctiveness consists in his being the *archetype* of all human nature. As archetype he is no mere exemplar, and furthermore, his full and complete humanity is preserved insofar as he *defines* what it means to be human. Schleiermacher notes that

the uniting divine activity [in the Origin of the Person of Christ] is also an eternal one, although only as in God there is no difference between resolve and activity, that means for us simply a divine decree, identical as such with the decree to create humankind and included therein.

(*CF* §97.2; *KGA* I.13,2 75; 401)

that makes its appearance gradually, and whose self-expression becomes stronger as Jesus matures. As such Schleiermacher hopes to make sense of the saying in Luke 2:52 that as a child Jesus "increased in wisdom and in favor with God and man" (*LJ* 98).

God's activity of uniting with humanity in the perfect God-consciousness of Jesus Christ is established in the original divine decree; the activity of the God-consciousness in human nature that has not yet been quickened by Jesus is but a prefigurement, in the form of potentiality, of its actualization in Jesus Christ. Therefore, the appearance of the Redeemer is already foreshadowed in the receptivity to the divine implanted in human nature from the beginning (*CF* §89.3; *KGA* I.13,2 31; 368). Schleiermacher clearly wants to affirm that human nature only becomes what it most truly is destined to be in *relation* to Jesus Christ. It is Jesus' presentation of himself to us "in word and deed" (*CF* §101.4; *KGA* I.13,2 119; 438) that quickens our God-consciousness. That this should be so was ordained at the very beginning. And this *relation* to Jesus, through which human nature arrives at completion, occurs within the historical arena.

A second key move allowing Schleiermacher to avoid the charge that his is a merely "empiricist" Christology has to do with his conception of perfected human nature. Schleiermacher points out that, "it has always been assumed in Christian faith that a union with God is possible in terms of man's essence" (*LJ*, 100). The essence of perfect human nature, according to Schleiermacher, just is to express the divine; there can therefore be no real duality between Jesus' perfect humanity and his divinity. The very structure of human consciousness guarantees that it is capable of receiving the divine impartation. Insofar as Jesus is the *archetype* of what it means to be most fully human, he both receives and expresses perfectly the divine love. This means that Jesus is no mere teacher of morality, but that what he mediates is a relation to the ground of being and love, and thereby to the transcendental ground of all true religion and ethics. Not only are we aware of the divine activity in the world through consciousness, but the principle way in which God imparts himself to the world as love is through consciousness. Schleiermacher notes that " 'Word' is the activity of God expressed in the form of consciousness" (*CF* §96.3; *KGA* I.13,2 69; 397). It is through his God-consciousness that Jesus mediates the divine to us, thereby bringing us closer to the perfection to which we were destined.

In order to understand just exactly how Schleiermacher understands it is possible that the activity of God can express itself in, and be mediated through, human consciousness, we need briefly to review some points made at the very beginning of *The Christian Faith* concerning the God-consciousness, which as Schleiermacher famously pointed out, is merely an abstraction from the reality of the Christian God-consciousness. First, the God-consciousness can only make its appearance along with the sensible self-consciousness. In self-consciousness, the self makes itself its own object, and can distinguish between itself and the world. However, the relation between self and world, its spontaneous and receptive existence, presupposes an original unity of consciousness, a moment given in pure immediacy, in which the two are one. It is this original unity of consciousness that makes possible the transition between the moments of spontaneity and receptivity. The consciousness of absolute dependence is given in this moment of pure immediacy, it is "the self-consciousness accompanying the whole of our spontaneity, and because this is never zero, accompanying the whole of our existence and negating absolute freedom" (*CF* §4.3; *KGA* I.13,1 38; 16). God is the "Whence of our active and receptive existence." (*CF* §4.4; *KGA* I.13,1 39; 16). As both Robert Adams and Manfred Frank have argued, however, for Schleiermacher consciousness of God is not directly given in the immediate self-consciousness.[13] What is given, rather, is a consciousness of the self as absolutely dependent, in particular in regard to its own spontaneous action in relation to the world. The consciousness of absolute dependence is a consciousness that "the whole of our spontaneous activity comes from a source outside us." (*CF* §4.3; *KGA* I.13,1 38; 16). Consciousness of the self as dependent arises from the consciousness of a "missing unity" in the river of the soul's life as it flickers from spontaneity to receptivity. As Frank argues,

Consciousness feels itself to be *absolutely* dependent on Being, and this dependence is indirectly represented as the dependence on the Absolute. When immediate self-consciousness (or feeling) flickers from one to the other pole of the reflexive rift, this does not shed light on the positive fullness of a supra-reflexive identity, but rather on its lack. Schleiermacher notes that in the moment of "transition" (286) from object to subject of

---

[13] Robert Adams, "Faith and Religious Knowledge," and Manfred Frank, "Metaphysical Foundations", in *The Cambridge Companion to Friedrich Schleiermacher*.

reflection, self-consciousness always traverses the space of a "missing unity" (*C*290, §LI). Since the self cannot attribute this lack to its own activity, it must recognize this lack as the effect of a "determining power transcending it, that is, one that lies outside its own power" (*C*290). The self can only ascribe to itself the ground of *knowledge* of this dependence. Schleiermacher can thereby say that the cause of this feeling of dependence is not "effected by the subject, but only arises *in* the subject" (*CF* §3.3). However, in feeling, the activity of the self is "never zero," for "without any feeling of freedom a feeling of absolute dependence would not be possible".   (*CF* §4.3)[14]

Consciousness comes to awareness of this missing unity only in reflecting upon the transcendental conditions of the possibility of the moments of self-consciousness, in which there is an antithesis between self and world. Consequently Schleiermacher emphasizes the point that the immediate self-consciousness, and consequently the feeling of absolute dependence, is only given along with the sensuous self-consciousness: "it is as a person determined for this moment in a certain way within the realm of the antithesis that he is conscious of his absolute dependence. This relatedness of the sensibly determined to the higher consciousness in the unity of the moment is the consummating point of self-consciousness" (*CF* §5.3; *KGA* I.13,1 46; 21).

How Schleiermacher understands the God-consciousness in general is key to how he conceives of the presence of the divine in Jesus and his mediation of it to humanity. Two points, already implied in the previous discussion, are especially important. First, the God-consciousness is *transcendental*. As Schleiermacher remarked to Dr. Lücke, "What I understand as pious feeling is not derived from a representation but is the expression of an *immediate* existential relationship" (*KGA* I.10: 318). Pious feeling is given only in and with the transcendental unity of both our receptive and spontaneous existence. As such, it cannot appear as content *for* consciousness. Insofar as Jesus shares a completely human consciousness like our own, the divine in him must be understood as something "that lies at the basis of the total consciousness" (*LJ* 97). Second, it is clear that Schleiermacher considers the consciousness of spontaneity in relation to the world key to the recognition of absolute

[14]   Manfred Frank, "Metaphysical Foundations," 31.

dependence. The importance of this point cannot be stressed enough. He notes:

> But the self-consciousness accompanying our entire spontaneity, and thereby also, our entire being (for this spontaneity is never at zero), and which negates absolute freedom, is already in and for itself a consciousness of absolute dependence, for it is the consciousness that our entire spontaneity comes from elsewhere. In the same way, were we to have had a feeling of absolute freedom with respect to it, it must have come entirely from us. However, without a feeling of freedom, a feeling of absolute dependence would not be possible.   (*CF* §4.3; *KGA* I.13,1 38; 16)

It is in and through the *activity* of consciousness that a person becomes aware of the reflective rift that must be traversed in order for the moments of spontaneity and receptivity to interpenetrate one another. Moreover, both self and world are brought to concepts, and can be thought of as a unity, only through the transcendental unity of consciousness. In §32.2 Schleiermacher speaks of the feeling of absolute dependence as a "co-positing of God as the Absolute undivided unity (*ein Mitgesetzsein Gottes als der absoluten ungeteilten Einheit*)." This ground of the unity between self and world co-posited along with the feeling of absolute dependence, however, is not one that can be given in a single representation to consciousness. It is, rather, accessible only through the transcendental unity of consciousness, itself accessible first and foremost through the *activity* of uniting representations. The co-positing of God as the unity underlying all the moments of the sensuous self-consciousness cannot, therefore, occur without the spontaneity of this transcendental activity. Moreover, Schleiermacher argues that the confusion of God with the world also entails the denial of freedom: were one to mistake the feeling of absolute dependence as referring to a dependence upon the world, one must "dispute the reality of the feeling of freedom, and do away with it entirely, for there is no moment in self-consciousness in which we do not posit ourselves as one with the world" (*CF* §32.2; *KGA* I.13,1 204; 133). In other words, insofar as we make ourselves our own object and think of ourselves as *part* of the world, we must think of ourselves as part of the nature system and as such completely determined by it. A failure to recognize the transcendental character of the feeling of absolute dependence and of the transcendent character of that to which it points goes hand and hand with the denial of the spontaneity of all thinking and willing, which must itself be a transcendental one.

The second point regarding the importance of spontaneity to access to the God-consciousness is especially important in understanding how Schleiermacher conceives of the consciousness of Jesus. Jesus is completely *dependent* in relation to God, and there is a very important sense, especially insofar as this concerns the moral and religious consciousness of Jesus, in which this complete dependence upon God entails a complete *spontaneity* in relation to the world. The consciousness of Jesus is completely original, which is to say that while Jesus certainly expressed himself in terms of the thought world of second temple Judaism, he was able to make use of the material given to him in his historical situation to express something completely new. The grounding principle of his reason and will was not in any way determined by previously existing material and social causes. In an important passage Schleiermacher notes that Jesus "cannot have come out of" the corporate life of sinfulness; rather, his appearance in human history must be recognized "as a miraculous fact (*eine wunderbare Erscheinung*)." This is because "his peculiar spiritual content . . . cannot be explained by the content of the human environment to which he belonged, but only by the universal source of spiritual life in virtue of a creative divine act which, as an absolute maximum, the conception of man as the subject of the God-consciousness comes to completion" (*CF* §93.3; *KGA* I.13,2 46–7; 381). In an earlier passage from §93.3 Schleiermacher aims his discussion against Kant, who had argued that unaided human reason is capable of constructing the ideal of perfect moral human being in the world, and posited Jesus as the greatest exemplar of such a rational ideal. Schleiermacher argues that once we postulate sin as a corporate act of the human race, there is no possibility that "an ideal could have developed out of this corporate life." This is true also of the notion that "the ideal might be produced by human thought and transferred more or less arbitrarily to Jesus." The reason for this is that "there is a natural connection between reason and will," (*CF* §93.3; *KGA* I.13,2 46; 380) so that if we affirm the universal and corporate character of sin, we must also affirm the corruption of reason: sin is not something that affects only the will, but affects the very core of the person, what earlier we referred to as the fundamental power of the soul. And if sin has obscured reason itself, then the ideal of the perfect man cannot have arisen in thought apart from the appearance of Jesus, which Schleiermacher considers a completely original event, *eine wunderbare Erscheinung.*

It is true that Schleiermacher argues that the development of Jesus' human consciousness was a purely natural one. By this, however, he means that his higher consciousness "developed gradually in human fashion" alongside of his sensuous self-consciousness. However, Jesus' sensuous self-consciousness is purely passive in relation to the higher consciousness, and this is how he differs from the rest of humanity caught up in the corporate life of sin. In §97 Schleiermacher notes that in Jesus "the divine alone is active or self-imparting and the human alone passive or in process of being assumed" (*KGA* I.13,2 70; 398) What this means is already explicated earlier, in §96.3:

... the being of God in the Redeemer is posited as his innermost fundamental power, from which every activity proceeds and which holds all moments together; everything human (in Him) forms only the organism for this fundamental power, and is related to it as the system which both receives and represents it, just as in us all other powers should relate to the intelligence. (*CF* §96.3; *KGA* I.13,2 69; 397)

By "everything human," Schleiermacher is referring to the sensuous self-consciousness. It is *passive* in relation to the higher consciousness: in the self-consciousness of Jesus no desire arises from the sensuous functions themselves, that is, simply in virtue of Jesus being affected from without. In *The Life of Jesus*, Schleiermacher claims that "not only was his moral development progress without struggle, but also his intellectual development was progress without error"[15] (*LJ* 107). Jesus' development is that from "complete innocence to an ever more perfect consciousness" (*LJ* 99); he "was always conscious

---

[15] That is, while his views concerning the nature of the physical world may have been similar to those of his contemporaries, he never asserted his certainty regarding them since a concern with them was not his task. For Schleiermacher error "emerges only when the desire for knowing is terminated before the truth is reached" (*LJ*, 110).

of being in relation to the divine will" (*LJ* 101) and throughout his development the sensual element never took preponderance over Jesus' God-consciousness (*LJ* 98–9) but rather "nothing was ever able to find a place in the sense-nature that did not instantly take its place as an instrument of the spirit" (*CF* §93.4; *KGA* I.13,2 49; 383).

Schleiermacher develops a sophisticated analysis of temptation and concludes that Jesus cannot have been genuinely tempted. Everything depends "on determining the point where sin begins." If Jesus' nature was a genuinely human one, he must have been susceptible to the difference between pleasure and pain. However, Schleiermacher does not think that this susceptibility could have involved him in any kind of moral struggle, since "the beginning of sin must lie between the moment at which pleasure and pain exist in this sinless way and that at which struggle begins." Hence, while Jesus felt pleasure and pain, these did not determine his incentives to action (*CF* §98.1; *KGA* I.13,2 91; 414–15). Genuine temptation involves the idea that an object of temptation is an object of desire, that is, that it is genuinely attractive. Temptation also involves the idea of struggle in the self: one struggles with the attractive force of the object of desire. But, Schleiermacher reasons, to think that the sensuous self-consciousness in Jesus was able, of itself, to determine something as attractive or repulsive in such a way that he had to struggle with it, is to posit the origins of sin, even if infinitely small, in Jesus. If the sensuous self-consciousness could, of itself, determine a course of action as *genuinely* attractive for him, this would mean that in him there was a moment of consciousness in which the sensuous self-consciousness was not just the organ of the expression of the Spirit, that is, of his God-consciousness. It is these doctrinal considerations that are the guiding thread in Schleiermacher's understanding of the life of the historical Jesus.

The fact that Jesus' sensuous self-consciousness is *passive* in relation to his higher consciousness has the further implication that Jesus is fully *spontaneous* in relation to the world. The humanity of Jesus "is only the organism for this fundamental power"; and his humanity "receives and represents it." Schleiermacher then makes the following very interesting analogy: the fundamental power is related to his humanity in just the same way that all of our powers should relate to our intelligence. Our intelligence, however, arises from our spontaneous activity (the activity of uniting representations). According to Schleiermacher's doctrine of the "preponderant synthesis," however, this spontaneous activity has the capacity to affect even the way that influences coming to us from the world are themselves received. This point is extremely important for Schleiermacher's understanding of the consciousness of Jesus, and how there can be a veritable existence of God in him. At §94.2 he notes that to ascribe to Christ "an absolutely powerful God-consciousness," and to "attribute a being of God in him, are wholly one and the same." He continues with the following very important argument:

> The expression "the being of God in any other" can always only express the relation of the omnipresence of God to this other. Since the being of God can only be grasped as pure activity, and each individual being is only an intermingling of activity and passivity—the activity being found apportioned to this passivity in all other individual being—there is so far no existence of God in an individual being, but only a being of God in the world. And only when the passive states of affairs are not purely passive, but are mediated through a vital receptivity standing over against the entirety of finite existence (that is, so far as we can say of the individual as a living creature that, in virtue of the universal reciprocity, it in itself represents the world) could we suppose an existence of God in it.   (*CF* §94.2; *KGA* I.13,2 55; 387)

The argument seems to be the following one. Schleiermacher asks: if God is omnipresent and must be apprehended as pure activity conditioning the entirety of the world, how is it possible for an existence of God to be found in a single individual other than God? Any single individual other than God is part of the world, and as such is both passive and active in relation to the world. How can God exist in it, that is, how can God exist in the finite individual, given that such an individual must also be passive in relation to the rest of the world? Schleiermacher answers: if we are speaking of mere things, there can be no existence of God in the individual, but only in the world taken as a whole, for mere things stand in a relation of both passivity and activity to the things that exist outside them. Rational nature, however, is a completely different matter. Through it human nature is *capable* of standing in an *active* relation to the whole of finite existence. The rational, conscious self stands in relation to the whole world in virtue of the universal reciprocity; rational nature takes up these influences and through them *represents* the world. Hence Schleiermacher concludes that "the being of God can be found only in the rational individual" (*CF* §94.2; *KGA* I.13,2 55; 387). Human beings are rational and as such stand, to differing degrees, in such an active relation to the world. However, this kind of *pure activity* in relation to the world can be found only in Christ. To be sure, the self-consciousness of Jesus is such that he receives impressions from the world through his sensuous functions. But Schleiermacher held that receptivity is thoroughly intermingled with spontaneity (there are no uninterpreted sense-data), so that the *way* that impressions are received is determined through spontaneity. Because Jesus' receptivity to the world is a perfectly *vital* receptivity, he receives the whole of the world as the object of the divine love. This vital receptivity then allows Jesus to reflect the world as loved by God. In an important passage Schleiermacher notes:

But our canon also compels us to think of the human nature of Christ not as moved for and through itself in such perceptions, but only as taken up in community with an activity of the divine in Christ. *This is just the divine love in Christ which, once and for all or in every moment—however one may express it—gave direction to His perceptions of the spiritual conditions of human beings.* In virtue of these perceptions, and in consequence of them, there then arose the impulse to particularly helpful acts. So that in this interrelation every original activity belongs solely to the divine, and everything passive to the human.   (*CF* §97.3, italics mine; *KGA* I.13,2 82; 407)

Insofar as Jesus expresses the divine, his self-consciousness is fully active in relation to the world, that is, he imparts his God-consciousness to others and thereby quickens the whole race. The perfect passivity of his self-consciousness in relation to God implies its perfect activity in relation to the world.

How is it possible that the divine love can be imparted perfectly to the self-consciousness of Jesus? How can his entire spontaneity and receptivity be so completely conditioned by the divine love? Schleiermacher's discussion in the *Dialectic*, explored above, provides the answer. The God-consciousness results from consciousness traversing a gap, a reflexive rift, as consciousness flickers from the pole of spontaneity to receptivity and back again. Insofar as consciousness comes to the recognition that it must traverse this gap, it recognizes that it is not itself the source of its own existence, but that it depends on something other than itself for its very being. In order for there to be a genuine divine *influence* on consciousness, however, it must occur at the moment that consciousness flickers from one pole to the other. It is in traversing the reflective rift that consciousness receives the divine influence, indeed, becomes one with it. Insofar as consciousness is open to this transcendental moment, each moment of the sensuous self-consciousness, both its spontaneous and receptive elements, is thereby conditioned by the divine love. The divine love thereby imparts itself to the human consciousness of Christ in the way of a *formal* cause.

From the above discussion it should be clear how Schleiermacher's Christology avoids the charge that it is a merely empirical one. By way of summary, let me reiterate the three principal points discussed in this section. First, Schleiermacher affirms an original divine decree according to which it was ordained that Christ should be the completion of human nature. Human nature achieves its perfection only in and through Christ. Second, the essence of perfect human nature just is to express the divine, so that the divinity of Jesus is given in and through his humanity, and there is a veritable presence of God in Christ. Third, and most importantly, while Jesus shares our humanity there is a fundamental difference between his consciousness and our own. The humanity of Jesus has been fully taken up by the divine and is completely the organ of this fundamental divine power. Only in Jesus is there the kind of *vital* receptivity that receives all the influences of the world as thoroughly conditioned by the God-consciousness. Through this vital receptivity Jesus stands in relation to the whole world, takes the world into himself, and then reflects it as the object of the divine love. The world is thereby divinized through the pure activity of Jesus and his vital receptivity.

MAGICAL VIEWS OF REDEMPTION

The other error that Schleiermacher identifies regarding the work of Christ is what he refers to as the "magical" view. There are two basic characteristics of such a view. First, it does not take into account the importance of the Christian community and the historical mediation of salvation. The influence of Jesus is understood in a "magical" sense when it is understood as "not mediated by anything natural, yet attributable to a person." Importantly, he notes that such a view is contrary to one of the fundamental principles of his own exposition, namely that "the beginning of the Kingdom of God is a supernatural thing, which, however, becomes natural as soon as it appears" (*CF* §100.3; *KGA* I.13,2 111; 430). Second, the magical view of redemption overlooks the *person-forming* character of the work of Christ, instead taking "the forgiveness of sins" to "depend upon the punishment which Christ suffered" and mistakes the impartation of blessedness to human beings "as a reward which God offers to Christ for the suffering of that punishment" (*CF* §101.3; *KGA* I.13,2 116; 435). Given that the person-forming activity of Christ takes place in every individual genuinely taken up into his life, such a magical view also does not recognize the importance of the ethical life of the community founded by Christ. It thereby does not understand the fundamental work of Christ as the founding of the Kingdom of God.

The beginning of the Kingdom of God is supernatural insofar as it owes its origin to the consciousness of Christ. As discussed above, this consciousness is one that is completely *passive* in relation to the divine, that is, all the moments of Jesus' sensuous self-consciousness are utterly conditioned by the divine influence. However, the passivity of Jesus' self-consciousness in relation to the divine guarantees its complete *spontaneity* in relation to the world. As such Christ takes up the world through his vital receptivity and reflects it as the object of the divine love. This reflection and expression of the world as the object of God's love, however, takes place in the historical arena, and for this reason the mediation of the work of Christ must be a purely natural one. It is in history that selves express not only themselves but also the way that they value other selves. Schleiermacher stresses that "there is no spiritual influence but the presentation of oneself in word and deed." Consequently, "the Redeemer could only enter into our corporate life by means of such self-presentation, thereby attracting men to himself and making them one with himself" (*CF* §101.4; *KGA* I.13,2 119; 438). Christ mediates God's love through his expression of himself (through his historical utterances) and his reflection of the world as the object of this love. He thereby brings others under his influence and establishes the Kingdom of God as the community in which persons know and love one another in and through the love of God.

Important in this regard is that impartation of the blessedness of Christ takes place first and foremost through his *person-forming* activity. This person-forming activity is itself something that takes place in the historical arena, which is also to say that it is something that takes place in the context of human *community*. Hence Schleiermacher notes that, one cannot "share in the redemption and be made blessed through Christ outside the corporate life which He instituted, as if a Christian could dispense with the latter and be with Christ, as it were, alone." Such a view fails to recognize that while the power of God in Christ has a divine origin, it "can nevertheless be received only as it appears in history, and also can continue to function only as a historical entity" (*CF* §87.3; *KGA* I.13,2 20; 360).

The magical view of the work of Christ, however, represents redemption as something that can take place in the life of the believer in isolation from other selves. It does so because it does not recognize the essential role that Christ's *person forming* activity plays in redemption. Such a view further ignores that personhood is not something that can be formed in isolation from other selves, but always takes place in community. Christ's redemptive activity "brings about for all believers a corporate activity corresponding to the being of God in Christ" (*CF* §101.2; *KGA* I.13,2 114; 433). Schleiermacher understood that if the essential character of human personhood is to be an image of the divine love, then one cannot realize this potential outside of one's being with others in community. Redemption and blessedness cannot occur outside the compass of the fulfillment of this potential for being an image of the divine.

Furthermore, magical views of redemption ignore the intrinsic connections between being taken up into the life of Christ and the forgiveness of sins. Such views "make the impartation of his blessedness independent of assumption into vital fellowship with him." On such a magical view, stress is laid upon the suffering of Jesus, which is thought of as a substitutionary atonement for the sins of the individual. The punishments of Jesus are viewed as a necessary condition for forgiveness, and blessedness "is presented as a reward which God offers to Christ for the suffering of that punishment." Guilt is supposed to cease "because the punishment has been borne by another." Schleiermacher argues that both the idea of the suffering of Christ and that of the forgiveness of sins "become magical when blessedness and forgiveness are not mediated through vital fellowship with Christ." When the two are not so mediated, their connection becomes an arbitrary one. Forgiveness is taken to mean that punishment will no longer be exacted, since it has been borne by another. However, since punishment can have to do only with an arrest of the sensuous functions, the *consciousness* of guilt, which is the properly ethical element in the forgiveness of sins, would still remain. Such a consciousness "would have to disappear as if conjured away, without any reason" (*CF* §101.3, *KGA* I.13,2 116–17; 435). Because magical views do not focus on the distinction between the consciousness of guilt and punishment, they blur the line between the two. Blessedness can thereby too easily be confused with mere happiness, that is, redemption reduced to the idea of a happy eternal life, vaguely conceived of in sensuous terms, but one devoid of any ethical content.[16] And lastly, the connection between the forgiveness of sins (in the sense of no longer having to suffer punishment) and the beginning of a new life would become singularly unclear. If forgiveness is understood principally in terms of the idea that punishment will no longer be meted out, how does this, by itself, affect a person's fundamental ethical disposition?[17] The properly ethical element in the forgiveness of

---

[16] While this idea is not explicitly argued for in §101.3, it follows as a consequence of his analysis.

[17] The very same problem is discussed at length by Kant in the *Religion within the Boundaries of Mere Reason*. There Kant notes that saving faith involves two elements, the first being faith that the debt that one has incurred due to sin has been atoned for, and the second, "faith in the ability to become well-pleasing to God in a future good

sins, the consciousness of deserving punishment, can only disappear
once the person has put on Christ, that is, made Christ's fundamental motive principle (which has to do with *how* one relates to God
and neighbor) their own. In an important passage Schleiermacher
notes:

Indeed Christ's highest achievement consists in this, that He so animates us
that we ourselves are led to an ever more perfect fulfillment of the divine
will ... The true view is that the total obedience—δικαίωμα—of Christ avails
for our advantage only insofar as through it our assumption into vital fellowship with Him is brought about, and in that fellowship we are moved

conduct of life." There arises a "remarkable antinomy of human reason with itself,"
which has to do with the question of how one faith "can be derived from the other,"
that is, whether "the faith in absolution from the debt resting upon us will elicit a
good life conduct, or the true and active disposition of a good life conduct—one
to be pursued at all times—will elicit faith in the absolution" (147) Kant concludes
his analysis by claiming that "the antinomy is therefore only apparent." He is able to
conclude this, however, through a bit of carelessness or sleight of hand, by substituting
the idea of the phenomenal, historical life of Jesus (taken as an ethical paradigm) for
the problematic notion of substitutionary atonement. Kant then argues that the active
principle attributed to the historical Jesus is the very same as the idea of the moral
archetype lying in our reason. The genuine "object of the saving faith is the prototype
lying in our reason which we put in him ... and such a faith is all the same as the
principle of a good life conduct" (149). Hence Kant concludes that "we do not
have two principles that differ in themselves ... but one and the same practical idea
from which we proceed: once, so far as this idea represents the prototype as situated
in God and proceeding from him; and again, so far as it represents it as situated in
us; in both cases, however, so far as it represents the prototype as the standard
measure of our life conduct" (149–50). In Schleiermacher, the idea of the need for
an atonement is replaced with the closely related idea of *the consciousness of guilt.* This
allows Schleiermacher to make the valid inference that consciousness of guilt is done
away with as soon as one is no longer guilty, that is, once one has become incorporated
into the divine life of Christ through fellowship with him. The idea of substitutionary
atonement thereby plays no role in Schleiermacher. Neither does it, in fact, in Kant. If
one focuses on Kant's *conclusion* regarding the "remarkable antinomy," rather than
on the way that he initially sets it up, there are fundamental similarities between
Kant's treatment and that of Schleiermacher. For both, true saving faith ultimately
involves a genuine transformation of the self. Kant allows that the moral archetype
can rationally be represented as "found in God and proceeding from him, and now,
as found in us," while Schleiermacher, of course, represents this transformation as
initiated through fellowship with the redeemer, in whom there is a veritable presence
of God. It is important to note, too, that Schleiermacher also stresses that adoption
of Christ's motive principle is something that must be done *freely* (this is one of the
principal themes of §100.1), and this, too, is one of Kant's main concerns. I present a
more in-depth discussion of Kant's antinomy in my article "Kant on Grace: A Reply
to his Critics."

by Him, that is, His motive principle becomes ours—just as we also share in condemnation for Adam's sin only in so far as we, being in natural life-fellowship with him and moved in the same way, all sin ourselves.

(*CF* §104.3; *KGA* I.13, 2 139–40; 456)

The total obedience of Christ becomes our own insofar as we adopt his fundamental disposition through our vital fellowship with him. As such, guilt disappears *because* one is no longer guilty. And because one is no longer guilty, whatever arrests to the sensuous functions that occur in virtue of the natural vicissitudes of life can no longer be *taken as* punishments. Hence, the correct view recognizes the impartation of blessedness as following *naturally* from incorporation into the life of Christ (*CF* §101.3), which is the divine love working in him. The removal of misery, and consequent impartation of blessedness, are achieved in the very same action in which the motive principle of Christ, namely, that of the divine love, becomes our own.

THE MYSTICAL VIEW OF THE WORK OF CHRIST AND THE IMPORTANCE OF THE HISTORICAL ARENA

A clear understanding of how Jesus redeems first presupposes a grasp of what it is that humans need redemption from, namely, sin. Schleiermacher understands sin as the result of inattention to the influence of the higher (transcendental) God consciousness upon moments of the sensible self-consciousness. The God-consciousness is always present and in relation to the sensible self-consciousness, which is the self's consciousness of itself as related to, and inter-acting with, the world. Insofar as the God-consciousness is allowed to be effective, it conditions every moment of the sensible self-consciousness. As transcendental, the God consciousness is like a light that casts its rays on how the world is understood, valued, and felt. As discussed above, insofar as the God-consciousness involves an element of *self*-consciousness, it is the consciousness that one is not the author of one's own existence. However, this "gap" in self-consciousness (through which one comes to the consciousness of one's dependence on the absolute) is also the place at which the power of God can shine through, so to speak, into the finite. If this gap remains completely open, so that the power of the divine can pass through it, the body and all the higher functions of the human psyche (such as intelligence, will, and the emotions insofar as they are informed by the former two), become the organs of the spirit. In Christ this is complete, and this is what Schleiermacher means when he notes that in Christ the divine is completely active and the human is completely receptive; in him the human has been taken up completely and become the organ of spirit.

While this gap in the self's consciousness of itself is always present, it can become obscured through the self's thinking of itself as independent. Schleiermacher notes that sin is "an arrestment of the power of spirit due to the independence of the sensuous functions" (*CF* §66.2, *KGA* I.13,1 408; 273). The "evil condition" from which humans need redemption is an "obstruction or arrest of the vitality of the higher-consciousness, so that there comes to be little or no union of it with the various determinations of the sensible self-consciousness..." (*CF* §11.2; *KGA* I.13,1 96; 54). In the state of sin the self shuts itself off from the power of God by thinking of itself as independent, as the source of its own existence. Hence sin is first and foremost "a turning away from the creator" (*CF* §66.2, *KGA* I.13,1 408; 273). Schleiermacher's understanding of the relation of God to human beings, and the results of the sundering of this relation is, at its core, Platonic and Augustinian.[18] There are, of course, important differences. But the similarities are fundamental. The right relation of the soul to God is one in which the soul allows itself to be infused with the power of the divine (the divine love); for Schleiermacher this happens through the feeling of absolute dependence. If the self mistakes itself as independent, it cuts itself off from the source of its true life. All sin is a result of this fundamental mistake, the authority problem in relation to God.

The belief that the self is independent has several important consequences. The first of these is the identification of the self with the body, that is, with the sensuous functions. As Schleiermacher notes,

---

[18] Augustine understood Plato as putting forth the ideal that "the supreme God visits the mind of the wise with an intelligible and ineffable presence," and that the "higher light, by which the human mind is enlightened, is God" (*In Joan. Evang.*, xv.19).

if the self thinks of itself as a body, then it will think that it can be harmed. If what conditions an experience is identification with the "flesh," then "every impression made by the world upon us and invoking an obstruction of our bodily and temporal life must be reckoned as an evil." As such, identification with the body brings fear. Second, as a result of its identification with the body, the self contracts in upon itself; it is ever vigilant lest it be harmed, and it stands in constant competition with others for what it believes are finite resources necessary for the sustenance of the body. If the supremacy of the God-consciousness is done away with, "what is a furtherance to one will often for that very reason become a hindrance to the other." Yet were the God-consciousness determinative of human existence, whatever opposition the world offers to the bodily life of human beings "could never have been construed by the corporate consciousness as an obstruction to life, since it could not in any sense act as an inhibition of the God-consciousness, but at most would give a different form to its effects" (*CF* §75.1; *KGA* I.13, 472–3; 316).

Key to Schleiermacher's understanding of redemption is that the belief system associated with sin is a corporate one having corporate effects. As noted above, this belief system contains three interrelated elements: first, belief that the self is independent of God, second, identification of the self with the body, and third, belief that since the self is a mere body, it is inherently independent of others and in competition with them for finite resources. All three ideas are inherently linked. They are not only beliefs of the individual self about the self, but are in general corporate. They are beliefs ensconced and reinforced in communities about what it means to be a self. Moreover, sin is itself always a corporate action. Schleiermacher notes that sin is "in either case common to all." Sin is

not something that pertains severally to each individual and exists in relation to him by himself, but in each the work of all, and in all the work of each; and only in its corporate character can it be properly and fully understood. This solidarity means an interdependence of all places and all times in the respect we have in view. The distinctive form of original sin in the individual, as regards its quality, is only a constituent part of the form it takes in the circle to which he immediately belongs, so that, though inexplicable when taken by itself, it points to the other parts as complementary to it. And this relationship runs through all gradations of community—families, clans, tribes, peoples, and races—so that the form of sinfulness in each of these points to that present in the other parts as complementary to it . . . and whatever of that power appears in the single unit, whether personal or composite, is not to be attributed to, or explained by, that unit alone.

(*CF* §71.2, *KGA* I.13,1 431–2, 288)

Sin is never an individual affair, but rather implicates ever-widening circles of community. What the self believes about itself (and hence the actions flowing from such a self-understanding), is never independent, but rather depends, to a great degree, on how the community constructs itself as a group as well as the individuals within it. Hence the sin of one individual is never fully understandable in isolation, but always points past itself. Understanding the corporate character of sin is key to an understanding of the work of Christ; Schleiermacher importantly notes that "the denial of the corporate character of original sin and a lower estimate of the redemption wrought by Christ usually go hand in hand (*CF* §71.3, *KGA* I.13,1 434, 289). It is because human beings are so interdependent with one another that the sin of one person implicates the whole race. More importantly, the converse is also true: it just this interdependence of human beings on one another that makes it possible for the salvation of the whole race to be accomplished in the historical life of one person.

Schleiermacher's understanding of the work of Christ can be broken down into two key moments. First, Jesus strengthens each individual's God-consciousness, enabling it to dominate each moment of the sensuous self-consciousness. In other words, Jesus awakens the God-consciousness and establishes the dominance of spirit over the flesh. Second, Jesus establishes the Kingdom of God. Both moments are interdependent, so that the awakening of the God consciousness occurs through the establishment of the Kingdom of God, and the Kingdom of God is established through the awakening of the God-consciousness. One is the vertical pole—the relation to God through Christ; the other the horizontal pole, the establishment of a Christian community. Schleiermacher notes that " . . . to believe that Jesus was the Christ, and to believe that the Kingdom of God (that is, the new corporate life that was to be created by God) had come, [are] the same thing . . . " (*CF* §87.3, *KGA* I.13,2 30, 360). There is no teaching about the Kingdom that is not at the same time a teaching about Jesus himself.[19] "The original activity of the Redeemer," Schleiermacher writes, is "that by means of which He assumes us into this fellowship of His activity and His life" (*CF* §100.1, *KGA* I.13,2 105, 425). This activity is the result of the divine love in Christ, which is communicated to all those who enter into fellowship with him. As a result of the communication of this divine love, "the redemptive activity of Christ brings about for all believers a corporate activity corresponding to the being of God in Christ." The love of Christ is communicated to the believer, and the believer in turn expresses Christ's love to the members of the community of Christ, both those already within the community and those yet to be incorporated into it. Insofar as the believer shares in the blessedness of the being of God in Christ, the "former personality dies, so far as is meant a self-enclosed life of feeling within a sensuous vital unity, to which all sympathetic feeling for others and for the whole was subordinated" (*CF*, §101.2, *KGA* I.13,2 114; 433). The love of Christ is a gift to each individual; once received the person is empowered to love others through the love of Christ. As such, the love of Christ for humanity founds the community of the Kingdom of God. The "will for the Kingdom of God" is "at once love to men and love to Christ and love to God," which is at the same time "Christ's love working in and through us" (*CF* §112.3, *KGA* I.13,2 224; 520–1). It is this founding of the Kingdom that is the principle work of Christ and the manner in which he redeems humanity.

Schleiermacher's understanding of the nature of the Kingdom of God and the corporate character of human sinfulness are intimately linked, for they are inverted images of each other. A proper grasp of the nature of each presupposes an understanding of the interdependent character of what it means to be a human being. Persons are destined to become members in the Kingdom of God, where each stands in the closest possible relation to the neighbor in virtue of the divine love that each is destined to reflect and express through the God-consciousness. Human wholeness thus always depends on the relation to the neighbor. Insofar as sin is a falling short of this

---

[19] The point is also made by Jack Verheyden in his introduction to *The Life of Jesus*, xxxiv–v.

ideal—a blocking of the God-consciousness and therefore a failure to express the divine love to others—the sin of one individual always points past itself, implicating ever widening circles of community. This is because sin is a failure in love. It is a failure to appreciate the other in and through the divine love, and to recognize the other as one that—in virtue of his or her God-consciousness—is also capable of expressing the divine love. To express the divine love *just is* to recognize the other in this way. If the God consciousness is blocked, this means that the person does not recognize others in this way. And *because* the individual does not recognize the value of the other, she cannot recognize her own real value, either. For it is only in *loving* the other—and this means recognizing them *as* loving (or at least as destined to love)—that the self can recognize *itself as* loving. The value that the self ascribes to itself is thereby dependent on the way that the self understands and values others.

The sin of the individual not only has communal effects, but it *implicates* others as well. When the God-consciousness is blocked, the person fails to properly appreciate *both self and neighbor*. The failure of the self to properly value the other often has the effect that the *other* then fails to properly value and understand him or herself and others as well. This is because it is only in virtue of being *recognized* that the capacity to express the divine love is capable of actualization. Hence while the God-consciousness can properly be understood as a kind of religious a priori in the sense that it is part of the pre-existing structure of human consciousness, the historical arena functions as the only locus where it can be actualized. The ability to love can be realized only *in relation to the other*, and hence in the way that persons express themselves to one another in history. As such, the proper functioning of the God-consciousness depends upon the relation to the other; as Schleiermacher notes " ... in this Kingdom of God ... the establishment and the maintenance of the fellowship of each individual with God, and the maintenance and direction of the fellowship of all members with one another, are not separate achievements, but the same" (*CF* §102.2; *KGA* I.13,2 122, 440).

It is only insofar as the self is recognized by others as capable of love that it can begin to love; this is because consciousness of self depends, to a large degree, not only on the way that the self relates to others, but also on the way that others view the self. This is why sin is always communal. When Schleiermacher tells us that original sin "though inexplicable when taken by itself... points to the other parts as complementary to it," (*CF* §71.2, *KGA* I.13,1 431, 288), he must be referring to this fact. The failure to love is too often the result of a failure of having been loved, and the failure to love often results in the failure of others to love as well. Significantly, Schleiermacher recognized that the way that selves express themselves, and the way that persons view and thereby "construct" one another (and thereby assign value to one another) is something that becomes embedded in language and in institutions. These then become *determinative* of human activity insofar as human activity occurs through them. In the *Hermeneutics* Schleiermacher notes

The individual is determined in his thought by the (common) language and can think only the thoughts which already have their designation in this language. Another new thought could not be communicated if it were not related to relationships which already exist in the language... language determines the progress of the individual in thoughts. For language is not just a complex of single representations, but also a system of the *relatedness* of representations.[20]

Because language serves to frame the way that self and others are understood and valued, it can be an expression of human communal sinfulness when it serves to solidify ideas devaluing individuals or groups. Language picks out the aspects of things that are to be of significance to us, and in doing so shapes our responses to them. It also shapes our responses to them by relating representations to one another, that is, by sedimenting the way that we understand persons and things to be related to one another.

Schleiermacher also recognized the ethical significance of property and institutions in shaping communal values. In the *Lectures on Philosophical Ethics* he notes, regarding the whole domain of "common possession and possessed community," that all "property is sociable, and all sociability property forming, all cognition language forming, all language cognition forming, everything which shapes the emotions depictional, and all depiction capable of moving the emotions."[21] Much is said in this one sentence regarding the role of

---

[20] Schleiermacher *Hermeneutics and Criticism and Other Writings*, 9.
[21] Schleiermacher *Lectures on Philosophical Ethics*, 23.

language, property, and, by extension, institutions in shaping the way that persons view and value one another and the world around them. In thinking we unite representations with one another. Through the concepts present in language ways of uniting representations and relating them to other representations are reproduced. Linguistic concepts are thereby a common property affecting the way that all that use the language view themselves and the world around them—language is thereby "cognition forming." Moreover, all sociability is "property forming" in that it is through the mechanisms of sociability that things such as knowledge and training are created and passed on. The upshot of this discussion is that the self-expression of individuals, both in terms of language and human products, become goods held in common which in turn both shape and limit individual self-consciousness and its self-expression. As such, sin can never be an individual affair because self-consciousness is never isolated. The self becomes conscious of itself and its capabilities in the context of a pre-existing social arena that sets the parameters for the self's understanding of itself, how it is to relate to others, and its capacities for actualization. And just as sin is never just an individual affair, so too, what Schleiermacher calls "blessedness" cannot be an individual affair, either. It always occurs in the context of the community founded by Christ expressing a new way of being in the world. This new way of being achieves expression in the Word of the New Testament and in the institution of the church. Both are common possessions that condition sociability and shape the emotions.

There are, then, two fundamental reasons why it is impossible to "share in the redemption and be made blessed through Christ outside the corporate life that he instituted." Both are intrinsically related. First, the self arrives at an understanding of itself in and through its relation to others. Its concept of itself cannot be divorced from how it expresses itself in its relation to others. For instance, I can know myself as a loving self only through the activity of loving. But I grasp myself as threatened and diminished when I view myself as principally competing with others. Second, Schleiermacher is keenly aware of the fact that a person's view of self and world depend to a large degree on what is common property, i.e., language and social institutions. Language shapes the views of self and world, and institutions shape and determine, to a large degree, the character of social interactions.

In entering into the historical life of the human race, and founding a community within it, Jesus communicates the God-consciousness and the activity of divine love. Schleiermacher notes that Jesus' "higher perfection" works "in a stimulating and communicative way upon the nature which is like His own, in the first place to bring to perfection the consciousness of sinfulness by contrast with itself, and then also to remove the misery, by assimilation to itself" (*CF* §89.2; *KGA* I.13,2 29; 367). This communication is one effected in history, which just *is* the arena of communicative praxis. What Jesus communicates is the divine love; even the significance of Christ's death lies in the fact that through his death Jesus' love for the world becomes "perfectly exhibited." In a significant passage Schleiermacher notes that

For in his suffering unto death, occasioned by his steadfastness, there is manifested to us an absolutely self-denying love; and in this there is represented to us with perfect vividness the way in which God was in him to reconcile the world to himself, just as it is in His suffering that we feel most perfectly how imperturbable was His blessedness...the high priestly value of his passive obedience consists chiefly in this, that we see God in Christ, and envisage Christ as the most immediate partaker in the eternal love which sent him forth and fitted him for his task.   (*CF* §104.4; *KGA* I.13, 2 142; 458–9)

Our assimilation into the divine life of Jesus is achieved through the communication of his words and deeds. Both are the divine love effective in history; both shape human self-consciousness and being in the world. The divine love manifest in the life of the historical Jesus brings a new way of envisioning what it means to be a human being, and what it means to be in community. Through the establishment of a community that embodies and furthers Christ's words and deeds, this new way of being in the world is passed from one generation to the next and communicated to the wider world. Because of our interdependence with one another, how we understand and value one another is determinative of how we understand and value ourselves. Jesus' vision of us through the divine love *changes our self-understanding*, thereby making operative our capacity (contained in the potentiality of our God-consciousness) to express the divine love.

It is in this way that his higher perfection "stimulates" our nature, which is "like his own" (*CF* §89.2; *KGA* I.13,2 29; 367). In this way we are incorporated into his life, such that his "motive principle becomes ours" (*CF* §104.3; *KGA* I.13,2 139–40; 456). This is the solution to the dilemma posed at the beginning of this chapter. Schleiermacher provides a coherent account of how it is that the self-expression of an historical individual can provide the actual *occasion* for the turning away from evil and the beginning of a new life. I have argued that he successfully integrates the idea that a historical event can be the occasion for human transformation with his account of the God-consciousness (the transcendental basis for all human knowing and willing) as the defining capacity for all human beings. His greatness as both theologian and philosopher lies in no small measure in this achievement.

8

Outpourings of the Inner Fire: Experiential Expressivism and Religious Pluralism

Thus far we have seen that Schleiermacher's highly original contribution to ethics lies in his understanding of (a) what constitutes individuality, (b) how language and social institutions shape self-consciousness, (c) the relation of the individual to the community, and (d) the way that individuals and communities can be the occasion for self-transformation. Yet, it is important to keep in mind that all of the mature Schleiermacher's highly original ethical insights are ensconced within a larger theory bearing the traces of a Platonic and Augustinian metaphysics of the self. The fact that Schleiermacher translated Plato is no doubt of significance here. But the traces of this metaphysical view also come to Schleiermacher through his Leibnizian inheritance. Schleiermacher's understanding of self-consciousness as grounded in an absolute that both transcends and establishes it is reminiscent of the way Leibniz conceived of the relation of the monads to God: they are preserved through the divine "fulgurations." For Schleiermacher, however, it is through the immediate self-consciousness that the self stands in direct relation to the absolute, and through it receives the divine influence. It is this metaphysics of the self that is the connecting link between Schleiermacher's ethical theory and his understanding of religion, for the divine influence infuses all elements of the psyche with transformative power. There is a sense, of course, in which the divine influence is always already present. For Schleiermacher, transformation has to do with opening oneself up to it. And as we have seen in the previous chapter, for Schleiermacher the *way* the self apprehends its relation to the absolute is inherently tied to the way the self apprehends the world and relates to others. In fact, Schleiermacher understands the relation of the self to God, and the relation of the self to the neighbor as so tightly interwoven that he can say "in this Kingdom of God...the establishment and maintenance of the fellowship of each individual with God, and the maintenance and direction of the fellowship of all members with one another are not separate achievements, but the same" (*CF* §102.2; *KGA* I.13,2 122, 440). This is why he understands the self-consciousness of Jesus, manifested principally in his love for humankind, as the medium through which our own God-consciousness is freed up. We become conscious of the divine influence in and through the love of neighbor made possible by the consciousness of Christ, for it is only in love of the neighbor that this influence finds expression.

In this final chapter I would like to explore the relevance of Schleiermacher's ethics and metaphysics of the self to a contemporary problem in the philosophy of religion, namely, the question of religious pluralism. In his book *An Interpretation of Religion*, John Hick claims there is a central spiritual reality to which all the major religious traditions point. Salvation, insofar as it is conceived in terms of being in relation with the Absolute Reality, is achievable from within the context of all the world's major faiths. In his book *On Religion*, Schleiermacher makes a similar kind of claim. There Schleiermacher tells us that

I invite you to study every faith professed by man, every religion that has a name and a character. Though it may long ago have degenerated into a long series of empty customs, into a system of abstract ideas and theories, will you not, when you examine the original elements at the source, find that this dead dross was once the molten out-pourings of the inner fire? Is there not in all religions more or less of the true nature of religion, as I have presented it to you? Must not, therefore, each religion be one of the special forms which mankind, in some region of the earth and at some stage of development, has to accept?[1]

---

[1] Friedrich Schleiermacher, *On Religion: Speeches to its Cultured Despisers*, translated by John Oman, 216. In this chapter, most references to *On Religion* will be to Oman's translation of the third edition (1821) of the *Speeches*. They will be contained in the body of the chapter, indicated by *OR* Oman, followed by the page number.

Yet there are significant issues raised by this kind of proposal. How can differing traditions, making competing truth claims about the human situation and how it relates to the transcendent, all point to a central spiritual reality? If they characterize it differently, how can we know it is the same ultimate reality to which they point, or which is being experienced? Moreover, it seems that insofar as these traditions are making competing truth claims, they cannot all be right, and their not getting the facts right about the nature of the absolute may translate into a failure in helping human beings achieve salvation. Can the claim that all the major world religions point to the same absolute be defended?

Both in the *Speeches* and in *The Christian Faith* Schleiermacher offers a comprehensive theory of the nature of religion grounding it in experience. In the *Speeches* Schleiermacher grounds religion in an original unity of consciousness that precedes the subject-object dichotomy.[2] *The Christian Faith* presents a similar analysis of religion: the feeling of absolute dependence is grounded in the immediate self-consciousness. In both accounts a fundamental experience grounds religion.[3] In *The Christian Faith* Schleiermacher explains

[2] The following passage from the *Speeches* illustrates this view: "Sense and object mingle and unite, then each returns to its place, and the object rent from sense is a perception, and you rent from the object are for yourselves, a feeling. It is this earlier moment, which you always experience yet never experience. The phenomenon of your life is just the result of its constant departure and return. It is scarcely in time at all, so swiftly it passess; it can scarcely be described, so little does it properly exist" (*OR* Oman, 43).

[3] The differences between Schleiermacher's analysis of religious experience in the third edition of the *Speeches* and *The Christian Faith* have to do principally with the question of Schleiermacher's Spinozism. By the time that Schleiermacher writes *The Christian Faith* he is careful to present a panentheistic position with respect to the relation of God and world. While God is immanent in the world, God as the Whence or ground of the world is more than the world. Schleiermacher revised the *Speeches* in order to stave off charges of Spinozism. However, traces of that position still remained even in the third edition (1831) of the book. For instance he there speaks of the "One in All, and All in One, an *object that knows no other bounds but the world*" (*OR* Oman, 7, italics mine). However, differences between the two works concerning the issue of the possible validity of differing religions have more to do with presentation than with substance. Both works ground the possibility of religious experience in an analysis of a unitary moment of consciousness preceding the subject–object split. Both recognize that all religions are grounded in that experience, although some religions will be more successful in expressing and therefore mediating it. And finally, both works consider Jesus as the mediator par excellence embodying the perfection of human nature. Hence in the *Speeches* Schleiermacher

that doctrines are expressions of this fundamental experience; Christian doctrines are, for instance, "accounts of the Christian religious affections set forth in speech" (*CF* §15; *KGA* I.13,1 127; 76). This view aptly has been labeled "experiential expressivism." I want to argue that Schleiermacher's theory offers a generally coherent account of how it is possible that differing religious traditions are all based on the same experience of the absolute. My account will attempt to show how Schleiermacher's program can respond successfully to some of the contemporary objections to religious pluralism noted above. My defense of Schleiermacher's view will revolve upon three different but related points.

First there is the question of the *nature* of religious doctrines. If doctrines are truth claims that seek adequately to describe reality as it really is, then their diverging claims as to the nature of the absolute and its relation to human beings can pose a threat to the coherence of idea that all the major faith traditions have validity. On the other hand, if the meaning and purpose of doctrines is to convey an experience, in particular when that experience is of something that transcends the categories of the mundane, then it seems that it is possible that two different systems of symbolic representation can be equally adequate vehicles conveying an experience of the absolute. In the first part of this chapter, I lay out the essential elements of Schleiermacher's experiential expressivism and explore the possibilities it offers for giving a coherent account of religious pluralism.

Second, related to this first issue is the issue of interpretation. What role does it play in the shaping of the religious experience itself? How does Schleiermacher envision this role? How might Schleiermacher respond to the critic arguing that cultural and linguistic categories are so central to the possibility of experiencing the transcendent that it is impossible to find a common experience across cultural boundaries? The key to Schleiermacher's response, I will suggest, lies in his understanding of the *immediate* character of religious experience and its *a priori* character.

---

calls Jesus "the true Founder of redemption and reconciliation" that must be acknowledged by every religious individual once "His whole efficacy is shown him" (*OR* Oman, 248).

Thirdly, because two or more systems of symbolic representations may be more or less adequate expressions of the experience of the absolute, it does not follow that all are. In fact, in *The Christian Faith* Schleiermacher clearly holds the position that only Christ has complete efficacy in freeing up the God-consciousness, and that consequently Christianity most perfectly expresses the feeling of absolute dependence. While it is questionable whether Schleiermacher is warranted in making this claim on the basis of his philosophical system,[4] it is nevertheless important to have criteria to distinguish those symbol systems that are more adequate vehicles for conveying the experience of the absolute from those that are inadequate. In the last part of this chapter I will discuss how Schleiermacher envisions these criteria.

ON THE NATURE OF DOCTRINE

It is well known that there are three basic models regarding what it is that religious doctrines are. On the first model, doctrines are a set of propositions that purport to make truth claims about human beings, the world in which they find themselves, and their relation to that which transcends the world. Doctrines are thereby informative of the nature of reality, and it is through the information they convey that they are able to guide human beings on their spiritual path towards salvation. If this is the nature and function of doctrine, then assertions that differ as to the nature of the world, ultimate reality, and their interrelations cannot all be correct. Either only one is correct, perhaps all are wrong, but two conflicting assertions cannot both be right. If the Muslim insists on the absolute Oneness of God, and the

---

[4] The experiential basis of Schleiermacher's philosophy and theology does not provide a warrant for some of his Christological claims, namely, those connected with the "original divine decree," explored in the last chapter, as well as Schleiermacher's claim concerning Christ's pre-eminence as the *only* perfect mediator of the feeling of absolute dependence. The Christian community is perfectly justified in testifying to its own experience of salvation through Christ. This does not, however, provide a warrant for the claim that the *only* way of salvation for other people is through Christ, or for the pre-eminence of Christ, since such claims move significantly beyond what is grounded in experience.

Christian insists that God is triune, both assertions cannot be true. Moreover, on this model the truth-functional status of a doctrine is usually thought to have a direct effect on how much of a help or a hindrance it can be in guiding persons in their quest for the ultimate.

On the second basic model, religious doctrines do not so much seek to describe the nature of ultimate reality as either to express or evoke an experience of that reality, or to reflect upon and systematize those expressions. At the core of this understanding of doctrine is religious experience. This religious experience is then expressed in aesthetic symbolic elements that point past themselves to the transcendent. As such, the expression of this experience is subject to the influence of cultural thought forms and patterns available to the individual expressing the experience.[5] On this model two or more different symbolic systems can be equally expressive and evocative of genuine religious experience. This occurs analogously to the way that two different paintings can both be beautiful. Moreover, here we move first, from the inner experience to the outer diverse forms, and then from the outer forms back to the inner experience to which they point. Experiences expressed by two differing forms can yet be experiences of the same absolute. This model has been aptly called "experiential expressivism" by George Lindbeck.[6] While there has been some controversy concerning the exact details of Schleiermacher's model of religious doctrines, there is no doubt that at its core his model contains the basic elements described here.

A compelling exposition of a third model, dubbed by George Lindbeck as the "cultural linguistic alternative", is provided in his book *The Nature of Doctrine*. One of the ideas driving this model is that there is no such thing as an uninterpreted datum of experience.[7] The experiencing self is always already equipped with cultural

---

[5] In the first edition of the *Speeches* Schleiermacher notes "belief in God depends upon the direction of the imagination. You will know that imagination is the highest and most original element in us, and that everything besides it is merely reflection upon it; you will know that it is imagination that creates the world for you, and that you can have no God without the world" *On Religion*, translated Richard Crouter, 53.

[6] See George Lindbeck, *The Nature of Doctrine*, 31.

[7] This is a neo-Wittgensteinian understanding of religion. On this understanding the "categories" or lens through which religious experience is understood is inherently

thought forms and linguistic categories through which it interprets its experiences. There is no innocent eye; the idea that there
are "given" experiences that form a common core of religion is
simply a myth, for it is these categories that *shape* the experience, and without them experience is simply not possible at all.[8]
Hence, "religions are producers of experience."[9] Here, in contrast
to the second model, we move from the outer forms to the inner
experiences.

While the second model (experiential expressivism) captures some
of the most essential features of Schleiermacher's understanding of
religion, Schleiermacher's views on doctrines and the religious experiences upon which they depend are extremely nuanced, and are
well equipped to deflect criticisms often made against this model
by proponents of other views. In what follows I will take a closer
look at Schleiermacher's understanding of the nature of religious
doctrines. How does his development of the nature of doctrine
help us to make sense of the diversity of religious expressions, and
what resources does it offer for dialogue amongst differing faith
traditions? How well does his model fare when compared with the
other two?

Doctrines, for Schleiermacher, are always derivative. In *The Christian Faith* he notes that revelation does not operate upon us as

tied to religious *practices*. Hence there is a significant sense in which one cannot
even understand the categories, and therefore the claims (made in terms of these
categories), of a particular religion unless one is on the inside, i.e. a participant in
that religion's practices. One of its earliest philosophical proponents was Peter Winch.
See, for instance, Winch's "Meaning and Religious Language," in *Reason and Religion*,
193–221.

[8] Lindbeck puts the matter quite clearly when he notes that "When one pictures
inner experiences as prior to expression and communication, it is natural to think
of them in their most basic and elemental form as also prior to conceptualization
or symbolization. If, in contrast, expressive and communicative symbol systems,
whether linguistic or non-linguistic, are primary—then, while there are of course
nonreflective experiences, there are no uninterpreted or unschematized ones. On this
view, the means of communication and expression are a precondition, a kind of quasi-
transcendental (i.e. culturally formed) a priori for the possibility of experience. We
cannot identify, describe, or recognize experience qua experience without the use of
signs and symbols. These are necessary even for what the depth psychologist speaks
of as "unconscious" or "subconscious" experiences, or for what the phenomenologist
describes as prereflective ones" Lindbeck, *The Nature of Doctrine*, 32.

[9] Ibid. 30.

cognitive beings, "for that would make the revelation to be originally and essentially *doctrine*" (*CF* §10.3, *KGA* I.13,1 90; 50). What is
revealed is not a proposition whose function is to mirror the structure
of what is known, but an experience. This does not imply that religious doctrines, being dependent upon that experience, are merely
subjective and reflective of states of the self.[10] As Rudolph Otto,
Schleiermacher's famous disciple and commentator notes, religious
experience has a peculiarly noetic quality, since what is experienced is
"felt as objective and outside the self."[11] Nevertheless, what it is that
is experienced cannot be adequately conveyed by propositions whose
structure corresponds to the known. This is because our *knowledge*
extends only to the phenomenal realm, that is, to what is given to
us through the five senses. What is intuited in religious experience,
however, is not given through the senses. It transcends the categories
through which ordinary sense experience is apprehended and organized and hence cannot be grasped in the same way. Schleiermacher
tells us that

any possibility of God being in any way given is entirely excluded because
anything that is outwardly given must be given as an object exposed to our
counter-influence, however slight this may be ... The transference of the idea
of God to any perceptible object, unless one is all the time conscious that it is
a piece of purely arbitrary symbolism, is always a corruption, whether it be

---

[10] The point has been made by George Behrens in his article "Schleiermacher *contra* Lindbeck on the Status of Doctrinal Sentences." There he notes that "All doctrinal
sentences are about God and the world *as we experience them*. Sentences of the first
form are not so much about feelings as they are about felt relations: they express the
experienced relation between God and the world ... ", 406.

[11] Rudolph Otto, *The Idea of the Holy*, 11. Later on in the book, commenting on
Schleiermacher's understanding of intuition, Otto notes that "Wherever a mind is
exposed in a spirit of absorbed submission to impressions of 'the universe,' it becomes
capable—so he lays down—of experiencing 'intuitions' and 'feelings' (*Anschauungen*
and *Gefühle*) of something that is, as it were, a sheer overplus, in addition to empirical
reality. This overplus, while it cannot be apprehended by mere theoretic cognition of
the world and the cosmic system and the form it assumes for science, can nevertheless
be really and truly grasped and experienced in *intuition*, and is given form in single
intuitions. And these, in turn, assume shape in definite statements and propositions,
capable of a certain groping formulation, which are not without analogy with theoretic propositions, but are to be clearly distinguished from them by their free and
merely felt, not reasoned, character. In themselves they are groping intimations of
meanings figuratively apprehended," 146.

a temporary transference, i.e., a theophany, or a constitutive transference, in which God is represented as permanently a particular perceptible existence.

(*CF* §4.4, *KGA* I.13,1 40; 18)

What is given through the five senses is material that is worked on by our own consciousness. This is what Schleiermacher means when he tells us that what is *given* as an object is "exposed to our counter-influence." On the other hand, what is experienced through the feeling of absolute dependence is not an object *alongside* of other objects. Schleiermacher tells us that it must be understood as "the *Whence* of our receptive and active existence . . . " and notes that, "this 'Whence' is not the world, in the sense of the totality of temporal existence, and still less is it any single part of the world" (*CF* §4.4; *KGA* I.13,1 39; 16). It is not finite or limited by space and time and it is not an object *set over against us*. As such it cannot be grasped or encompassed by the mind and eludes apprehension through concepts; it is best apprehended through the symbol. In paragraphs 15 and 16 of *The Christian Faith* Schleiermacher notes that the original expressions of piety are the poetic or rhetorical. These contain aesthetic and symbolic elements pointing past themselves to a transcendent reality. Doctrines are the result of reflection upon these primary forms; they are "derivative and secondary" (*CF* §16.1; *KGA* I.13,1 131; 79), that is, second order propositions that are a result of reflection and systematization of first order expressions.[12] Hence, unlike the feeling of absolute dependence itself, they have been mediated and worked through by consciousness. "Dogmatic propositions," Schleiermacher notes, arise out of "logically ordered reflection upon the immediate utterances of the religious self-consciousness" (*CF* §16.3; *KGA* I.13,1 133; 81). They are the result of a process of dialectical reflection through which inconsistencies are weeded out and central tenets of the faith are given a controlling influence over subsidiary ones (*CF* §16.3, *KGA* I.13,1 132–2; 80).

---

[12] This is one of the central points of Behrens' article. He notes: "Doctrinal sentences are not themselves 'accounts' of pious self-consciousness, but the products of dialectical inquiry proceeding from such accounts to claims about God, the world, and the relation between the two" Behrens, "Schleiermacher *contra* Lindbeck on the Status of Doctrinal Sentences," 413.

If Schleiermacher is right in his characterization of religious experience as transcending ordinary experience, then there are good reasons why we cannot think of doctrines as propositions whose structure ontologically corresponds to the structure of the real. At the heart of ultimate reality is *mystery* transcending all our cognitive capacities. Hence we can only express or point to both what is intuited and its relation to the self that intuits through symbols that gesture past themselves. The symbol, like the aesthetic object, has an overplus of meaning to which no concept is ever adequate. As such only it is suited to point to the absolute, which cannot be captured in concepts but can only be alluded to through symbolic elements of the imagination. The purpose of doctrine is not to mirror the real but to give logical coherence to a system of symbols. If this is the case, then it is possible that two differing religious systems of symbolic representation and the second order doctrines that systematize them can both be valid expressions of the experience of ultimate mystery.

On the other hand, if the purpose of religious doctrines is to present an isomorphism between the "structure of knowing and the structure of the known,"[13] then insofar as two religious doctrines are *not* in agreement, they cannot both be right. As Keith Ward puts it, "To think that it [a proposition] is true is to affirm that reality is as it is described by that proposition ... Thus an affirmation by its nature excludes some possible states of affairs; namely one which would render the proposition false."[14] This is not to say that distinct religions might not be right on different points, so that no single religion has a monopoly on truth. Nonetheless, if doctrines are propositions, then the ultimate purpose of inter-religious dialogue would have to be either to convert others to the true religion, or to discover the elements of truth in each tradition. The symbolic system of rites and religious practices of each tradition would have worth only insofar as they reflected propositions deemed to be true. On this model, for instance, it would be difficult for a Christian to ascribe validity to the Muslim practice of the recitation of the Koran since the Muslim faith is at odds with Christianity on many doctrinal points.

---

[13] This is the way that Bernard Lonergan puts it in *Insight*, 399; quoted by Lindbeck in *The Nature of Doctrine*, 47.

[14] Keith Ward, "Truth and the Diversity of Religions," 110.

THE INTERPRETATION OF RELIGIOUS EXPERIENCE

Before more can be said about the resources Schleiermacher's model of religion offers for inter-religious dialogue and a sympathetic understanding of other religions, his exposition of the interplay between religious experience and culture needs to be discussed in more depth. An exploration of this point will also allow us to compare Schleiermacher's model of the nature of doctrine with so-called cultural–linguistic approaches. The first and most important point that must be made in this regard is the fact that the feeling of absolute dependence is *immediate*, that is, it is not mediated by the work of consciousness. As noted above, it is not given in sensuous experience in such a way that we could exert our counter-influence (through the interpretive work of consciousness) upon it. If we were to exert such a counter-influence, then the feeling would not be of *absolute* dependence. This means, then, that the foundational religious experience remains pure, that is, it is unaffected by cultural and linguistic categories. These come into play only when the experience is being *expressed*. This is the fundamental point of difference between Schleiermacher's model of religion and the cultural–linguistic model. On the latter view, *all* experience is subject to the work of consciousness and as such is interpreted. There can be no such thing as an *immediate* self-consciousness or an unmediated feeling of absolute dependence. Hence strictly speaking we cannot posit a fundamentally similar experience at the ground of different religious symbols since *all* experience has been shaped and molded by historically determined and contingent cultural categories.

Note that in insisting on the *unmediated* character of the feeling of absolute dependence, Schleiermacher avoids one of the principal difficulties faced by John Hick in his attempt to link diverse religious traditions to the experience of a single ultimate. According to Hick, all religious experience is interpreted and the Real in itself is unknown and unknowable in our present state.[15] As pointed out

---

[15] This is the position that Hick seems to advocate in his *An Interpretation of Religion*. There he writes: "It follows from this distinction between the Real as it is in itself and as it is thought and experienced through our religious concepts that we cannot apply to the Real *an sich* the characteristics encountered in its *personae* and *impersonae* . . . None of the concrete descriptions that apply within the realm of

by many of Hick's critics, however, on this view there is a problem in linking the phenomenal manifestations of religion to the Real in itself.[16] If all experience is interpreted, how are we to know that diverse religious traditions all point to the same Ultimate? Strictly speaking we cannot, since we have no access to that Ultimate as it is in itself. Schleiermacher, on the other hand, insists that the feeling of absolute dependence is immediate. As such, it is an experience not subject to the interpretive work of consciousness. But if it is immediate, what thematic access do we have to it?[17] And insofar as we are able to represent it thematically, then do not all the facts concerning the conditioned nature of the interpretation of experience again apply?

Although the foundational religious experience is immediate, Schleiermacher has a good deal to say about the relation of the feeling of absolute dependence to the *activity* of consciousness, and hence to the categories through which consciousness interprets and appropriates experience. Very much like transcendental Thomists such as Rahner,[18] Schleiermacher insists that while the feeling of absolute dependence is itself unmediated, it can only really make an appearance when what he calls the sensible self-consciousness has been fully developed. Shortly after introducing the feeling of absolute dependence in *The Christian Faith*, he discusses three grades of consciousness: (1) the confused, animal grade of consciousness; (2) the consciousness of an antithesis between the self and the world; and (3) the higher consciousness, that is, the consciousness of absolute dependence. In the confused, animal grade of consciousness there is no clear distinction between "the objective and introversive, or feeling

---

human experience can apply literally to the unexperienceable ground of that realm," 246.

[16] See, for instance, George A. Netland, "Professor Hick on Religious Pluralism." The problem is also discussed at length by Sumner B. Twiss in "The Philosophy of Religious Pluralism: A Critical Appraisal of Hick and His Critics." Phil Quinn discusses a similar problem in his "Toward Thinner Theologies: Hick and Alston on Religious Diversity."

[17] This is, of course, the main challenge put forward by Hegel to Schleiermacher's system. On this point see Richard Crouter, "Hegel and Schleiermacher at Berlin: A Many Sided Debate," in *Friedrich Schleiermacher: Between Enlightenment and Romanticism*, 70–97.

[18] See Karl Rahner, *The Foundations of the Christian Faith*.

and perception" (*CF* §5.1, *KGA* I.13,1 42; 18), precisely because there is no *self*-consciousness. In other words, in order to be able to distinguish between self and world, consciousness must be able to make itself its own object. Only then can it distinguish itself from what is other than itself. This is precisely what is lacking in this confused animal grade of consciousness. In the second grade of consciousness there is self-consciousness, and hence a grasp of the antithesis between the self and the world. The third grade of consciousness is the higher consciousness, which we have already noted is *immediate*. Now interestingly enough Schleiermacher claims that it is only in relation to the sensible self-consciousness that the higher consciousness can make an appearance:

It is impossible to claim a constancy for the highest self-consciousness, except on the supposition that the sensible self-consciousness is always conjoined with it...It means rather a co-existence of the two in the same moment, which, of course, unless the Ego is to be split up, involves a reciprocal relation of the two. It is impossible for anyone to be in some moments exclusively conscious of his relations within the realm of the antithesis, and in other moments of his absolute dependence in itself and in a general way; for it is as a person determined for this moment in a particular manner within the realm of the antithesis that he is conscious of his absolute dependence. This relatedness of the sensibly determined to the higher self-consciousness in the unity of the moment is the consummating point of the self-consciousness.

(*CF* §5.3, *KGA* I.13,1 46; 21)

This passage is important in several regards. First it allows us to understand what Schleiermacher means by the *immediate* self-consciousness, a term which, unaccompanied by further explanation, seems to make little sense. What can this possibly mean, since *self*-consciousness must always be mediated? Unless Schleiermacher is simply confused, he must be referring to the higher consciousness, which is itself always immediate, but which can only develop when consciousness recognizes the realm of the antithesis between self and world and is therefore *self*-conscious. This higher consciousness is transcendental, and as such can never become an object *for* consciousness. Insofar as it is the *whence* of both our active and receptive existence, it is always in the background. Nonetheless, the individual must be conscious of the antithesis between self and world in order thereby to intuit the unity of the ground of both activity and receptivity.

Second, this passage provides the basis for Schleiermacher's claim that religion must always be positive. The claim is made both in *The Christian Faith* and in the fifth Speech of *On Religion*. In the latter Schleiermacher notes that "the positive religions are just the definite forms in which religion must exhibit itself... in the positive religions alone a true individual cultivation of the religious capacity is possible" (*OR* Oman 217). The reason why this is so is explained in the passage given above from *The Christian Faith*. The higher consciousness can only exist insofar as it is related to the antithesis of the sensible self-consciousness between self and world. Hence there can be no development of the higher consciousness that is not *situated*, that does not develop in relation to the sensible self-consciousness. Schleiermacher tells us that this relation between the higher consciousness and the sensible self-consciousness is "the consummating point of self-consciousness." It is in the realm of the sensible self-consciousness, however, that there is a distinction between subject and object. Objects are given to consciousness through perception, but consciousness must take them up and make sense of them through interpretive categories. Many of these categories are contingent and develop historically; religious symbols are one of the products of the work of consciousness on the material given to it. As Schleiermacher notes in the *Speeches*, even the consciousness of the individual in whom the activity of the higher consciousness is most developed has an historical development influencing the expression of religion:

Is not then a characteristic personality born with the religious life? There is a definite connection with a past, a present and a future. The whole subsequent religious life is linked in this way to that moment and that state in which this feeling surprised the soul. It thus maintains its connection with the earlier, poorer life, and has a natural, uniform development.   (*OR* Oman 227)

The diversity of religious expression is thereby inevitable.[19]

---

[19] Schleiermacher notes that "you must abandon your vain and foolish wish that there should only be one religion" and "lay aside all repugnance of its multiplicity" *OR* Oman, 214.

Schleiermacher's account is subtle and nuanced; as such it can accommodate many of the insights of the cultural–linguistic approach to understanding religion and doctrine. Religions have a historical development and as such are subject to the influence of linguistic, cultural, sociological and psychological factors. There is an important sense in which they provide interpretive categories through which religious feelings (at the level of the antithesis) are understood. Moreover, many of the criticisms leveled against experiential expressivism do not apply to it. Lindbeck, for instance, hints that on this model one can be "religious in general"[20] and sees this as a drawback. It should be clear by now that this is not Schleiermacher's position. For Schleiermacher the experience of religion always takes place in a given context. Only thus can it be a genuinely *human* experience. While there is no doubt that for Schleiermacher there is a religious *a priori*, this a priori does not become operative in a vacuum. Given that we are concrete socio-historical individuals, there is no "view from nowhere" in religion. Each experience is a *situated* experience of the transcendent; that situatedness cannot be abstracted from the experience. In the fifth Speech Schleiermacher notes that "as long as we occupy a place there must be in these relations of man to the whole a nearer and a farther, which will necessarily determine each feeling differently in each life" (*OR* Oman, 217). However, the fact that religious experience is always situated does not imply that believers from two differing traditions are not experiencing the same thing. My perception of any given object will be situated from a given perspective, and that perspective will be different from yours; it does not follow, however, that *what* is experienced is different. The situation is analogous with respect to religious experience.

SCHLEIERMACHER'S CRITERIA OF GENUINE RELIGIOUS EXPERIENCE

Two things must be noted about Schleiermacher's use of the terms "a nearer and a farther" in relation to the transcendent. First, his

[20] Lindbeck, *The Nature of Doctrine*, 23.

use of this language makes it clear that the religious experience is *of* something and hence religious language, while necessarily symbolic because of the nature of its object, is about *something* and hence has a noetic quality. It is not merely about the feeling states of the subject. Second, given that the religious experience is first and foremost a transcendental one, Schleiermacher's language of a "nearer and a farther" must be understood metaphorically; there is no thematized *object* relating to a subject. Nevertheless, it is clear that what Schleiermacher means to say is that some religious experiences are better manifestations of the feeling of absolute dependence than others.

We have already pointed out the transcendental character of the highest self-consciousness through which the feeling of absolute dependence is experienced. The transcendental nature of this experience further implies that it is given *a priori*. Schleiermacher tells us in *The Christian Faith* that "The highest self-consciousness is in no wise dependent on outwardly given objects which may affect us at one moment and not at another. As a consciousness of absolute dependence it is quite simple, and remains self-identical while all other states are changing" (*CF* §5.3, *KGA* I.13,1 45; 21). Moreover, the consciousness of absolute dependence "accompanies our whole existence" and "is never zero" (*CF* §4.3, *KGA* I.13,1 38; 16). All religious phenomena are in one way or another grounded in this religious *a priori*. Even the religions "of the lower levels" are expressions, howsoever flawed and limited they may be, of piety. Hence Schleiermacher insists that "we must never deny the homogeneity of all these products of the human spirit, but must acknowledge the same root even for the lower powers" (*CF* §8.4; *KGA* I.13,1 72; 38).

Since the feeling of absolute dependence is always self-identical, it cannot, of itself, account for the diversity of religious expressions. The difference between them lies in how this feeling of absolute dependence actualizes itself in a given moment through its relation to a moment of the sensible self-consciousness. Given that the moments of the sensible self-consciousness are infinitely various, there is infinite variety in the expression of piety (*CF* §5.4; *KGA* I.13,1 47–9; 22, see also §9.1). Nonetheless, each moment of the sensible self-consciousness is in principle related to the higher consciousness.

The question is the degree to which that relation to the higher consciousness dominates the moment. Hence sin is understood as "God-forgetfulness," and is defined as the blocking of the influence of the higher (transcendental) consciousness upon moments of the sensible self-consciousness.[21] Yet even in the case of God-forgetfulness, the feeling of absolute dependence is never at zero, for if it were "the lack of a thing which lay outside one's nature could not be felt to be an evil condition" (*CF*§11.2, *KGA* I.13,1 96; 54). Characteristic of the religious a priori is thus a kind of élan pushing it towards its fullest self-realization in its relation to the sensible self-consciousness. Schleiermacher would no doubt agree with Augustine's pithy statement that "our hearts are restless until they rest in Thee," that is, the arrest of the God-consciousness is felt as an *evil condition*, and as such spurs consciousness on to its remedy, namely the freeing up of the God-consciousness.

Given what has been said so far, it is clear that for Schleiermacher the difference between religions lies principally in the *degree* to which they are able to manifest the feeling of absolute dependence. In a telling passage he notes that "since Christianity affirms that only perfect love casts out all fear, it must admit that imperfect love is never entirely free from fear." Likewise even those polytheistic religions in which idols serve as protectors are manifestations of imperfect love; they are adaptations, "corresponding to imperfect love, of the feeling of absolute dependence" (*CF* §8.4; *KGA* I.13,1 71; 38). Noteworthy here are two things important to Schleiermacher's criteria for the adequacy of religions. First, the feeling of absolute dependence is related to the Christian understanding of love, and as such these criteria are going to be associated in important ways with the moral fruits that each religion yields. Second, the criteria for the adequacy of religions must therefore be able to gauge differences in the *degree* to which they convey the feeling of absolute dependence.

Before Schleiermacher divides religions into two major kinds, the aesthetic and the teleological, he provides a general account of the

---

[21] Schleiermacher notes that "the evil condition can only consist in an obstruction or arrest of the vitality of the higher self-consciousness, so that there comes to be little or no union of it with the various determinations of the sensible self-consciousness, and thus little or no religious life." *CF* §11.2, *KGA* I.13,1 96; 54.

causes for differences in how religious objects are conceived. He notes that there are two major factors influencing how the religious object is thought: first, the *extensiveness* of the self-consciousness, and second, the clarity with which the difference between the lower and the higher self-consciousness is held in view. If an individual identifies him or herself with only part of the world, he or she will think of only *part* of the world as dependent upon a correspondingly limited deity, and hence "his God will remain a fetish" (*CF* §8.2; *KGA* I.13,1 67–8; 36). On the other hand, if the higher self-consciousness is not clearly distinguished from the lower, that to which the feeling of absolute dependence corresponds will mistakenly be taken to be the world or an object in it instead of that which fully transcends it.[22]

This analysis has implications for Schleiermacher's major division of religions into the teleological and the aesthetic. Key to his distinction between the two kinds of religion are the concepts of passivity and spontaneity. To be passive is to be affected from without; in being conscious of my passivity I think of my character and habits as the result of intra-worldly causes. I am what I am because something outside me has made me that way. Schleiermacher links an emphasis on such passivity to the aesthetic type of religion. This kind of religion develops when the higher self-consciousness is not distinguished from the lower; hence the individual sees him or herself as dependent upon intra-worldly objects or causes. Schleiermacher notes that "It [an aesthetic form of faith] will reduce both these arrestments and continued developments of the God-consciousness, as indeed every other change in man's experience, to passive states, and represent them consequently as the effects of external influences in such a manner that they will appear simply to be appointed events" (*CF* §63.1; *KGA* I.13,1 395; 262). In teleological religion, on the other hand, all passive states are simply occasions for *spontaneous* activity. Such activity is *not* the result of intra-worldly causes and thus is linked with genuine human freedom. Schleiermacher associates this

---

[22] So Schleiermacher: "Idol-worship proper is based upon a confused state of the self-consciousness which marks the lowest condition of man, since in it the higher and the lower are so little distinguished that even the feeling of absolute dependence is reflected as arising from a particular object to be apprehended by the senses" *CF* §8.2, *KGA* I.13,1 67; 35.

spontaneous activity with that which transcends the subject-object dichotomy (and thus anything that appears *in* the world) and which can only be given in the immediate self-consciousness, that is, with the Whence of our active and passive existence. He explicitly notes that "no one can doubt that the results of free activity take place in virtue of absolute dependence" (*CF* §49.1, *KGA* I.13, 1 295, 190). It is only insofar as we are absolutely dependent on the ground of all that is that we are able to recognize ourselves as free, that is, as not determined by intra-worldly causes. Moreover, we can only achieve the feeling of absolute dependence insofar as we are freely acting agents. Schleiermacher notes that "the God-consciousness surely... has a content which relates exclusively to human freedom and presupposes it" (*CF* §62.2; *KGA* I.13,1 393; 260). Freedom, in the sense of independence from intra-worldly causes, is a condition of the possibility the God-consciousness. Freedom and absolute dependence mutually condition and imply one another.

In Christianity, considered by Schleiermacher the teleological religion par excellence, "the consciousness of God is always related to the totality of active states in the idea of a Kingdom of God" (*CF* §9.2; *KGA* I.13,1 78–9; 43). Moreover, this freedom is closely associated with morality; in teleological religion "a predominating reference to the moral task constitutes the fundamental type of the religious affections" (*CF* §9.1; *KGA* I.13,1 77; 42). In aesthetic religion, on the other hand, an individual's actions are taken as resulting from "a determination of the individual by the whole of finite existence, and thus as referred to the passive side ... " (*CF* §9.1; *KGA* I.13,1 78; 42). It is interesting that Schleiermacher considers Greek polytheism the religion most clearly antithetical to Christianity, since in it even the beauty of the soul is "the result of all the influences of Nature and world" (*CF* §9.2; *KGA* I.13,1 79; 43).

Schleiermacher's distinction between spontaneity and passivity was no doubt influenced by Kant's ethics, which sharply differentiated between heteronomy and autonomous moral action.[23] In heteronomous action the individual allows his actions to be determined

---

[23] As discussed in the first chapter, the distinction is developed by Kant both in the *Groundwork for the Metaphysics of Morals*, and in the second *Critique*. In the second *Critique* Kant notes that "autonomy of the will is the sole principle of all moral laws and of the duties conforming to them; *heteronomy* of choice, on the other hand, not

by what Kant calls the lower faculty of desire, itself constituted by our receptivity and hence by how we can be *affected* from without. Autonomous moral action, on the other hand, is possible only insofar as we are free, that is insofar as our motives for action are not determined by intra-worldly causes. Not only is freedom the *ratio essendi* of the moral law,[24] but the free will of necessity stands under the obligation of the moral law. Moreover, insofar as an individual's actions are not merely *reactions* to how s/he has been affected by outside causes, s/he acts morally, for there is only one categorical imperative that the will as practical reason can *give itself*.[25] In the *Religion within the Boundaries of Mere Reason* Kant notes that the "very incomprehensibility of this predisposition [i.e. to be moved to action by the moral law] proclaiming as it does a divine origin, must have an effect on the mind, even to the point of exaltation, and must strengthen it for the sacrifices which respect for duty may perhaps impose on it."[26] In *The Conflict of the Faculties* he tells us that "grace is none other than the nature of the human being in so far as he is determined to actions by a principle which is intrinsic to his own being, but supersensible (the thought of his duty)."[27]

Now while the later Schleiermacher emphasizes the autonomous character of religion, distinguishing it from metaphysics and morals, his thinking about religion still has important points of contact with that of Kant: teleological religion is characterized through its emphasis on *spontaneity* and this spontaneity implies a reference to the moral task. While Schleiermacher's early ethical writings espoused a deterministic empirical psychology in which previous states of

---

only does not establish any obligation but is opposed to the principle of obligation and to the morality of the will," *KprV* 5:33; 33.

[24] In the *Critique of Practical Reason* Kant famously notes that "though freedom is certainly the *ratio essendi* of the moral law, the latter is the *ratio cognoscendi* of freedom," *KprV* 5:5; 4.

[25] This is Kant's reciprocity thesis, developed in the second *Critique*. There Kant claims "freedom and unconditioned practical law reciprocally imply one another," *KprV* 5:30; 29.

[26] Immanuel Kant, *Religion within the Boundaries of Mere Reason* 6:50, in *Religion and Rational Theology*, 93–4.

[27] Immanuel Kant, *The Conflict of the Faculties* 7:43, in *Religion and Rational Theology*, 268.

consciousness determine later ones,[28] by the time he writes *The Chris-tian Faith* he no longer holds this view. There he quite clearly notes, "every original ideal which arises in the soul, whether for an action or for a work of art, and which can neither be understood as an imitation nor be satisfactorily explained by means of external stimuli and *pre-ceding mental states*, may be regarded as a revelation" (*CF* §10.2; *KGA* I.13,1 91; 51, italics mine). Hence a revelation, which can include both moral and aesthetic elements, is something original in that it cannot merely be explained as a result of intra-worldly causes or previous states of consciousness; in revelation that which transcends the world breaks into consciousness through the immediate consciousness of the absolute.

For Schleiermacher spontaneity is the condition of one's becoming conscious of one's absolute dependence. Love is a function of the feeling of absolute dependence: the more conscious one is of absolute dependence, the more perfect is one's love. Hence the best measure for gauging a religion's effectiveness in freeing the God-consciousness lies within the realm of ethics. When the feeling of absolute depen-dence on that which transcends the world is blocked, one is in a state of captivity or constraint. Associated with this captivity or constraint is an understanding of oneself as merely receptive, that is, as simply reacting to intra-worldly causes. As a result of the confusion between the higher and lower consciousness, the individual understands her-self as passive, as under the control of *outside* influences that have led her to be what she is. On the other hand, when the distinction between the higher and lower consciousness is properly maintained, the individual comes to understand herself as absolutely dependent on that power which *transcends* the world while yet being immanent to it. This leads the individual to understand herself as *free* vis à vis the world and empowers her to accomplish the moral task set to her as a member of the Kingdom of God. In fact, even the idea of such a Kingdom is defined by Schleiermacher in terms of the *activity* of its subjects (*CF* §9.2; *KGA* I.13,1 78–9; 43).

The connections between the constraint of the God-consciousness, the view of oneself as *merely receptive* and therefore dependent upon the world, and the blocking of love in a systematic fashion are

---

[28] On this point see Chapter 1.

explored by Schleiermacher in his discussion of sin. In what ways does
the understanding of oneself as merely passive lead to fear, the opposite of love? What are the connections between self-transcendence,
spontaneity, and love towards one's fellow human beings? In his discussion of sin Schleiermacher makes use of the Pauline distinction
between flesh and spirit. The flesh is our bodily nature subject to
corruption and determination by intra-worldly causes. The spirit,
on the other hand, is associated with the God-consciousness. Sin
is "an arrestment of the determinative power of spirit, due to the
independence of the sensuous functions." This view of sin is "certainly
reconcilable with those explanations which describe sin as turning
away from the creator" (*CF* §66.2, *KGA* I.13,1 408; 273). In giving
free rein to the sensuous desires one invests the limited and bodily
with worth, ignoring what transcends the world and is of true worth.
Hence sin is associated with an identification of oneself with the
sensuous functions, that is, with the body. As such, anything that
threatens the body and everything associated with it will be perceived as a real threat and will engender fear. Schleiermacher notes
that if

the predominant factor is not the God-consciousness but the flesh, every
impression made by the world upon us and invoking an obstruction of our
bodily and temporal life must be reckoned as an evil, and the more so, the
more definitely the moment of experience terminates solely in the flesh apart
from the higher consciousness.   (*CF* §75.1; *KGA* I.13,1 472; 316)

On the other hand, were every moment of our existence determined
by the God-consciousness, the relative opposition between the external world and the temporal life of man "could never have been
construed by the corporate consciousness as an obstruction to life,
since it could not in any sense act as an inhibition of the God-
consciousness, but at most would give a different form to its effects"
(*CF* §75.1; *KGA* I.13,1 472; 315). Identification of the self with the
higher consciousness has three effects, all interrelated with each other.
First, not to identify oneself with the body results in freedom from
the bondage of the fear of death (*CF* §75.1; *KGA* I.13,1 472; 316),
since one has identified oneself with spirit, which is incorruptible and
cannot be threatened. Second, to see oneself as absolutely dependent
on the ground of being, which transcends the world, allows one to

understand oneself as subject to a higher destiny and t
free in relation to the world. Third and most importantl
one's absolute dependence on the Whence of our existenc
to transcend ourselves. We are no longer bound to identify
with the body, which has a particular causal history and particular
sensuous desires associated with that causal history.[29] Insofar as we
must also recognize others as capable of becoming conscious of their
absolute dependence, we must value them as we value ourselves. In
this way identification with the spirit engenders a completely different
attitude to the world and others in it than identification with the
body.

Thus far I have discussed how Schleiermacher envisions the nature
of doctrines, issues linked to the problem of the interpretation of the
religious experience, and Schleiermacher's criteria for the adequacy
of religions. Given what has been said so far, we need to take a
closer look at how this model accommodates religious pluralism and
dialogue among different religious traditions. I have shown that for
Schleiermacher at the core of all religions is an *unmediated* experience
of the ground of all that is (the whence of our active and receptive
existence). Differences in religions amount to the extent to which they
can adequately convey the experience of absolute dependence upon
this ground; they are differences in degree, not in kind. It is because
there *is* a single, fundamental experience to which all the world's
religions are related that there can be meaningful and significant
dialogue among them. The alternative is to think of the relations
between world religions as "family resemblances." On this view categories of religious thought may be so different across religions that
they may not even be equipped to pick out the same things. If, on the
other hand, there is a fundamental human experience grounding religion, then the question is how well the different religious traditions
express it and facilitate that experience's influence on all aspects of
life.

It might be asked: if the foundational religious experience is immediate, then how are we to gauge the adequacy of a religious tradition? We have no *thematic* access to this experience, and hence it is

---

[29] As Schleiermacher notes, "the flesh has to do with the particular only and knows
nothing of the general ... " (*CF* §68.1, *KGA* I.13,1 413; 276).

impossible to reflect upon that experience in its immediacy. How then are we to understand how well a religious tradition expresses this experience and how are we to compare religions? Do we not need to be able to reflect on *both* the initial experience and its expression in order to measure the adequacy of a religious tradition's expression of the experience? If so, then it would seem that it would be impossible to make these kinds of judgments. Problems similar to those plaguing John Hick's understanding of the absolute as a thing in itself would then seem to crop up again in a different guise. In what sense can we *know* this experience and that to which it points? Is not all knowledge thematic?

Schleiermacher's resources for answering these questions lie in his systematic discussion of why religions must always be positive. As noted above his analysis hangs on a transcendental theory of consciousness: such a consciousness exists only in relation to the sensible self-consciousness. In fact, only *as such* can it be transcendental. States of the sensible self-consciousness to which we do have thematic access therefore reflect relations to the higher (transcendental) consciousness. Hence Schleiermacher tells us that "...the world will be a different thing to a man according as he apprehends it from the standpoint of a God-consciousness completely paralyzed or of one absolutely paramount" (*CF* §64.2; *KGA* I.13,1 400; 267). While the experience of absolute dependence is immediate and transcendental, how one understands the world is dependent upon the relation of the God-consciousness to the sensible self-consciousness. This is because the transitions between all moments of the sensible self-consciousness take place in the immediate self-consciousness, through which the self stands in direct relation to the absolute. Schleiermacher concludes "it will accordingly be possible to distinguish in the Christian life itself between what in our conception of the world is to be placed to the account of sin, and what to the account of grace. The like holds good also of the results of man's action upon the world as far as these are realities to himself and come within his consciousness" (*CF* §64.2; *KGA* I.13,1 400; 267). Because transitions between the moments of self-conscious life are susceptible to the divine influence, how one acts in the world and treats others will be dependent upon the strength of the God-consciousness. Hence Schleiermacher importantly notes that the works of the second table of the law, which have to do with the treatment of the neighbor, "are in no sense external or carnal; they are truly spiritual works, and are possible only in virtue of an efficacious and purified God-consciousness" (*CF* §70.3; *KGA* I.13,1, 426; 285). Without the God-consciousness action in accordance with the second table of the law might indeed invoke "the most consummate self-renunciation of the individual." This, however, would only be "the self-love of the nation or the country as a composite person," which may very well be combined with "animosity and injustice of all kinds towards those who are outside the group" (*CF* §70.3; *KGA* I.13,1 426; 284–5).

Schleiermacher's transcendental analysis of consciousness allows him to provide criteria of adequacy for religious traditions: it is insofar as they adequately reflect human transcendence and freedom that they can also thereby adequately point to the ground of all that is. While the experience of absolute dependence is immediate and no thematic access can be had to it, whether or not one is open to the higher consciousness has concrete manifestations on the level of the sensuous self-consciousness. These have to do with how one views oneself and one's relation to the world around one. Religious symbol systems reflect these views. Principal among the questions reflected therein are whether one should identify oneself with the body and the effects of the material world on it, or whether one should identify oneself with that which transcends the world. To understand the self as only a body will engender fear because the body can be destroyed. Such an understanding, moreover, implies a denial of the possibility of self-transcendence. On the other hand, identi-fication of the self with that which transcends the body, the finite and the particular, is a condition of the possibility of genuine love. In viewing others as one views oneself, as loci of self-transcendence, one values them precisely because they have the possibility of recognizing their absolute dependence on the Whence of all that is. As such it is through the higher consciousness that genuine love of the neighbor is possible. In an important passage Schleiermacher notes that if the God-consciousness is perfectly dominant

Just as little again could the action of one person prove a hindrance to another's life, since, in virtue of the God-consciousness that was supreme in all, each could not but acquiesce in the other's every action. But if that supremacy is done away, there emerges opposition between the individual beings, and what is a furtherance to one will often for that very reason become a hindrance to the other.   (*CF* §75.1; *KGA* I.13,1 473; 316)

If the idea of self-transcendence and freedom from determination by intra-worldly causes yields a concrete ethic, namely one of love, then Schleiermacher's theology provides the basis for a theoretical justification of how an individual's relation to the absolute affects his/her relation to others and vice versa. As such his theology provides a concrete proposal for comparing and gauging the adequacy of different traditions. Religious traditions are adequate vehicles expressing the God-consciousness insofar as they affirm (1) the self-transcendence of the individual (2) the individual's freedom from complete determination by the world (3) love of the neighbor as one loves oneself. These should not be understood as mere theoretical propositions. Their true efficacy lies in the practical realm, in how they determine our understanding of ourselves, of others, and of the world. This understanding in turn determines how and what we will value, and therefore how we will act.

Schleiermacher's theology allows us to understand how different historically situated religious traditions can provide access to the absolute. Moreover, because God cannot be an *object* of our experience, the idea that we can simply have propositional knowledge of God and God's relation to the world is beset with difficulties. Yet Schleiermacher's philosophical theology provides a coherent account of how it is that the absolute can be experienced and talked about if this is the case. Because genuine religion is based on immediate experience, which must be interpreted through the imagination— itself shaped by history, culture, and language—it is impossible to arrive at a universal theology. It may, however, be possible to arrive at a universal *praxis*. Working from there we may be enabled to measure the adequacy of religious traditions in reflecting upon this experience.

Concluding Remarks

As I have shown in this book, Schleiermacher's ethics cannot be separated from his metaphysical commitments. His vision is a holistic one integrally relating the way that the self relates to the transcendent ground with the way that the self relates to others. The two domains cannot be separated without seriously compromising either one. Without a grasp of how the self relates to the transcendent ground, ethics ignores the source of the fundamental energy that informs and transforms the self, and which makes genuine communication between persons possible. However, without an understanding of how this energy is to be redirected into the world, an exploration of the self's relation to the transcendent degenerates into an empty mysticism bearing no ethical fruit.

Schleiermacher's vision is a powerful one. It recognizes both the reality and importance of religious experience, but places this experience in the context of human finitude. His philosophical ethics emphasizes that it is *individuals*—in all their finitude and historically conditioned particularity—who are the essential building blocks of community. A grasp of the historically conditioned particularity of both the self and the groups with which it identifies is a precondition for genuine dialogue with others. Only in this way is an acknowledgement and valuation of the culturally and religiously different other possible. Otherwise the self must either withdraw from others or attempt to impose its own vision of the world on them, for without the recognition of the role that finitude plays in all our cognitions, we can too easily come to the conclusion that if we are to be right, then others must be wrong. This is especially the case with respect to religion, which plays such a large role in many of the crises we face today.

Religion can too easily lead to violence when historically conditioned apprehensions of the absolute are mistaken for the absolute itself, and when these claims to absolute truth are then taken as an excuse either to engage in outright violence or to seize political power in order to impose a particular religious agenda on others. The same dangerous dynamic is found in religious fundamentalisms of all stripes, from Christian Reconstructionism, to Islamic fundamentalism, to Hindutva.

Ironically, religious fundamentalism is only abetted by those who espouse a closed naturalism and trenchantly deny the validity of religious experience altogether. It is well known that fundamentalism is a reaction to modernity and post-modernity; among other things, many fundamentalists are often trying to find meaning in their lives given both what they find to be the bewildering pronouncements of modern science as well as their contact with radically different others. Many are drawn to fundamentalist systems since such systems at least recognize the validity of their religious experience. Without a nuanced view such as Schleiermacher's, which both recognizes the validity of this experience and yet puts it in the context of human finitude, too many persons can be easily lured by what fundamentalism has to offer. Schleiermacher's philosophy is not only significant for his account of religious experience and its foundational role in religion, however. As I have argued in this book, his metaphysics of the self and account of self-consciousness also provide the foundations of an ethical system that stands as a powerful alternative to the usual ethical fare. It is my hope that this book will interest others in his work.

Bibliography

Primary Sources

Fichte, Johann Gottlieb. *Fichte: Early Philosophical Writings.* Edited and translated by Daniel Breazeale. Ithaca: Cornell University Press, 1988, 2nd edn., 1993.

—— *The Vocation of Man.* Edited by Roderick Chisholm. Indianapolis: Bobbs-Merrill, 1956.

—— *Wissenschaftslehre nova methodo* (student lecture transcripts, 1796–9). *Foundations of Transcendental Philosophy (Wissenschaftslehre) nova methodo.* Edited and translated by Daniel Breazeale. Ithaca: Cornell University Press, 1992.

Hume, David. *A Treatise of Human Nature.* Edited by L. A. Selby-Bigge, with revised text by P. H. Nidditch. Oxford: Oxford University Press, 1978.

Jacobi, F. H. *F. H. Jacobi: The Main Philosophical Writings and the Novel Allwill.* Includes complete major texts from original editions, with original pagination, historical and critical notes, extensive bibliography, and a complete list of Jacobi's publications. Translated and edited by George di Giovanni. Montreal and Kingston: McGill-Queen's University Press, 1994.

—— *Werke.* Edited by F. Roth and F. Köppen. Leipzig: G. Fleischer, 1815. Reprint, Darmstadt: Wissenschaftliche Buchgesellschaft, 1968.

Jaucourt, Le Chevalier de. "Histoire de la Vie et des Ouvrages de L'Auteur." In Leibniz, *Essais de Theodicée.*

Kant, Immanuel. *Critique of Pure Reason.* Translated by Paul Guyer and Allen W. Wood. Cambridge: Cambridge University Press, 1998.

—— *Critique of Practical Reason.* Translated by Lewis White Beck. New York: Macmillan Publishing, 1993.

—— *The Conflict of the Faculties.* Translated by Mary J. Gregor and Robert Anchor, in di Giovanni and Wood, eds., *Religion and Rational Theology,* pp. 235–327.

—— *Groundwork for the Metaphysics of Morals.* Edited and translated by Allen W. Wood. New Haven: Yale University Press, 2002.

—— *Kants gesammelte Schriften,* herausgegeben von der Königlich Preußischen Akademie der Wissenshaften, 29 vols. (Berlin: 1902–83; 2nd edn., Berlin: De Gruyter, 1968, for vols. i–ix).

250 *Bibliography*

Kant, Immanuel. *Lectures on Ethics*. Translated by Louis Infield. Indianapolis: Hackett, 1963.

—— *Lectures on Logic*. Edited and translated by J. Michael Young. Cambridge: Cambridge University Press, 1992.

—— *Prolegomena to any Future Metaphysics*. Translated by Lewis White Beck. Indianapolis: Bobbs-Merrill, 1950.

—— *Religion within the Boundaries of Mere Reason*, translated by George di Giovanni, in di Giovanni and Wood, eds., *Religion and Rational Theology*, pp. 39–215.

—— *Religion and Rational Theology*. Edited and translated by George di Giovanni and Allen W. Wood. Cambridge: Cambridge University Press, 1996.

—— *Theoretical Philosophy, 1755–1770*. Edited and translated by David Walford. Cambridge: Cambridge University Press, 1992.

Landau, Albert, ed. *Rezensionen zur kantischen Philosophie 1781–87*. Bebra: Albert Landau Verlag, 1991.

Leibniz, G. W. *Essais de Theodicée sur la Bonté de Dieu, la Liberté de L'Homme et L'Origine du Mal par M. Leibniz*. Edited by Le Chevalier de Jaucourt. Amsterdam, 1747.

—— *Leibnitii et Bernouilli Commercium philosophicum et mathematicum*. Editor unknown. Lausanne/Genf, 1745.

—— *Leibniz: Opera omni*. 6 vols. Edited by Louis Dutens, Genf, 1768.

—— *Die Leibniz-Handschriften der Königlichen Öffentlichen Bibliothek zu Hanover*. Edited by Eduard Bodemann. Hanover: Hahn, 1889; reprinted Hildesheim: Georg Olms, 1966.

—— *Philosophical Essays*. Translated by Roger Ariew and Daniel Garber. Indianapolis: Hackett, 1989.

—— *Philosophical Writings*. Edited and translated by Mary Morris and G. H. R. Parkinson. London: Dent, 1973.

Lessing, Gotthold Ephraim. *Lessing: Philosophical and Theological Writings*. Translated and edited by H. B. Nisbet. Cambridge: Cambridge University Press, 2005.

Pistorius, Herman Andreas. Review of *Erläuterungen über des Herrn Professor Kant Critik der reinen Vernunft* von Joh. Schulze. In *Algemeine deutsche Bibliothek* 66 (1): 92–123. Reprinted in Landau, ed., *Rezensionen zur kantischen Philosophie 1781–87*.

Plato. *Timaeus*. Translated by Donald J. Zeyl, in Cooper, ed., *Plato: Complete Works*, pp. 1224–91.

—— *Plato: Complete Works*. Edited by John M. Cooper. Indianapolis: Hackett Publishing Company, 1997.

Schleiermacher, Friedrich. *Aus Schleiermachers Leben. In Briefen.* Edited by Wilhelm Dilthey. 4 Volumes. Berlin: Reimer, 1860.

—— *Brouillon zur Ethik/Notes on Ethics (1805/1806).* Translated by John Wallhausser. *Notes on the Theory of Virtue (1804–1805).* Translated by Terrence Tice. Lampeter: Edwin Mellen, 2003.

—— *The Christian Faith.* Translated by H. R. Mackintosh and James Stewart. Edinburgh: T. and T. Clark, 1928. Reprint, with a foreword by B. A. Gerrish, 1999.

—— *Der christliche Glaube nach den Grundsätzen der evangelischen Kirche im Zusammenhange dargestellt (1821–22).* Edited by Herman Peiter. Berlin: De Gruyter, 1980 (*KGA* I.7, 1 and 2).

—— *Der christliche Glaube nach den Grundsätzen der evangelischen Kirche im Zusammenhange dargestellt (1830–31)* Edited by Rolf Schäfer. Berlin: De Gruyter, 2003 (*KGA* I.13, 1 and 2).

—— *Dialektik* (1814/15). *Einleitung zur Dialektik* (1833). Edited by Andreas Arndt, Philosophische Bibliothek, vol. 387, Hamburg: Felix Meiner, 1988.

—— *Dialektik.* Edited by Manfred Frank. Frankfurt am Main: Suhrkamp, 2001.

—— *Dialektik: Aus Schleiermachers handscriftlichem Nachlasse.* Edited by L. Jonas. Berlin: Reimer, 1839.

—— *Dialektik.* Edited by Rudolf Odebrecht. Unveränd. reprograf. Nachdruck der Ausgabe Leipzig 1942. Edn. Darmstadt: Wissenschaftliche Buchgesellschaft Abt. Verlag, 1976.

—— *Hermeneutics and Criticism and Other Writings.* Edited by Andrew Bowie. Cambridge: Cambridge University Press, 1998.

—— *Lectures on Philosophical Ethics.* Translated by Louise Adey Huish. Edited by Robert B. Louden. Cambridge Texts in the History of Philosophy. Cambridge: Cambridge University Press, 2002.

—— *The Life of Jesus.* Translated by S. Maclean Gilmour. Edited by Jack C. Verheyden. Lives of Jesus Series. Philadelphia: Fortress Press, 1975; reprint Mifflintown: Sigler, 1997.

—— *On Freedom.* Translated by Albert L. Blackwell. Lewiston: Edwin Mellen Press, 1992.

—— *On the Highest Good.* Translated by H. Victor Froese. Lewiston: Edwin Mellen Press, 1992.

—— *On Religion: Speeches to its Cultured Despisers.* Translated and edited by Richard Crouter. Cambridge: Cambridge University Press, 1988, 1996.

—— *On Religion: Speeches to its Cultured Despisers.* Translated by John Oman. New York: Harper and Rowe, 1958.

Schleiermacher, Friedrich. *On What Gives Value to Life*. Translated by Edwina Lawler and Terrence N. Tice. Lewiston: Edwill Mellen Press, 1995.

—— *Schleiermacher Kritische Gesamtausgabe: Jugendschriften 1787–1796*. Edited by Günter Meckenstock. Berlin: De Gruyter, 1983 (*KGA* I.1).

—— *Schleiermacher Kritische Gesamtausgabe: Schriften aus der Berliner Zeit 1796–1799*. Edited by Günter Meckenstock. Berlin: De Gruyter, 1984 (*KGA* I.2).

—— *Schleiermacher Kritische Gesamtausgabe: Schriften aus der Berliner Zeit 1800–1802*. Edited by Günter Meckenstock. Berlin: De Gruyter, 1988 (*KGA* I.3).

—— *Schleiermacher Kritische Gesamtausgabe: Schriften aus der Stopler Zeit 1802–04*. Edited by Eilert Herms, Günter Meckenstock, and Michael Pietsch. Berlin: De Gruyter, 2002 (*KGA* I.4).

—— *Schleiermacher Kritische Gesamtausgabe: Theologische-dogmatische Abhandlungen und Gelegenheitsshriften*. Edited by Hans-Friedrich Traulsen, 1990.

—— *Schleiermacher Kritische Gesamtausgabe: Briefwechsel 1774–1796*. Edited by Andreas Arndt and Wolfgang Virmond. Berlin: De Gruyter, 1985 (*KGA* V.1).

—— *Schleiermacher Kritische Gesamtausgabe: Briefwechsel 1799–1800*. Edited by Andreas Arndt and Wolfgang Virmond. Berlin: De Gruyter, 1992 (*KGA* V.3).

—— *Schleiermacher's Soliloquies*. Translated by Horace Leland Friess. Open Court Publishing Companay, Chicago: 1957.

Schmid, Carl Christian Erhard. *Wörterbuch zum leichtern Gebrauch der Kantischen Schriften nebst einer Abhandlung*. Jena, 1788.

Scholz, Heinrich. *Die Hauptschriften zum Pantheismusstreit zwischen Jacobi und Mendelssohn*. Berlin: 1916.

Spinoza, Benedict de. *A Spinoza Reader: The Ethics and Other Works*. Edited and translated by Edwin Curley. Princeton: Princeton University Press, 1994.

Strauss, David Friedrich. *The Christ of Faith and the Jesus of History*. Edited by Leander E. Keck. Philadelphia: Fortress Press, 1977.

Secondary Sources

Adams, Robert Merrihew. "Faith and Religious Knowledge." In Mariña, ed., *The Cambridge Companion to Friedrich Schleiermacher*, pp. 35–51.

—— *Leibniz: Determinist, Theist, Idealist*. Oxford: Oxford University Press, 1994.

Albrecht, Michael. *Kants Antinomie der praktishen Vernunft.* Heldesheim: G. Olms, 1978.

Allison, Henry. *Lessing and the Enlightenment.* Ann Arbor: University of Michigan Press, 1966.

——*Kant's Theory of Freedom.* Cambridge: Cambridge University Press, 1990.

——*Kant's Transcendental Idealism: An Interpretation and Defense.* New Haven: Yale University Press, 1983, 2004.

Ameriks, Karl, ed. *The Cambridge Companion to German Idealism.* Cambridge: Cambridge University Press, 2000.

——"Kant's Deduction of Freedom and Morality," *Journal of the History of Philosophy* 19 (1981): 53–79.

——*Kant's Theory of Mind.* Oxford: Oxford University Press, 1982, 2000.

Barth, Karl. *The Theology of Schleiermacher: Lectures at Göttingen, Winter Semester of 1923–24.* Edited by Dietrich Ritschl. Grand Rapids: Eerdmans, 1982.

Barth, Ulrich. "Der ethische Individualitätsgedanke beim frühen Schleiermacher." In G. Jerouschek and A. Sames, eds., *Aufklärung und Erneuerung: Beiträge zur Geschichte der Universität Halle im ersten Jahrhundert ihres Bestehens (1694–1806),* pp. 309–31.

Behrens, George. "Schleiermacher *contra* Lindbeck on the Status of Doctrinal Sentences," *Religious Studies,* 30 (1994): 399–417.

Beiser, Frederick C. *The Fate of Reason: German Philosophy from Kant to Fichte.* Cambridge: Harvard University Press, 1987.

——"Moral faith and the highest good." In Guyer, ed., *The Cambridge Companion to Kant and Modern Philosophy,* pp. 588–629.

——"Schleiermacher's Ethics." In Mariña, ed., *The Cambridge Companion to Friedrich Schleiermacher,* pp. 53–71.

Bennett, Jonathan. *A Study of Spinoza's Ethics.* Indianapolis: Hackett, 1984.

Berner, Christian. *La Philosophie de Schleiermacher: Herméneutique, Dialectique, Ethique.* Paris: Cerf, 1995.

Birkner, Hans-Joachim. *Schleiermachers Christliche Sittenlehre im Zusammenhang seines philosophisch-theologischen Systems.* Berlin: Alfred Töpelman, 1964.

Blackwell, Albert. *Schleiermacher's Early Philosophy of Life: Determinism, Freedom, Phantasy.* Harvard Theological Studies 33. Chico: Scholars Press, 1982.

Boehm, Gottfried and Enno Rudolph, eds. *Individuum: Probleme der Individualität in Kunst, Philosophie, und Wissenshaft.* Klett-Cotta: Stuttgart, 1994.

Bowie, Andrew. "Introduction." In Bowie, ed., *Schleiermacher: Hermeneutics and Criticism And Other Writings,* pp. vii–xl.

Brown, Stuart, ed. *Reason and Religion*. Ithaca: Cornell University Press, 1977.

Brunner, Emil. *Die Mystik und das Wort. Der Gegensatz zwischen moderner Religionsauffassung und christlichen Glauben*. Tübingen: J. C. B. Mohr, 1924.

Corrigan, John, ed. *The Oxford Handbook of Religion and Emotion*. Oxford: Oxford University Press, forthcoming.

Crossley, John. "Schleiermacher's Christian Ethics in Relation to his Philosophical Ethics," *Annual Society of Christian Ethics* 18 (1998): 93–117.

—— "The Ethical Impulse in Schleiermacher's Early Ethics." *Journal of Religious Ethics* 17, No. 2, 1989: 5–24.

Crouter, Richard. *Friedrich Schleiermacher: Between Enlightenment and Romanticism*. Cambridge: Cambridge University Press, 2005.

Curley, Edwin. *Behind the Geometrical Method: A Reading of Spinoza's Ethics*. Princeton: Princeton University Press, 1988.

Denis, Lara. "Kant's Conception of Virtue." In Guyer, ed., *The Cambridge Companion to Kant and Modern Philosophy*, pp. 505–37.

di Giovanni, George. *Freedom and Religion in Kant and His Immediate Successors*. Cambridge: Cambridge University Press, 2005.

Dole, Andrew. "Schleiermacher and Otto on Religion." *Religious Studies* 40 (2004): 389–413.

Englehardt, Paulus, ed. *Sein und Ethos: Untersuchungen zur Grundlegung der Ethik*. Mainz: Matthias-Grunewald-Verlag, 1963.

Frank, Manfred. "Einleitung." In Frank, ed., F. D. E. Schleiermacher, *Dialektik*, pp. 10–119.

—— "Metaphysical Foundations: A Look at Schleiermacher's *Dialectic*." in Mariña, ed., *The Cambridge Companion to Friedrich Schleiermacher*, pp. 15–34.

—— *The Philosophical Foundations of Early German Romanticism*. Translated by Elizabeth Millán-Zaubert. Albany: State University of New York Press, 2004.

Franks, Paul W. *All or Nothing: Systematicity, Transcendental Arguments, and Skepticism in German Idealism*. Cambridge: Cambridge University Press, 2005.

Gerrish, Brian. *Tradition and the Modern World*. Chicago: University of Chicago Press, 1977.

Grier, Michelle. *Kant's Doctrine of Transcendental Illusion*. Cambridge: Cambridge Univeristy Press, 2001.

Grove, Peter. *Deutungen des Subjekts: Schleiermachers Philosophie der Religion*. Berlin: De Gruyter, 2004.

Guyer, Paul, ed. *The Cambridge Companion to Kant and Modern Philosophy*. Cambridge: Cambridge University Press, 2006, 588–629.

—— "The Rejection of Kantian Dualism." In Ameriks, ed. *The Cambridge Companion to German Idealism*, pp. 37–56.

Helmer, Christine, Marjorie Suchocki, and John Quiring, eds. *Open Systems in Dialogue: Schleiermacher and Whitehead*. Berlin: Walter de Gruyter, 2004.

Henrich, Dieter. "The Concept of Moral Insight." Translated by Manfred Kuehn. In Velkley, ed., *The Unity of Reason: Essays on Kant's Philosophy*, 55–87.

—— "Identity and Objectivity." Translated by Jeffrey Edwards. In Velkley, ed., *The Unity of Reason: Essays on Kant's Philosophy*, 123–208.

—— "Das Problem der Grundlegung der Ethik bei Kant und in Spekulativen Idealismus." In Englehardt, ed., *Sein und Ethos: Untersuchungen zur Grundlegung der Ethik*.

—— "On the Unity of Subjectivity." Translated by Günter Zoeller. In Velkley, ed., *The Unity of Reason: Essays on Kant's Philosophy*, 19–54.

Herms, Eilert. *Herkunft, Entfaltung, und erste Gestalt des Systems der Wissenschaften bei Schleiermacher*. Gütersloh: Gütersloher Verlaghaus, 1974.

Hick, John. *An Interpretation of Religion*. New Haven and London: Yale University Press, 1989; second edition: New York: Palgrave Macmillan, 2004.

Kasprzik, Wolfgang. "Monaden mit Fenstern? Zur Konzeption der Individualität in Schleiermacher's *Dialektik.*" In Gottfried Boehm and Enno Rudolph, eds., *Individuum: Probleme der Individualität in Kunst, Philosophie, und Wissenshaft*, pp. 99–121.

Jerouschek, Günter and Arno Sames, eds. *Aufklärung und Erneuerung: Beiträge zur Geschichte der Universität Halle im ersten Jahrhundert ihres Bestehens (1694–1806)*. Hanue/Halle: W. Dausien, 1994.

Lamm, Julia. *The Living God: Schleiermacher's Theological Appropriation of Spinoza*. University Park: Pennsylvania State University Press, 1996.

—— "The Early Philosophical Roots of Schleiermacher's Notion of Gefühl, 1788–1794." *Harvard Theological Review* 87, no. 1 (1994): 67–105.

Lindbeck, George. *The Nature of Doctrine*. Philadelphia: Westminster Press, 1984.

Lonergan, Bernard. *Insight*. New York: Harper and Row, 1978.

Longuenesse, Beatrice. *Kant and the Capacity to Judge*. Princeton: Princeton University Press, 1998.

Mariña, Jacqueline, ed. *The Cambridge Companion to Friedrich Schleiermacher.* Cambridge: Cambridge University Press, 2005.

—— "A Critical-Interpretive Analysis of Some Early Writings by Schleiermacher on Kant's Views of Human Nature and Freedom (1789–1799) with Translated Texts." *New Athanaeum/Neues Athenaeum* 5 (1998): 11–31.

—— "Kant on Grace: A Reply to his Critics." *Religious Studies* 33 (1997): 379–400.

—— "Making Sense of Kant's Highest Good," *Kant-Studien* 91, Heft 3 (2000): 329–55.

—— "The Religious Significance of Kant's Ethics," *American Catholic Philosophical Quarterly* 75, No. 2 (2001): 179–200.

—— "On Some Presumed Gaps in Kant's Refutation of Idealism." In Rameil, ed., *Metaphysik und Kritik,* pp. 153–66.

—— "Schleiermacher Between Kant and Leibniz: Predication and Ontology." In Helmer, Suchocki, Quiring, eds., *Open Systems in Dialogue: Schleiermacher and Whitehead,* pp. 59–77.

—— "Schleiermacher on the Outpourings of the Inner Fire: Experiential Expressivism and Religious Pluralism." *Religious Studies* 40 (2004): 125–43.

—— "Schleiermacher on the Philosopher's Stone: the Shaping of Schleiermacher's Early Ethics by the Kantian Legacy," in the *Journal of Religion* 79, No. 2 (April 1999): 193–215.

—— "Schleiermacher's Christology Revisited: A Reply to his Critics." *Scottish Journal of Theology* 49, no. 2 (1996): 177–200.

—— "Transcendental and Phenomenological Analyses of Religious Feeling: Friedrich Schleiermacher and Rudolf Otto." In *The Oxford Handbook of Religion and Emotion,* edited by John Corrigan. Oxford: Oxford University Press, forthcoming.

—— "Transformation and Personal Identity in Kant," *Faith and Philosophy* 17, No. 4 (2000): 479–97.

Meckenstock, Günter *Deterministische Ethik und kritische Theologie.* Berlin: De Gruyter, 1988.

—— "Schleiermacher's Auseinandersetzung mit Fichte." In Sergio Sorrentino, ed., *Schleiermacher's Philosophy and the Philosophical Tradition,* pp. 27–45.

Moretto, Giovanni. "The Problem of the Religious in Fichte and Schleiermacher." In Sergio Sorrentino, ed., *Schleiermacher's Philosophy and the Philosophical Tradition,* pp. 47–73.

Munzel, G. Felicitas. *Kant's Conception of Moral Character: The Critical Link of Morality, Anthropology, and Reflective Judgment.* Chicago: University of Chicago Press, 1999.

Netland, George A. "Professor Hick on Religious Pluralism." *Religious Studies* 22 (1986): 249–61.

Niebuhr, Richard R. *Schleiermacher on Christ and Religion: A New Introduction.* New York: Charles Scribner's Sons, 1964.

Otto, Rudolph. *The Idea of the Holy.* London: Oxford University Press, 1950.

Paton, H. J. *The Categorical Imperative.* Chicago: University of Chicago Press, 1948.

Quinn, Philip and Kevin Meeker, eds. *The Philosophical Challenge of Religious Diversity.* Oxford: Oxford University Press, 2000.

—— "Toward Thinner Theologies: Hick and Alston on Religious Diversity." In Quinn and Meeker, eds., *The Philosophical Challenge of Religious Diversity,* pp. 226–42.

Rahner, Karl. *The Foundations of the Christian Faith.* New York: Crossroad, 1978.

Rameil, Udo, ed. *Metaphysik und Kritik.* Berlin: De Gruyter, 2004.

Ravier, Emile. *Bibliographie des Oeuvres de Leibniz.* Hildescheim: Georg Olms, 1966; originally published Paris, 1937.

Reath, Andrews. "Hedonism, Heteronomy, and Kant's Principle of Happiness." *Pacific Philosophical Quarterly* 70 (1989): 42–72.

Rutherford, Donald. *Leibniz and the Rational Order of Nature.* Cambridge: Cambridge University Press, 1995.

Schmidt, Sarah. *Die Konstruktion des Endlichen.* Berlin: De Gruyter, 2005.

Scholz, Gunter. *Ethik und Hermeneutik: Schleiermachers Grundlegung des Geisteswissenschaften.* Frankfurt: Suhrkamp, 1995.

Sockness, Brent. "The Forgotten Moralist: Friedrich Schleiermacher and the Science of Spirit." *Harvard Theological Review* 96, no. 3 (2003): 317–48.

—— "Schleiermacher and the Ethics of Authenticity." *Journal of Religious Ethics* 32, no. 3 (2004): 477–517.

—— "Was Schleiermacher a Virtue Ethicist? *Tugend* and *Bildung* in the Early Ethical Writings." *Zeitschrift für Neuere Theologiegeschichte/Journal for the History of Modern Theology* 8, no. 1 (2001): 1–33.

Sorrentino, Sergio, ed. *Schleiermacher's Philosophy and the Philosophical Tradition.* Schleiermacher Studies and Translations. Lewiston: Edwin Mellen, 1992.

Thandeka. *The Embodied Self: Friedrich Schleiermacher's Solution to Kant's Problem of the Empirical Self.* Albany: State University of New York Press, 1995.

Twiss, Sumner B. "The Philosophy of Religious Pluralism: A Critical Appraisal of Hick and His Critics." *The Journal of Religion* 70 (1990): 553–68.

Vallée, Gérard. *The Spinoza Conversations between Lessing and Jacobi,* Lanham: University Press of America, 1988.

Velkley, Richard L., ed. *The Unity of Reason: Essays on Kant's Philosophy.* Cambridge: Harvard University Press, 1994.

Wallhausser, John. "Schleiermacher's Critique of Ethical Reason: Toward a Systematic Ethic." *Journal of Religious Ethics* 17, No. 2, 1989: 25–39.

Ward, Keith. "Truth and the Diversity of Religions." In Quinn and Meeker, eds., *The Philosophical Challenge of Religious Diversity*, pp. 109–38.

Wilson, Margaret. "Leibniz and Materialism," *Canadian Journal of Philosophy* 3 (1974): 495–513.

Winch, Peter. "Meaning and Religious Language." In Brown, ed., *Reason and Religion*, 193–221.

Wood, Allan W. "Kant's Compatibilism," In Wood, ed., *Self and Nature in Kant's Philosophy*, pp. 73–101.

Wood, Allan W., ed. *Self and Nature in Kant's Philosophy*. Ithaca and London: Cornell University Press, 1984.

Zöller, Günter. "German Realism: The Self-Limitation of Idealist Thinking in Fichte, Schelling, and Schopenhauer." In Ameriks, ed., *Cambridge Companion to German Idealism*, pp. 200–38.

—— " 'On revient toujours.' Die transzendentale Theorie des Wissens beim letzten Fichte," *Fichte Studien*, Vol. 20, Teil III.

Index

Absolute, the, 3–5, 11, 17, 23, 33, 38, 59,
    69, 109, 114–116, 119, 120n, 131,
    138n, 139, 149n3, 179, 180,
    180n, 181, 198, 200, 221–225,
    241, 244, 246, 248
  beginning, 18, 20, 36–37
  dependence, 3, 107, 109, 145, 149,
    179, 180, 198–201, 221, 223, 225,
    225n, 229, 231, 232, 233, 236,
    237, 238, 238n, 239, 241, 242,
    243, 244, 245
  knowledge, 119, 162, 176
  philosophy, 175
  worth, 21, 23
Acknowledgement, 141, 174, 180
Act attribution, 37–39
Activity, expressive, 11, 146
Agency, 24, 36–39, 43, 136
Agent, 24, 37–39, 43, 79
An Interpretation of Religion (Hick), 222,
    231
Analogies of experience, 36, 51, 52, 54,
    56, 76, 89, 90, 91, 123
Animal/animals, 79, 82, 91, 93, 101, 137,
    139, 232, 233
*Anthropology from a Pragmatic Point of
    View* (Kant). *See* Immanuel
    Kant: works
Antinomy, 36–40, 210, 210n
  of agency, 36–39
Appearances, 9, 51, 52, 55n, 57, 58,
    61–65, 68, 70–72, 88, 95, 98, 99,
    101, 102, 104, 105n, 107, 124,
    124n, 126, 128, 129, 136, 149,
    151
Apperception, 74, 74n, 82, 83n, 84, 84n,
    85, 89, 94, 103, 177
  immediate, 112, 134, 139
  transcendental unity of, 74–75,
    83–85
Apprehension/apprehensions, 52, 54,
    56, 63, 64, 72, 90, 131–132, 141,
    178, 229, 248

Archetype, 190n, 192, 196, 197, 210n
Atheism, 45–46
Atonement, substitutionary, 209, 210n
*An Attempt to Introduce the Concept of
    Negative Magnitudes into
    Philosophy* (Kant). *See* Immanuel
    Kant: works
Augustine (Saint), *City of God*, 169, 212n
Autonomy, 189, 190, 239–240. *See also*
    Freedom

Barth, Karl, 191
Blessedness, 161–162, 207–209, 211,
    215, 218–219
Bliss, 160
Body, 7, 18n, 19n, 25n, 28n, 59, 73, 92n,
    99, 101, 118, 122n, 132, 162, 165,
    176, 181, 212, 213, 222n, 223,
    242–243, 245
Bourget, Louis, 47

Categorical Imperative, 16, 20, 29,
    157–159, 164, 166, 167, 240. *See
    also* Immanuel Kant: works
    (*Groundwork of the Metaphysics
    of Morals*)
Categories, 11, 62, 83–86, 95n, 97,
    105, 105n, 117, 224, 226n,
    227n, 228, 231, 232, 235,
    243
Causality, 4n, 10, 21, 36, 38, 40n, 103n,
    108, 159n, 169
  finite, 113, 114n
  absolute, 113, 114n, 147
  of reason, 108
Character, 16, 35, 37–39
Choice, 29–34, 38, 40, 239n
Christ, 7, 12
  divinity of, 195–196, 206
  complete humanity of, 188, 195–7,
    203–204, 206
  consciousness of, 191–192, 194–195,
    197–198, 201–207, 222

Christ (*cont.*)
  empirical view of the work of,
    188–191
  magical view of the work of, 207–211
  mystical view of the work of, 188, 191,
    211–220
  person and work of, 186, 188, 191,
    196, 207, 208, 211, 214, 215
  person-forming activity of, 12, 188,
    207–208
  redemptive activity of, 190, 215
The Christian Faith (Schleiermacher).
    See Friedrich Schleiermacher:
    works
Christological doctrine, 187–188
Clarke, Samuel (correspondent with
    Leibniz and supporter of Sir
    Isaac Newton), 38
City of God (Saint Augustine), 169,
    169n. *See also,* Augustine
Cognition, 86, 89, 105, 116, 117n,
    170–173, 175–176, 182, 186, 193,
    217, 228n
Common root, 116–118, 120, 159
Community, Christian, 7, 12, 47, 48, 51,
    52, 118, 120, 120n, 132–133, 134,
    187, 207, 214, 225n
Compatibilism, 8–9, 18–19, 25, 34–37,
    40, 41
Concept, 18, 41, 54, 58, 62, 72, 73, 74,
    78, 80, 81, 83–86, 95, 98, 99, 103,
    104, 105, 115, 117, 117n, 130,
    151, 156, 157, 171, 172, 174,
    190n, 230
  analytic unity of, 81
  complete, 119, 121, 122, 122n,
    124–125, 139
  immediate, 71–74
Conflict of the Faculties (Kant). *See*
    Immanuel Kant: works
Consciousness:
  analytic unity of, 78, 80–82, 85,
    90–91, 94–95, 106
  animal grade of, 232–233
  bundle theory of, 84
  higher, 198, 202, 203, 212, 232–234,
    237, 242, 245
  identity of, 88, 97, 98, 102, 104, 106

  of Jesus, 191–192, 194–195, 197–198,
    201–207, 222
  lower, 241
  of identity, 80–1
  of unity, 82
  original unity of, 198, 223
  synthetic unity of, 82, 94, 106
  transcendental unity of, 11, 80–84,
    93, 94n, 106, 128, 129, 200
  transitions in, 120, 198
Corporate life, 201, 202, 208, 214, 218
Creatio ex nihilo, 66
Creation, 70, 110, 112–114, 122n,
    125–126, 133, 140–142, 196
Creature/Creatures, 48n, 110, 113–114,
    122n, 124–25, 138n, 152, 204
Critique of All Previous Ethical Systems
    (Schleiermacher). *See* Frierich
    Schleiermacher: works
Critique of Practical Reason (Kant). *See*
    Immanuel Kant: works
Critique of Pure Reason (Kant). *See*
    Immanuel Kant: works
Culture, 141, 142, 245
Cultural linguistic alternative, 226
Cultural and linguistic categories, 226,
    227, 231, 235

Death, 143, 219, 242
Decree, original divine, 196, 206, 225
Descartes, René, 59, 122
Desire/desires, 8, 9, 16, 19, 22, 24,
    27–34, 35–36, 40–42, 43, 58, 72,
    99–102, 106–108, 114, 136, 137,
    147–152, 157–159, 161, 162, 167,
    175, 194, 202–203
  empirically conditioned, 12, 23, 41,
    107, 147, 150, 154, 159–161,
    164–165, 167
  lower faculty of, 24, 136–137, 144,
    149, 165–166, 240
  harmony of, 156–157
  therapy of, 35, 36, 40
Determinism, 9–10, 14, 17, 22, 34, 36,
    40–44, 77, 97–108, 130–131. *See
    also* Freedom
Dialectic (of Kant's first *Critique*), 83n,
    84

Dialectic (of Kant's second *Critique*), 149, 149n

Dialectic. See Schleiermacher: works

Dialogue, 4, 12, 25–27, 55n, 227, 230, 231, 243, 247

Discourse on Metaphysics (Leibniz). *See* Gotfried Wilhelm Leibniz: works

Disposition/dispositions:
  as active, 210n
  as fundamental/pre-existing, 1, 26, 34n, 35, 38, 66, 211
  as inner, 188
  power/powers and, 139
  as unique, 128, 130, 130n
  as virtuous (good, or moral), 50, 152, 167, 189–190, 209

Divine:
  causality, 147
  decree, 196, 197, 206, 225
  influence, 114, 131–132, 139, 206–207, 221, 222, 244
  love, 4, 6, 12, 144, 146, 195, 197, 205–208, 211–212, 215–216, 219

Divinity of Christ. *See* Christ, divinity

Doctrine:
  Christological, 188
  of freedom of the will, 35
  nature of, 224, 225, 226–229, 230, 230n, 231, 243
  of necessity, 35, 39

Dogmatic propositions, 229

Dualism, 99, 120n, 171, 172n, 178, 181, 186, 187

Eberhard, Johann August, 120n, 193, 194, 194n

Efficient cause, 43, 66–67. *See also* Causality

Embodiment, 66, 176, 181

Empiricism, 17, 128–129

Ensouling (of human nature by reason) 11–12, 157–163, 167

Eschatology/eschatalogical, 11, 147

Ethical solipcism, 126

Ethics, early views, and Kantian influence upon, 4–9, 6, 15–34

and language, 134, 147
of personal identity and individuality, 8, 11, 77, 136, 148, 164–169, 176, 247
in relation to knowledge of self communally and in the world, 175, 181
in relation to religion, 7, 14, 221–222, 239, 241
as response to Kantian deontological and eudaimonistic, 155, 157–158, 162

Exemplar, 190, 194, 196, 201

Experience, 37, 47, 49, 53n, 54, 55n, 64, 74–76, 79, 83, 84, 86–89, 90–95, 95n, 104, 105, 107, 119, 123, 126, 134, 139, 156
  analogies of, 51, 56, 76, 89
  objective, 49, 51–56, 64, 90, 91
  outer, 49, 54, 134
  religious, 13, 194, 213, 223–232, 235, 247–248
  religious, criteria for a genuine, 235–246

Expressivism, experiential, 221, 224, 226, 227

Extension, 41, 57, 59, 67, 88, 88n, 98–102

Eudaimonism, political, 166–167

Fact of reason, 105, 107, 147

Faculty, faculties, 22, 32, 35, 103, 150, 159, 171, 194, 240
  of cognition (*see* Cognition)
  common origin of, 117
  of desire, 8, 22–24, 28–32, 149, (*see* Desire)
  of sensation 26–27 (*see* Sensation)
  of representation, 32–34, 62–64
  of understanding, 19, 22, 50, 51, 54, 55, 57, 63, 76, 104, 105

Fatalism, 36, 45

Faith/faiths, 45, 169, 222, 224, 227, 230, 238
  Christian, 187–220

Family resemblances, 243

Feeling/feelings, 6, 16, 17n, 19, 20, 21,
    22n, 23, 24, 25–28, 33, 35, 42,
    55n, 71, 72, 73, 98, 99, 115, 116,
    120n, 129, 130n, 149, 154, 157,
    170, 171n, 172, 173, 176, 183,
    212, 215
  of absolute dependence, 109,
    179–180, 199–201, 212, 223,
    223n, 225, 228n, 229, 231–232,
    234–239, 241
  of freedom, 35, 199–200
  moral, 19
Fichte, Johann Gottlieb, 8, 15, 46n, 116,
    118, 127, 127n, 128n, 129, 130n,
    133, 157, 164, 165, 176–180
  Wissenshaftslehre, 176
Finite and infinite (relation between),
    67–70, 100–101, 111–113,
    111–115, 115n, 126–127, 131,
    132, 137, 138–140, 143
First person point of view, 89–91, 93. *See
    also*, I think
Flesh, 242, 243
Fonds, 112, 121n
Forgiveness, 130, 207, 209
Freedom, 7–10, 33, 35–40, 43, 44n, 45,
    47, 97, 108, 111, 128, 128n,
    129–134, 136, 137, 164, 164n,
    165–166, 189, 190, 193n,
    198–200, 238, 240, 240n, 242,
    245, 246
  absolute, 198
  human, 9, 20, 33, 34, 133, 134, 238,
    239
  intelligible, 11, 97, 98, 102, 104
  logical, 107n
  positive, 107, 108, 166
  transcendental, 8, 11, 15–16, 18–20,
    34n, 35–37, 41, 42, 43, 44n, 104,
    105, 107, 107n, 108, 190
Friendship, 128, 142–143
Fulgurations, 110n, 113–114, 221

God, 48, 50, 65–73, 92–93, 109, 110,
    111, 112, 113, 112–114, 121,
    124–126, 131, 138
  consciousness, 12, 134–136,
    144–145
  forgetfulness, 237
  as transitive cause, 65

immanent cause, 65
  and the world (relation between),
    114–120, 125–126
Good principle, 189
Grace, 169n, 191–192, 240, 244
Ground/grounds:
  of action/will's acting, 16, 20, 32,
    33–34, 34n, 38
  of appearances, 63, 64, 70, 99–105
  of endurance or subsistence, 48
  of individuation, subjective, 51, 51n
  logical, 69–71
  noumenal, 68–70, 76
  of both self and world, 48, 49, 110,
    115
  real, 69–71, 172
  of unity of the soul/self, 96, 120
Groundwork of the Metaphysics of Morals
    (Kant). *See* Immanuel Kant:
    works
Guilt, consciousness of, 209–210

Happiness:
  distinction from blessesdness, 209
  empirical, 149, 156, 160
  maximizing, 26, 155–160
  proportioning of virtue to, 148–149,
    150–155
  relation to Categorical Imperative,
    166–167 (*see also* Categorical
    Imperative)
Harmony (of desires) 162
  of principles of action, 157
  of thought and physiological
    processes, 99–103
Hegel, Wilhelm Georg Friedrich, 116,
    118, 144, 171, 175, 232n
  Phenomenology of Spirit, 144
Hermeneutics, 4n, 184, 193n, 217n
Heteronomous action, 6, 239–240
Heteronomy, 6, 150n, 239–240
Hick, John, 231, 239
  An Interpretation of Religion, 222
Highest Good, 5, 11–12, 17n, 28n,
    146–147
  Schleiermacher's early understanding
    of, 148–155
  in Schleiermacher's later thought,
    155–163, 184, 190
  as a synthetic concept, 149

History, 5, 119, 136, 188, 191, 201,
    207–208, 216, 219, 243, 246
  historical arena, 144, 190–191, 197,
    207–208, 211, 216
Holiness, 53, 189
Holy will, 152
Human nature, 6, 11, 12, 22, 87n, 188,
    189, 192, 194, 206, 223
  ensoulment by reason, 148, 150, 159,
    162, 171n
  Jesus as perfect fulfillment of,
    196–197
Hume, David, 37, 55, 84
  Treatise on Human Nature, 84
Hypothetical Imperative, 19, 20, 22n,
    29. *See also* Kant: works
    (*Groundwork of the Metaphysics
    of Morals*)

I think, 81, 82, 85–87, 94, 103n. *See also*
    Unity of consciousness
Idea of the Holy (Otto), 228n. *See also*
    Rudolph Otto
Idealism, critical, 52, 53, 69, 101, 136
  German, 68
  transcendental, 9, 39, 44, 53, 56, 63,
    70, 71, 99
  double aspect view of, 62–66
  Fichtean, 115, 130, 136
  two world view of, 64–67
Identity of consciousness. *See*
    consciousness
Identity of self-consciousness. *See*
    self-consciousness
Identity, of persons, 43, 76–108
  of the subject, 80, 81, 82, 88, 94, 95n,
    106
  of self, 76–108
  of substance, 92–96
  of things, 9, 43, 48–61
Imagination, 25, 51, 53, 57, 130–133,
    142, 145, 226n, 230, 246
  moral, 142
Immediacy, 10, 28, 72, 116, 171, 173,
    177, 179, 180, 198, 244
Impression/impressions, 3, 27, 30, 32,
    39, 103n, 113–114, 117n,
    128–130, 133, 153, 157, 159,
    181, 205, 213, 227n, 228,
    242

Impulse, 28–33, 35–36, 42, 170, 174, 205
  boundlessness of, 33
Incentive/incentives, 16–22, 22n, 24,
    28–33, 42, 190
  to/for action, 42, 108, 190, 203
  to/for the will, 16, 18, 28–29
Inclinations, 6, 20, 22n, 28, 36, 66, 98,
    147, 149, 150, 152, 155, 161,
    163
Incompatibilism, 18, 40
Incorporation thesis, 31, 33–34
Individuality, 7, 12, 46n, 48, 109, 110,
    135, 137, 138, 139, 140, 143, 144,
    157, 165, 168, 170, 174, 183, 187,
    221
Individuation, 9, 44, 45, 48, 49–61
Infinite, 48, 48n, 61, 65, 66, 67, 68, 69,
    72, 79, 96, 96n, 100, 101, 102,
    111, 113, 115, 115n, 125, 126,
    131, 131–140, 143, 169, 179, 183,
    183n, 226
Infinite causality. *See* Causality: absolute
Inner experience, 54, 226
Inner fire, 12, 114, 115, 221–222
Inner sense, 12, 51, 52n, 55n, 56, 72, 76,
    88n, 99, 102
Intelligible freedom. *See* Freedom,
    intelligible
Intelligible order, 150, 152
  substance/substances, 77, 86, 97, 103,
    108
  world, 60n, 96n, 107, 108, 135, 136,
    151, 159–161, 173n
Inter-subjective knowledge, 112, 132
Intellect, 97, 98, 172
Interpretation of Religion (Hick), 231.
    See also John Hick
Intrinsic properties. *See* Properties,
    intrinsic
Intuition, 62, 69, 70, 85, 88n, 93, 98,
    105, 105n, 115, 116, 117, 118,
    171, 172, 174, 176, 228n
  empirical, 69, 178
  forms of, 62, 69, 70, 71, 99
  inner, 88, 89
  intellectual, 64, 105, 117, 178, 179
  manifold of, 10, 64, 94
  moral, 162
  outer, 56, 89, 90, 98, 99
  of representations, 98

Intuition (*cont.*)
  of self, 85
  sensible, 62, 99

Jacobi, Friedrich Heinrich, 8, 15, 43–46,
    53–56, 61, 65–66, 77, 79–80, 96,
    99, 100–101
  works:
    *David Hume on Faith, or Idealism
      and Realism, a Dialogue*, 55
    *On Spinoza's Doctrine in Letters to
      Moses Mendelsohn*, 45–46
John, Gospel of, 132
Judgment, 15, 19, 22, 23, 83, 83n, 84, 86,
    86n, 87, 87n, 100, 101, 104n,
    107n, 117n, 142, 145, 168n

Kant, Immanuel, vii, 2, 3, 5, 8, 9, 11,
    12, 13, 15–18, 19–24, 26, 31n,
    33, 33n, 34, 35, 37, 38, 39,
    40n, 41, 43, 44, 46, 52, 53, 54,
    56, 62, 63, 69, 70, 71, 72, 74,
    77, 78, 81, 83, 83n, 84, 89–95,
    97, 99–108, 116, 118, 123, 124,
    130, 147–152, 154, 155–161,
    187–190, 192, 194, 209n, 210,
    239, 240n
  works:
    *An Attempt to Introduce the Concept
      of Negative Magnitudes into
      Philosophy*, 172
    *Anthropology from a Pragmatic
      Point of View*, 8, 16, 18, 16, 21,
      40, 40n, 158n, 168n, 188, 192
    The Conflict of the Faculties, 240
    Critique of Pure Reason (First
      Critique), 10, 18, 54, 62, 69, 75,
      77–96, 172
    Critique of Practical Reason (Second
      Critique), 19n, 40n, 70, 105,
      107n, 240n
    *Groundwork for the Metaphysics of
      Morals*, 107, 107n, 159, 161,
      167–169, 190n, 239n
    Jäsche Logic, 123
    Nova Delucidatio, 123, 123n
    *Prolegomena to any Future
      Metaphysics*, 63
    *Religion within the Bounds of Mere
      Reason*, 145, 158n

Kingdom
  of ends, 157, 166, 169
  of God, 207, 208, 214, 215
  of grace, 169n
Knowledge, 9, 10, 117, 135, 141, 144,
    182, 218, 228, 244, 246
  conditions of, 2, 3, 4, 74, 76, 178, 184,
    194n
  social construction of, 4, 133
  divine, 125
  of individuals, 51, 55, 57, 176
  impossibility of absolute, 119, 162,
    176
  as infinite perception, 125
  inter-subjective, 4, 132, 147, 174
  object/objects of, 103n, 139, 173, 180,
    182, 183
  perspectival character of, 12, 141, 170,
    174, 176, 184
  possibility of, 3n, 75, 119
  self-, 110, 139, 143, 145, 154, 188
  of self, 143
  unavoidability of beginning in the
    middle, 119

Language, 14, 124, 134–135, 139, 171,
    181, 186, 217, 218, 221, 227, 236,
    246
Law of cause and effect, 52, 54
Law of humanity, 137
Laws of nature, 36, 38, 148
Leap of faith, 45
Lectures on Philosophical Ethics
    (Schleiermacher), 217. *See also*
    Friedrich Schleiermacher,
    works
Leibniz, Gottfried Wilhelm, xii, 8,
    10–11, 15, 37, 38, 43–51, 53, 56,
    61, 66, 67, 101, 109, 110, 110n,
    111–113, 118, 119, 121n,
    122–124, 126, 132, 138n, 139,
    146, 168–170, 221
  works:
    Discourse on Metaphysics, 50, 110n,
      111, 112, 121
    Monadology, 50, 66–68, 110, 110n,
      168, 169
    *New System of the Nature and
      Communication of Substances*,
      110n, 111

Principles of Nature and Grace, 110, 121, 168
Lessing, Gotthold Ephraim, 45–46
   On the Reality of Things Outside God, 73
Limitation/Limitations, 64, 112, 113, 132, 138n, 142, 145, 153, 180
Lindbeck, George, *Nature of Doctrine*, 226, 235
Logical unity, 78, 85, 86, 90, 91, 96n
Love, 5, 142–145, 154, 169, 185, 197, 217, 222, 237, 241, 242, 245
   divine. *See* Divine love
   self. *See* Self love
Lower faculty of desire. *See* Desire: lower faculty of

Manifold, of sensible intuition 49–50, 55–57, 61, 62, 64, 72, 84, 85, 87, 88, 94
   of representations, 27, 131
Material of willing, 158
Matter, 2, 48, 56, 59, 98, 99, 101, 193
Maxim, 26–28, 33, 34, 149, 150, 151, 157–159
Mechanism of nature, 40n, 44n, 77, 97–108, 151, 193
Mendelsohn, Moses, 45–46
   Morgenstunden, 45
Metaphysics, 8, 61, 76, 97, 120, 193, 221, 240, 248
   of the self, 76–108
Mode, 11, 36, 48, 51, 59, 62–64, 96, 98, 102, 130
Monadology (Leibniz). *See* Gottfried Wilhelm Leibniz: works
Monad/monads, 46, 46n, 47–51, 61, 68, 76, 88n, 96, 102, 110n, 113, 114, 119, 120n, 123–125, 133, 135, 139, 146, 169, 186, 187, 221
   Infinite, 72–74
Monadic individualism, 11, 108, 186, 187
Monadic properties. *See* Properties, monadic
Monologen (Schleiermacher). *See* Friedrich Schleiermacher: works
Moral:
   agent/agents, 157, 166
   disposition, 152, 167, 189–190

feeling, 19
ideal, 145, 189
insight, 107–108
law, 9, 18–22, 22n, 23–28, 31, 41, 42, 106, 107, 108, 137, 144, 149, 151, 152, 156, 159–161, 164, 166, 167, 169, 190, 239, 240
motivation, 26–28, 35, 41
obligation, 22, 31
principle, 15, 16, 19, 190
subject, 23, 106
Mysticism, 113, 248

Nature system, 192, 200
Nature of Doctrine (Lindbeck), 226. *See also* George Lindbeck
Neighbor, duty to, 6, 59, 210, 215, 216, 222, 245, 256
New System of the Nature and Communication of Substances. See Gotfried Wilhelm Leibniz: works
Nicolas of Cusa, 112n
Niebuhr, Reinhold, 13
Non-moral motivation, 23–24
Non-transposable/Non-transposability, 7, 168, 170, 173–175
Notes on Ethics (*Ethics*). *See* Friedrich Schleiermacher: works
Noumena, 9, 48, 60–65, 68–69, 76–79, 95–96, 98–99, 104, 105, 136
   positive conception of, 105
   noumenal self, 106
Nova Delucidatio (Kant). *See* Immanuel Kant: works

Objects of experience, 51, 52, 79, 83, 86, 87, 88, 105
Obligation, 22, 28, 31, 240
Omnipotence, 112, 125
On Freedom (Schleiermacher). *See* Friedrich Schleiermacher: works
On Religion: Speeches to its Cultured Despisers (Schleiermacher). *See* Friedrich Schleiermacher: works
On What Gives Value to Life (Schleiermacher). *See* Friedrich Schleiermacher: works
Organic, development, 146, 163
   function, 171

Organization, 162, 183, 184, 187
Organ/organs:
   formation of, 181
   of our embodiment, 181
   of cognition, 175–176, 181–182
   of sensation, 173–176
   of spirit, 212
Otto, Rudolph, 228
   Idea of the Holy, 228n
Ought. *See* Moral: obligation
Outer sense, 76, 88, 88n, 98, 102
Outline of a Critique of Previous Ethical Theories (Schleiermacher). *See* Friedrich Schleiermacher: works

Panentheism, 65
Pantheism, 45, 46n, 65n, 66, 96n
Paralogisms, 10, 76–99, 102, 107n, 136
Perception/perceptions, 49, 51–53, 56–58, 84, 112, 116, 125, 171, 182, 223, 233–235
Perfect human nature. *See* Human nature, perfect fulfillment of
Person, 77–80, 89, 91–92, 97, 102
   forming activity of Christ (*see* Christ, person-forming activity of)
   imperative for treatment of as ends, 164–183
Personal identity, 7, 10, 76–108
Personhood, complete, 77–78
Personality, 77–97, 102, 165, 195
   principle of, 77–80, 92–93
   unity of, 8–9, 15, 195n
Perspective, 4, 5, 7, 12, 40, 131, 138, 140, 145, 162, 163, 173, 235
   transcendental, 131n
   uniqueness of, 174–176, 180, 181, 183
Phenomena, 9, 48, 50–57, 60–61, 71, 76, 79, 94–96, 104–106, 116, 236
Philosopher's stone, 15–16, 18–25, 144
Philosophy of religion, 3, 5, 8, 13, 14n, 191, 222
Pistorious, Hermann Andreas, 96n
Piety, 13, 112n, 229, 236
Plato, 5, 58–59, 212, 212n, 221
   Timaeus, 58
Pleasure, 23–26, 149–150, 165, 203
Pleasure and pain, susceptibility to, 25, 149, 150, 203

Pluralism, religious, 13, 115n, 221, 222, 232, 243
Practical reason, 6, 9, 19, 21, 33, 40, 42, 70, 77, 97–108, 148, 149, 149n, 152, 159, 160, 166, 240
Pre-established harmony, 47, 50–51, 125
Preponderant synthesis, 130, 188, 204
Preservation, 106, 114. *See also* Creation
Principium diudicationis, 15–16, 23.
   See also principle of discrimmination
Principium executionis, 15–16, 23.
   See also principle of execution
Principle/Principles:
   Christ's motive, 210, 210n, 211, 220
   of discrimination, 15–16, 19, 23–24, 26–28
   of execution, 15–16, 23–4, 26–8
   ensouling-, 162, 176, 182
   of God-likeness, 162
   of identity, 79
   of individuation/individuating, 9, 43–44, 48–61, 67, 75–79, 96, 165
   moral, 15, 16, 19, 156, 190
   of personality, 77–80, 92, 93
   rational, 16, 23
   of sufficient reason, 38
Principles of Nature and Grace (Leibniz).
   See Wilhelm Gottfried Leibniz: works
Property/properties:
   intrinsic, 11, 102–103, 122–124, 125
   monadic, 88, 102
   relational, 71, 88, 95, 122–124
Punishment, 207, 209, 211

Rational psychology, 78–96, 110, 121, 127, 139, 144, 186
Realm of ends, 169–170. *See also* Kingdom of ends
   of grace, 169n
Realism, 44n
   direct, unmediated, 53, 55, 55n, 56
   empirical, 55
   German, 180
   transcendental, 71
Reason:
   and nature, bifurcation between, 12, 147, 151, 152, 158n, 159, 161

causality of, 108
  influence on will, 17–18, 20–22,
    25–29, 31n, 42
  practical, 6, 9, 21, 23, 24, 28, 33,
    97–108, 107n, 148–149, 152,
    159–160, 240
  theoretical, 45, 49, 107
Receptivity, 6, 9, 22, 26, 102, 103, 113,
    114, 117, 119, 120, 130, 133, 136,
    149, 150, 179, 181, 182, 193, 195,
    197, 198, 200, 234, 240
  vital, 204–207
Reimarus, Elise, 45
Reciprocity thesis, 105–106
Recognition, 2, 42, 108, 150, 154, 165,
    178, 187, 190, 199, 206, 216–220,
    247
Redeemer, 191, 196, 197, 202, 208, 210,
    215
Redemption, 194–196, 207–209,
    212–214, 218, 224n
Refutation of idealism, 52, 54, 180n. *See
    also* Immanuel Kant: works
    (*Critique of Pure Reason*)
Relation/relations:
  between appearances and things in
    themselves, 62, 63
  of God to self, 111 (*see also* Self:
    relation to the Absolute)
  between individuals, 168, 170
  outer, 134, 136, 146, (*see also* Self:
    relation to world)
  real, 112, 140, 172, 181, 181n
  social, 139
  between substance and accidents, 87,
    103n
Relational properties. *See* Properties,
    relational
Religion, 1, 13, 247–8
  aesthetic, 239
  philosophy of (*see* Philosophy of
    religion)
  positive, 254–255
  teleological, 238–240
*Religion within the Boundaries of Mere
    Reason* (Kant). *See* Kant: works
Religious experience. *See* Experience:
    religious
Religious pluralism. *See* Pluralism,
    religious

representatio per notas communes, 171
representatio singularis, 171
Representation /Representations:
  faculty of, 8, 9, 32, 34, 52, 54, 61, 62,
    64, 102
  mode of, 62–64
  immediate, 62, 171
  symbolic, 224, 225, 230
Respect (for moral law), 20, 25
Revelation, 54, 192, 227, 241

Salvation, 207, 214, 222, 225, 225n
Schleiermacher, Friedrich
  works:
    The Christian Faith, 3, 11, 13, 15,
      44n, 114, 119, 145, 177, 179, 181,
      188, 191, 198, 223, 225, 227, 229,
      234, 236, 241
    Dialectic, 3n , 4n, 11, 74, 74n, 119,
      120n, 171, 171n, 181, 184, 193,
      206, 232
    Dialogues on Freedom, 8, 16, 25, 29
    Hermeneutics, 184
    Lectures on Philosophical Ethics, 217
    Life of Jesus, 195, 202, 210n, 219
    Monologen, 10, 11, 44, 108, 110,
      111, 120, 126, 127, 131, 133, 135,
      137, 140, 144, 146, 154, 186, 187
    On Freedom, 8, 16, 17n, 19, 22n, 25,
      27, 28, 32, 37, 41n, 42, 43, 136,
      194
    On the Highest Good, 17n, 28, 148,
      149, 153
    *On Religion: Speeches to its Cultured
      Despisers*, 4, 13, 44, 114, 120n,
      144, 222n, 226n, 234
    On What Gives Value to Life, 153
    Notes on Ethics (*Ethics*), 5, 11–12,
      14n, 17n, 19, 19n, 147n, 148,
      155, 155n, 156, 157, 161–163,
      165–168, 170, 171n, 173, 174,
      174n, 176, 177, 181–184, 186,
      187, 217
    *Outline of a Critique of All Previous
      Ethical Systems* (*Critique of all
      Previous Ethical Systems*), 12, 13,
      17, 145, 155, 165, 166, 187
    *Short Presentation of the Spinozistic
      System*, 9, 43, 44, 48, 59, 60, 72,
      76, 110, 135

Schleiermacher, Friedrich (*cont.*)
  Works (*cont.*)
    Spinozism, 9, 43–108, 110, 127, 130,
      131n, 135
Schmid, Carl Christian Erhard,
  Wörterbuch zum leichten
  Gebrauch der kantischen Schriften
  nebst eine Abhandlung, 77
Self:
  empirical, 88–89, 110, 129, 134, 136,
    180n
  inner, 76, 88, 143, 144, 186
  knowledge of, 76, 110, 139, 143, 145,
    154
  metaphysics of, 120n, 121, 133, 221,
    247
  moral development of, 141–145
  as noumenon, 10, 77–78, 79, 96n,
    106–107
  outer, 76, 88, 134, 186
  relation to the Absolute/Divine/God,
    3, 6, 7, 11, 13, 58, 109, 112, 124,
    184, 201, 205, 212, 214, 221, 244,
    246
  relation to world, 2, 10, 11, 77, 120,
    127, 129–132, 146, 176, 186, 198,
    242, 245, 246
  substantiality of, 77, 79, 83, 106
  transcendence, 252, 245, 246
  transformation of, 221
  and world, 2, 54, 55, 77, 115, 116, 118,
    119, 120, 121, 179, 181, 195, 198,
    200, 218, 233, 234
Self conceit, 20, 21
Self love, 20, 21, 245
Self-consciousness, 7, 12, 54, 80, 103,
    134, 233, 244
  identity of, 77, 80, 88–90, 97, 103, 106
  immediate, *see* immediate
    self–consciousness
  reflective, 10
  sensuous, 13, 199, 200, 202, 203, 205,
    207, 214, 245
Sensation, 52, 53, 55–57, 63, 64, 76, 87,
    101, 117, 118, 129, 159, 171, 173,
    173n, 174–176
  faculty of, 26, 27
Sensibility, 25, 62, 63, 90, 98, 103n, 105,
    115, 116, 117n, 145, 171, 172,
    173

Sensitiveness, 141, 143
Short Presentation of the Spinozistic
  System (Schleiermacher). *See*
  Schleiermacher: works
Sin, 134, 191, 192, 201–218, 237, 242,
    244
Sociability, 5, 217, 218
Social institutions, 186, 217, 218, 221
Solipcism, ethical, 126
Soul, 111–114, 116, 121, 122, 124n, 126,
    128, 129, 131, 140
  as mirror of the world, 11, 121,
    125–126
  depths of (*fonds*), 112, 121n
  ground of, 120n, 131, 134
  simplicity of, 78, 79, 83, 85–87
  substantiality of, 77–80, 83, 86. *See*
    also: Self, substantiality of
Space, 39, 52, 53, 58, 59, 59n, 69–72,
    72n, 88, 98, 99, 117, 119, 120n,
    123, 124, 173, 173n, 199, 229
  as form of intution, 69, 70, 71
  ideality of, 70, 71
Spinoza, Baruch/Benedict, 9, 10, 15,
    31n, 43, 44n, 45, 46, 46n, 47,
    48, 48n, 49, 59, 59n, 65, 66n, 68,
    68n, 69, 71, 73, 96n, 99–101, 103,
    105, 114, 120, 122, 135, 136, 156
  Ethics, 65
Spinozism, 9–10, 44–48, 61–73, 76, 95,
    96, 96n, 101, 122–124, 187
Spirit, 7, 11, 45–47, 100, 101, 127–135,
    142–144, 178, 179, 181, 203, 212,
    214, 228, 236, 242, 243, 245
Spontaneity, 9, 19n, 20, 22, 34, 97–98,
    103–104, 104n, 107, 116, 130,
    150, 198, 199, 200, 201, 205, 206,
    207, 238–240, 242
  of the intellect, 97, 98
  and receptivity, 6, 9, 22, 119, 120n,
    150, 181, 193, 195, 198, 200
  of theoretical reason, 107
  of thought, 99, 103, 104, 107, 118
Standpoint/standpoints, 1, 7, 9, 12, 40,
    66n, 69, 79, 89, 101, 127, 141,
    142, 150, 168, 170, 173, 175, 176,
    182, 184
  causal, 42
  empirical, 40, 89, 90, 91, 92
  epistemic, 76

Kantian, 49, 76
transcendental, 40
ultimate (God-consciousness), 110, 244
Subjectivity, 2–6, 3n, 8, 10, 32, 76, 77, 121, 171, 171n
Substance/substances, 43, 47, 48, 49–53, 57, 59n, 65–71, 75, 79–81, 83, 85, 86–88, 90, 91, 92, 95, 96n, 98, 102–104, 108, 110n, 111, 113n, 119, 121–126, 130, 131, 139, 169, 172, 223
  category of, 11, 86, 87, 102, 108
  corporeal, 46n
  identity of, 92, 93, 95
  independent, 49, 110n 122, 125
  intelligible, 11, 77, 86, 97, 98, 108
  individual, 79, 121, 124, 125
  simple, 50, 85, 113, 126, 169
  single, 47, 90, 91
Substitutionary atonement, 209
Substrate, 56, 58, 59n, 67, 71, 80, 81, 87, 90, 98, 100, 104, 106. *See also* Substratum
Substratum, 52, 58, 80, 83, 98. *See also* Substrate
Sufficient reason/reasons, 37, 38, 39, 41, 42, 67, 68
Symbol, 135, 225, 227, 229–231, 245
Synthesis:
  empirical, 69, 70
  of the imagination, 51, 53, 57, 69, 70, 86
  of the manifold of intuitions, 10, 85, 86, 94
  of representations, 94, 96n
Synthesis speciosa, 87n

Tathandlung, 179
Teleological religion. *See* Religion: teleological
Temptation, 33, 203
Teresa of Avila (Saint), 112n
terminus ad quem, 119–20, 147
terminus a quo, 119–20
Theology, 2, 4, 12, 13, 14, 147, 187, 225, 246
Thing/things:
  identity of, 43

in itself/in themselves, 50–56, 57, 60–64, 63, 63n, 70, 70n, 71, 88, 95, 98, 99, 105n, 118, 124, 136, 178, 224
Third analogy (of the *Critique of Pure Reason*), 52, 123
Third antinomy (of the *Critique of Pure Reason*), 36–39
Third person point of view, 79, 89, 91–92
Thought, discursive character of, 64, 67, 76, 81, 92, 93, 98–102, 133, 135
  relation to material substrate, 100–104
Time, 52, 52n, 54, 59, 69–72, 89, 90, 93n, 95, 96n, 98, 99, 101, 117, 118, 121, 122n, 128, 131n, 159n, 189
  determination, 54, 96
  as form of intuition, 69–71, 89
  ideality of, 70, 71
Traditions, 13, 17, 22, 223, 224, 227, 231, 232, 235, 243, 245, 246
Transcendent, 1, 2, 5, 74, 74n, 75, 120, 149, 193, 201, 223, 224, 226, 229, 235, 247
Transcendental:
  Deduction, 10, 81, 94, 97
  Freedom, 15–16, 19–20, 34–43, 77, 97, 98, 104–108, 132, 164n, 190, 193
  I (of apperception), 78, 80–89, 91, 93, 94, 108, 177
  Illusion, 70, 83n
  unity of apperception. *See* Apperception: transcendental unity of
  unity of consciousness. *See* Unity of consciousness
Truth claims, 223–225

Unconditioned. *See* Absolute
Understanding, 19, 20, 22, 50, 51, 54, 57, 62, 63, 72, 76, 81, 83, 104n, 105, 116, 117n, 149, 159, 168, 171, 242. *See also:* understanding, faculty of
Unity of consciousness, 80, 81, 82, 91, 94
  analytic, 78
  original 198, 223

Unity of consciousness (*cont.*)
  synthetic, 106
  transcendental, 81–82, 93, 106, 129,
    200
Unity of experience, 37, 90, 94n
Unity of self-consciousness, 77–82,
    87–90, 92, 93, 94, 102, 107
Uniqueness, 170, 172–175
Unknown root, 116, 159, 171, 193. *See
    also* Common root

Value
  of the individual, 7, 165–167
  of will, 164
Vinculum, 46, 46n, 51, 61, 76, 78, 96, 98
Virtue, 6, 25, 26, 148–154, 157, 158n,
    160–163, 166, 167n
Vital receptivity, 204–207

Whence, 6, 119, 179, 180, 193, 198,
    223n, 229, 233, 239, 243, 245
Wissenshaftslehre. See Johann Gottlieb
    Fichte: works
Work of Christ:
  as person forming, 188–211
  empirical views of, 188–191
  magical view, 207–211
  mystical view, 211–220
World:
  as mirror of the soul, 118, 119, 121,
    126
  relation to God, 111, 112n, 113
  relation to self, 111, 115, 116,
    118–129
  social construction of, 133. *See also*
    Knowledge: social construction
    of